FORGOTTEN
LAND

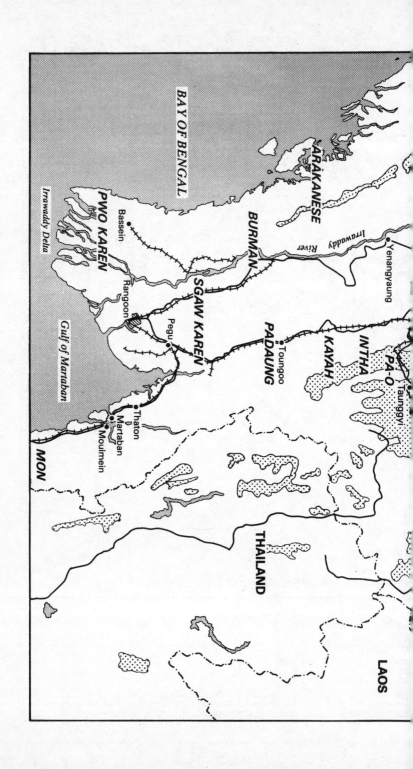

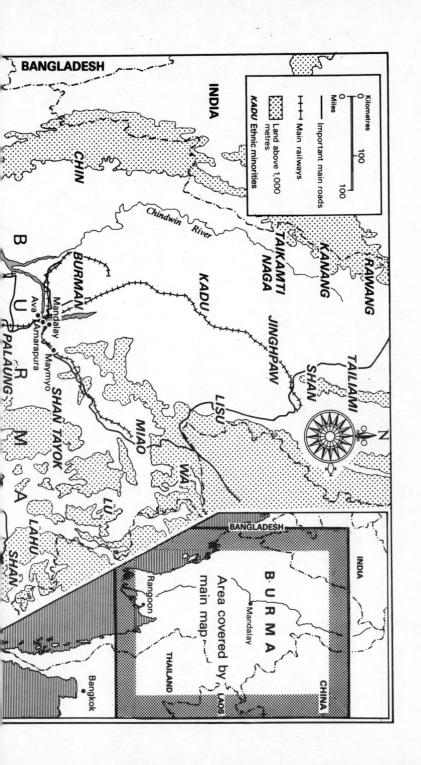

FORGOTTEN LAND

A REDISCOVERY OF BURMA

Harriet O'Brien

MICHAEL JOSEPH   LONDON

MICHAEL JOSEPH LTD
Published by the Penguin Group
27 Wrights Lane, London W8 5TZ, England
Viking Penguin, a division of Penguin Books USA Inc.,
375 Hudson Street, New York, New York 10014, USA
Penguin Books Australia Ltd, Ringwood, Victoria, Australia
Penguin Books Canada Ltd, 2801 John Street, Markham, Ontario, Canada L3R 1B4
Penguin Books (NZ) Ltd, 182–190 Wairau Road, Auckland 10, New Zealand

Penguin Books Ltd, Registered Offices: Harmondsworth, Middlesex, England

First published in Great Britain 1991

Copyright © Harriet O'Brien 1991

Printed in England by Clays Ltd, St Ives plc
Filmset in 11/13 pt Plantin Light

A CIP catalogue record for this book is available from the British Library
ISBN 0 7181 3426 5

CONTENTS

List of Illustrations

Copyright holders are indicated in italics

INTRODUCTION

The morning mist hung lazily on the water, blurring outlines and softening the contours of the landscape. The river twisted quietly through dense greenery. Great jungle vegetation reached right down to the banks and large forest-clad hills stretched up beyond. Dotted between the trees and the foliage, a few thatched settlements blended into the scenery while wispy trails of wood smoke from small cooking fires left lingering signs of human activity. It was at first difficult to appreciate that in the midst of this lushness life was hard, a battle of survival over jungle diseases, lack of food and the constant threat of warfare.

This was the borderland of Burma. Just across from Thailand, it was an area under the control of the Karen rebel army, one of the strongest of Burma's many insurgent groups. Over the hills distant fighting sporadically took place between Karen troops and battalions of the Burmese army. It was a jungle war that had been going on for over forty years.

The long boat nosed past dark-green leafage and stopped immediately below a settlement of scattered huts. We made our way up on foot. The sun began to beat down, driving the mist away and as the heat of the day broke through, jungle noises from the outlying vegetation quietened. A smiling young man came out to greet us, always pleased to welcome visitors, anxious that they should learn about the situation in the hinterland of Burma. His was not a Karen village but a camp for about 200 exiles from the cities of Burma. Racially, ethnically and culturally they were very different from the Karen people in whose territory they had taken sanctuary.

Maung Tin had been a medical student at university in the capital of Burma, Rangoon. Along with thousands of others, he had fled from the government controlled area of the country after Burma's mass movement for democracy was suddenly and violently checked by the army clampdown back in 1988. He had come from a relatively comfortable urban environment to live in rough shelters where there was no running water, no electricity and only a poor and sparse supply of food. He had been in the jungle for nearly two years.

His story, like that of many others, was a sad reflection of the hope and the waste that characterize the recent history of Burma. 'I was just a young and carefree student,' Maung Tin said wistfully. 'I was only in my third year at university and I thought I had many years ahead of me before becoming a fully qualified doctor. I was often told I'd have to work harder to pass my exams. Of course all that changed dramatically after the uprising when so many of us escaped to jungle areas. Now I find that I'm the only person here who is even vaguely qualified to be in charge of a clinic and medically I'm responsible for two hundred people.' He looked earnest and worried, almost overwhelmed by his sense of responsibility and the play of life and death that had abruptly forced him to grow up.

Maung Tin took me to his clinic, a thatched shelter at the far end of the camp. Outside, a series of little bushes had been carefully planted out to spell HOSPITAL in English. Inside it was spotlessly clean. About ten patients lay listlessly on bamboo platforms that served as beds. 'Most of us go down with malaria about once every two months. So long as we have supplies of quinine and other medicines people normally recover, but quite a number have died since we first arrived.'

He showed me their supplies books, all carefully written out in English for the few relief agencies who provided a certain amount of aid. Medicines: ampicillin, quinine, vitamin B complex, penicillin, novalgin, needles, syringes (they had difficulty in keeping equipment fully sterilized), plasters, bandages. Food: rice, lentils, fish paste, cherries, vegetables (when available), garlic. (I was puzzled by the cherries until I realized they meant dried chillies). These were people who had nothing and had little opportunity or possibility of improving their lot.

The camp was just one of several similar settlements along the Burma–Thai border and there were many other young, educated people living as exiles: students of engineering, maths, physics, chemistry, the arts and the humanities. There were also Buddhist monks, a few lawyers and other professional people and there were several schoolteachers. Some of them had arrived in the jungle with entire classes of teenage schoolchildren. In addition, a handful of young soldiers from the Burmese army had defected to join those in the jungle. Whatever future these exiles had depended largely on events back home where, with a sense of mounting tension, the people of Burma waited and hoped that the military regime would allow the first democratically elected government to come to power after more than twenty-eight years of army rule. Only then would it be safe for the exiles to return.

Burma had briefly become front-page news when nationwide demonstrations in 1988 had looked set to change the course of more than a quarter century of military rule. I had subsequently read with mounting horror of the shooting and killing with which the movement was put down and the authority of the army aggressively reasserted. The country had then slunk back into obscurity and only a few reports about the predicament of those who fled from the military had reached the international Press.

Burma's isolation is at once historical, cultural and political; locked away from external influence, it has pursued its own course, ignoring the events and movements in the international world beyond. In turn the wider world has had little opportunity or cause to show anything other than a passing, baffled interest in the country.

My parents lived in Burma in the 1970s and, to a large extent, I grew up there. I have fond, bittersweet memories of the place. I first arrived in Burma aged about thirteen. At that stage a few scheduled flights still went direct from England (a final hangover from colonial ties) and as the BOAC VC10 came in to land the airline steward looked at me and my sister with some sympathy and said 'good luck'. We were the only passengers stopping there. The plane had circled over acres of flat sodden land that from above had looked dank and unappealing. Hot, humid air engulfed us as we walked across the tarmac to Rangoon airport. It was the monsoon. We spent the next couple of months in the stickiness of Rangoon, unable to travel anywhere because of the internal problems and because the rains left many roads up country in a near-treacherous condition. It seemed a depressing, sultry place, marked by repression and an underlying sense of threat. I can't remember precisely when or why that changed and at what stage I fondly began to think of the country as home. Perhaps it was because of the prettiness that emerged as the rains abated, perhaps it was because of the delightful charm and wit of Burmese friends and perhaps I just became hooked on Burma's rich history and curious timelessness. After some years of travelling in and out of the country I found myself left, above all, with a lingering sense of the sad plight of the Burmese people and their struggles to improve their lot. It is a beautiful, mesmerizing country whose people and whose problems have made little impact on the rest of the world.

In 1988 it seemed that at last things might change in Burma. Since then there have been surges of great optimism tempered by periods of extreme gloom. I wanted to see things for myself, to try to understand what has happened to the country, what has gone wrong and what might possibly happen next. In the early part of 1990 I returned to see friends and places I had known well. Then I went to the borderland to learn more about those who were living in exile in the jungle. For foreigners this particular region is only accessible from Thailand, owing to the fierce civil war that started shortly after Burma's independence from the British in 1948 and that has continued ever since. In visiting the area I also began to understand more about the struggles of Burma's ethnic minority groups, the rebel Karen, Kachin, Shan, Chin, Mon and others, who for years have been fighting the Burmese army in a bid for some degree of federalism within the country.

Burma's problems are complex and confusing, character-ized by years of tension and unrest. There are numerous ethnic divisions within the country and a history of warfare and skirmishes between them. Set against this is the more recent movement for democracy and the divisions between the Burmese people themselves and their repressive army. The people have made it abundantly plain that they no longer wish for military rule. They have been shot and bullied as a result. Yet a movement has been set in train which makes it likely that the system will change. How and when this will be achieved is a matter of speculation. Democracy is certainly one answer to Burma's current problems. But it is only a start. The task of implementing a new political system, of uniting all the war-torn regions and of dragging the country out into the twentieth century beyond is beset with obvious difficulties. If a civilian, democratically elected government does succeed in coming to power it will probably have to work with the army under a continual threat of military takeover. This is a very real danger; after years of army government there is no infra-structure for anything else and until recently there was no obvious opposition to provide a viable alternative.

But during the demonstrations in 1988 a strong, popular opposition leader unexpectedly emerged. The dramatic story of Aung San Suu Kyi, daughter of Burma's almost legendary independence hero, has given the people a new sense of optimism. Despite the attempts on the part of the military to silence her and blend the memory of her struggle into muted obscurity, she remains the hope for Burma's future.

Yet for all the bloodshed and the unease, Burma remains an enticing place. A land of jewels, rivers and forests, enigmatic and richly remote. Its self-imposed isolation has lent it an air of romantic seclusion and, although a country of forty million people, it seems to have been almost forgotten by the rest of the world. Having spent much of my adolescence there, I have been both horrified and fascinated by the country ever since. In the 1970s, it felt that little had developed since the days of the British. The same feeling pervades even today. It is at once charmingly nostalgic and depressingly stagnant; a Waiting for Godot land where nothing seems to happen. Time evaporates while things slide into slow deterioration and measures of brutality gradually escalate.

It is a country of contradictions: for all the harsh measures of the army, the people are gentle and generous (perhaps too gentle and too generous). Despite the political xenophobia of the military government, individually the Burmese themselves are welcoming and hospitable. But perhaps most marked of all is the juxtaposition between Burma's potential wealth and the country's current-day poverty. This almost fairytale land of golden pagodas and pretty people is now one of the poorest nations in the world.

But Burma remains a land of enormous possibilities. Its natural resources alone could still make it one of the richest countries in Southeast Asia. There are fertile farmlands and forests of valuable hardwood. There is oil and tin below the ground (to say nothing of the great wealth of gems such as rubies, sapphires and jade) and along Burma's extensive coastline there are territorial waters rich in fish and also in pearls. The Burmese themselves are well aware of their potential wealth; Burma for them is still the 'golden land'.

It seemed, when we lived there, that the ambition of a great many Burmese people was simply to leave the country. Friends would often try to find places for their sons in the merchant navy (it was relatively easy to get out from there), while others would go abroad for further training and academic studies. Having left, many would never return. But for all that, they proudly remained Burmese and they frequently clung to a hope of going back, given a different political climate. If it was difficult for them to get out, it was equally difficult for foreigners to get in. For years tourists have been limited to visits of one or two weeks, while the foreign community in Rangoon (and sometimes Mandalay and a very few other places) has remained small and severely restricted.

In terms of the repression and the fear generated by military rule, Burma is not dissimilar to Romania before the fall of Nicolae Ceausescu. It is a country of rumour and suspicion. It is difficult to get at facts, to ferret through the stories and find answers to the puzzle of the place. The country is no longer even called Burma any more – in 1989 it was renamed Myanmar, but the change has largely been ignored by the world outside.

I wanted to write an explanation of this strange, wistful country, a sort of testimony for past generosity and kindness and also all the sadness I have shared with Burmese friends. What I have subsequently written is purely a personal view; I am not an expert or an academic. I was fortunate in having a rare opportunity to get to know something of the country not simply as an outsider but as someone who was involved. I owe much to a great many friends who have helped to explain the country's inner story.

For a while I thought that perhaps I should do things officially, that I should contact the Burmese authorities and tell them I wanted to write about their country. I was advised against this. It would be very limiting, I was told. But in any case I did not want to be forced into saying nice things about a government that shoots its own people. Equally, I did not want to cause problems for anybody within the country. 'You must write the book; it would be good for more people to know about our country. But please, you must not mention names or even too many places,' one friend said to me. In some instances I have therefore used false names and except in a few, safe, cases I have avoided identifying people fully. Burmese names are, in any event, fiendishly difficult and the Anglicized spelling of the language looks disturbingly obscure ('ky' is pronounced 'ch', 'gy' is 'dj').

At the moment the country is in a state of limbo; the bid for democracy is held in check and the people wait to see what will happen next. It may be that for the moment nothing will happen, that the military will hang on to power and at best concede only the semblance of democratic rule; in which case I have tried to provide an adequate rundown as to why this would happen. It may be that Burma will change radically and that the people will start to have some real say in how they want to be governed. For years the country has been tucked away from world view but as a fully democratic nation it could open up dramatically. It would need help and investment; with a British colonial past the country could (at a pinch) look to the West, or it might (more realistically) stay firmly within its Asian context. There would inevitably be transitional difficulties in becoming part of the world outside. But above all else, Burma has had very little experience of democracy and federalism, the ideals to which the majority of the people aspire. I have tried to identify what sort of problems the country would face with a new, liberal political system.

I have put together a perspective on the history, the military politics and the people: the history because so many of Burma's difficulties relate to ethnic, age-old divisions while other, more recent problems date back to Burma's struggle for independence from the British; the military politics because this goes some way in explaining the current predicament; and the people because they are what it is all about.

'We must keep in touch, although sometimes I feel we are on different planets,' a friend recently wrote. I hope it won't be too long before such an overwhelming sense of our differences begins to disappear.

PART ONE

CHAPTER ONE

KINGDOM AND COLONY

A truck bumped and rattled its way down the dusty road towards our hotel. It carried a group of about twenty dishevelled people who sat at the back of the uncovered van staring blankly out at the scene around them. These were the model workers of Burma. Selected for their hard work and productivity, they were being trundled round the country on a special tour. It was really a public relations exercise on the part of the government, as much to establish that there were indeed model workers as to reward these individuals for their efforts. They were unsophisticated rural people chosen from different parts of the fertile rice plains and packaged off on a tour of the country to meet the local workers' cooperatives and to see the sights and cities of Burma. The government-controlled Press provided regular coverage of what inadvertently sounded like a rough trip. Roads in Burma are not good and the sort of transport that manages to survive the wear and tear of these conditions is usually ancient and extremely uncomfortable. By the time we came across the model workers they must have been about halfway through their trip; and they looked it. They were weary, crumpled and were covered in dust.

It was 1975 and my first trip to Central Burma. We had travelled up from Rangoon, the capital city, to see Pagan. This is the ancient capital of the Anawrahta dynasty of Burmese kings. Built on the banks of the great Irrawaddy

River about 200 miles inland from the Delta, it is an astonishing place. Devoid now of much contemporary life and activity, Pagan is a bit of a ghost town but between the eleventh and thirteenth centuries it was the centre of a cultured and extensive kingdom. To glorify Buddhism, and themselves, the eleven kings of the dynasty built thousands of pagodas that still stretch out silently across the surrounding plains. The architecture, the reliefs, the wall paintings and the sheer variety of pagodas all contribute to the enormous historical and visual richness of the place. White pagodas, golden pagodas, vaulted, painted, terraced, they bear testimony to a skilful craftsmanship and a religious reverence that still exists today. Huge, gracious temples punctuate the horizon and between them smaller pagodas sit quietly crumbling into the outlying paddy fields.

As if in sharp contrast to the archaeological atmosphere of Pagan, the Thiripyitsaya Hotel where we were staying still proudly offers Burma's most modern and prestigious tourist accommodation. It is tastefully constructed as a series of bungalows with basic but clean and comfortable furnishings. It has air conditioning in every room. Each bedroom has an adjoining bathroom with hot and cold running water. By most international expectations the hotel is hardly luxurious, but by Burmese standards it is something of a miracle.

The model workers' truck stopped outside the main reception area and the bemused workers shuffled out. Assuming a proud, proprietorial air, one of the hotel staff came rushing out to greet them and ushered them off on a guided tour of all the facilities. They looked with awe and glazed curiosity at the simplest of features: the beds, the showers, the cupboards, even the shelves. The model workers had not come to stay, they had merely been given a chance to look at this wonder of modern technology and efficiency before being bundled off on the next leg of their journey.

I got the impression that this visit to Pagan was one of the highlights of the model workers' tour. But it seemed that they came not so much to look at the pagodas and to muse over the finery that once was, as to see the modern

hotel and to take a look at the Western tourists there. I
suppose by some bizarre leap of logic the authorities deemed
that the model workers would gain from the experience. It
was a curious juxtaposition that while we had come to
explore their past, they had come to see our present lifestyle;
one that afforded us the luxury of bothering about their
history and art.

My own interest in Burma's past lies principally in what
it reveals about the country today. Rather than putting
forward a comprehensive account of Burmese history, my
focus is on what it amounts to in terms of the current
situation. There is a pattern of events, of wars and power-
play, that is the necessary background to a proper understanding of the residue of racial tension that has run through
successive generations. Pagan seems a neat place to start
because it was from here that the Burmese kings and their
people began to dominate the outlying regions and tribal
peoples of the area that was to become an ostensibly united
Burma. And for those wretched model workers, Pagan was
certainly where it all really started; the beginning of the
very first Burmese Empire.

In the ninth and tenth centuries Mongol tribes from
Tibet and other mountainous areas to the north entered the
plains of Burma in successive waves, forcing many of the
earlier settlers up into the surrounding hills. These aggressive intruders were the Burmans. They settled in the fertile
lowlands and by about 1044 had established the first Burmese capital at Pagan under their king, Anawrahta. He
reigned for about thirty-three years and brought under his
control a substantial part of what is now known as Burma.

Anawrahta's kingdom took in areas previously governed
by other ethnic groups; part of Arakan to the west, the
foothills of the Shan States to the east and all of the Mon
territory which runs along the south-east leg of the country.
These ethnic groups: that make up Burma have totally
distinct and separate identities, a fact which underlies much
of the racial tension in the country, even today. The history
of Burma reflects the struggle for control between the

different cultural and racial groups and until the eighteenth century the three most powerful were the Burmans, the Mon and the Shan. On a wider scale, though, foreign invasion or interference has been very limited. Until the arrival of the British, who variously governed Burma between 1826 and 1947, the country was largely cut off from the outside world and outside influence.

The geographical positioning and make-up of the country go a long way in explaining how Burma became so isolated – and why it continues to remain so isolated today. It lies to the west of Laos, Thailand and China, east of India and Bangladesh. A range of fairly substantial hills surrounds the fertile plains of Burma in a sort of horseshoe shape and provides an effective barrier against these potentially intrusive neighbours. Although Burma has an extensive coastline, this is largely tucked away in the Bay of Bengal and so historically the major trade routes between the tip of India and the Indonesian archipelago passed the country by. Until the eighteenth century Burma remained a fairly unknown quantity, dominated to a great extent by the Burman people of the plains whose power was intermittently challenged by the other tribes and groups of the area.

My own awareness of Burma's cultural mix developed from a childish appreciation of the visual impact made by the rich variety of different ethnic dress; the weaves of cloth, the colours and the ornaments. Neat and well scrubbed, the people of the plains wear *lungyis*, lengths of material which are wrapped round as skirts and tied at the front, for men, or tucked in at the side, for women. (This form of dress is now widely worn throughout the country, but the tribal peoples have their own additions and variations.) Traditionally Burmese men have checked lungyis over which they wear white shirts and well pressed jackets with small stand-up collars. On formal or ceremonial occasions they wear on their heads *gaungbaung* which are, very loosely speaking, a sort of turban, faintly reminiscent of tied-up handkerchiefs but rather more elegantly styled than the traditional British seaside variety. The Burmese women wear plain or patterned lungyis with beautifully matching *engyis*, long-sleeved tops modestly fastened with tiny buttons at the neck and above and below the bust. The practice of tatooing has long since diminished but at least until the turn of the century the Burmese men would be fantastically decorated on their arms and thighs with figures, birds, lizards, symbols and other mystic designs.

While the plains people are pretty and elegant, I found the tribal minorities particularly exotic, the Shan, Chin, Kachin, Karen, Karenni (or Kayah) and other smaller groups with intriguing-sounding names – like the wild Wa who come from northern Burma. (The wild Wa were at one time headhunters, as opposed to the tame Wa who did not indulge in such bloodthirsty pursuits.) Up in the area bordering China the Kachin wear ceremonial black and red. The jackets of the women are strikingly decorated with ornaments that look like great breastplates made of chains and badges of silver. 'Terribly expensive', I was told. 'All those badges are solid silver.'

The Karen hills people to the east are brightly but less fiercely dressed: a shirt once given to me by a Karen friend was delicately embroidered with tiny, vividly coloured flowers. It was made of fine cotton, sleeveless, with tassles of bright ribbon hanging down from a V at the front and back and also, slightly disconcertingly, from under the arms.

Strange and perhaps most interesting of all are the giraffe-necked women of the Padaung, a small tribe who live mainly within the Karenni area. At a young age girls in the tribe are given gold or brass rings which they wear round their necks, and sometimes round their ankles and legs. Every year a new ring is added so that by the time the girls reach adulthood their necks look elongated and distorted, their chins perching at the top of long coiled cylinders of metal. I am told that the stack of rings does not in fact stretch the women's necks; their shoulders, though, are pushed down and crushed by the weight of all the metal. It all looks very uncomfortable but also intriguingly and richly tribal. I believe the custom originally started as a way of dissuading other marauding tribes from carrying off the Padaung women, but for obvious health reasons the tradition is now dying out. In the 1930s, during the days of British rule in Burma, the Bertram Mills Circus used to bring over giraffe-necked Padaung women who were displayed as freaks at their show in Earls Court in London.

The largest of the hill tribes are the Shan, whose area was formerly divided into independent and separate states. Until 1959 each state was governed with varying degrees of autonomy by its own *sawbwa* or hereditary ruler. Shan friends showed me photographs of the jewelled, wonderfully clad rulers and their courtiers; it seemed a world apart from life today, but these pictures are lovingly kept by people for whom such days are still a living memory. Now, out of necessity, many of the jewels are sold and the Shan sawbwas have effectively relinquished their power.

In comparison with the bygone splendours of the courts, ordinary Shan dress is neat but simple; the men, though, are notable in that below their loose jackets they wear very baggy trousers. Out of context such ethnic dress can lead to confusion. One of the sawbwas spoke with some amusement of his very first visit to England during the 1930s. The Shan were generally on good terms with the British and as a schoolboy he was sent off halfway round the world to be educated in Britain. Clad in ordinary Shan dress, he arrived by ship in Liverpool on a damp grey day after a trip of about six weeks. His British guardians waiting to greet him at the port saw a small figure standing shivering on the deck. This, it transpired, was their charge. They gave him a warm welcome but were a little puzzled by his appearance; why, they asked him, had he come to England wearing his pyjamas? He said it took a long time to live that one down.

The Shan, together with the Mon, were the largest, fiercest and most sophisticated of the different indigenous peoples to oppose Burman rule. Ethnographically the Shan are Shan-Tai people related to the Thais (the term 'Shan' closely echoing 'Siam', the ancient kingdom of Thailand).

The Mon, meanwhile, are Mon-Khmer people in origin, like the Cambodians and the Vietnamese.

Long before Anawrahta's rule and the formation of a unified Burma, the Mon had established themselves in the southern part of the country around the Irrawaddy Delta and down the south-east coast. They are known to have developed a cultured kingdom with interests and contacts reaching a long way overseas. Thaton, their capital, was a busy port on the coast through which the Mon developed particularly close ties with India. Significantly, it was from India, and through the Mon, that Theravada Buddhism was introduced to Burma – a religion and philosophy that lies at the heart of much of Burmese culture and thought today. It was also from India that the Mon imported and adapted an alphabet which was later absorbed by the Burmans and became the national script. It is ironic, though, that this flurry of cultural activity effectively led to the undoing of the first Mon kingdom.

The neighbouring Burman king, Anawrahta, was not just a fierce warlord; he was a good statesman. His acquisitive intrusions into other territories were not always entirely land and power grabbing activities. The story goes that in about 1054 one Shin Arahan, who was a *pungyi*, or Buddhist monk, came on a mission to the court at Pagan. He very successfully converted King Anawrahta who became a devout Buddhist and marshalled his people into accepting this new teaching. At that stage the Burmans had been largely animist, or spirit worshippers. Anawrahta displayed some wisdom in handling these various somewhat violent spirits; rather than being tossed aside, they were adapted to the Burmese Buddhist philosophy. Even today the Burmese remain a very superstitious people and their thirty-seven *nats*, or spirits, which pre-date King Anawrahta, are very much in evidence. Nat images sit in little enclaves around the precincts of pagodas and are regularly and actively appeased.

Encouraged by Shin Arahan, King Anawrahta sought to learn and to understand more about the teachings of

Gautama Buddha. A long way inland, the court at Pagan was introspective and had little means of communicating with the world beyond, so Anawrahta despatched special envoys to the Mon court at Thaton where there was known to be greater learning and greater contact with far-away cultures. He was particularly interested in the thirty complete sets of the Tripitaka, the sacred Buddhist scriptures the Mon had acquired. Much to Anawrahta's infuriation, though, the Mon court ignored all his royal requests so he got together his army and moved in on the Mon, conquering their Kingdom and seizing their king and his retinue.

Anawrahta took back to Pagan the Mon King Manuha, his entire court complete with white elephants (which were to develop a particular regal significance) and, most importantly of all, the Theravada Buddhist scriptures that the Mon had held. In this way not only the teachings of Theravada Buddhism but also the Mon culture itself were captured and absorbed by the Burmans.

According to ancient chronicles, King Manuha suffered an ignominious fate: after a short time at the Pagan court he and his family were dedicated as pagoda slaves to the great golden Shwezigon pagoda just outside Pagan. Their duties to sweep, clean and generally look after the pagoda do not on the face of it sound too bad, but they and all their descendants were forever bound to tend the pagoda and as such became the lowest of the low, outcasts of society.

I was amazed and puzzled to learn about pagoda slaves. It was only by looking through historical accounts of the social set-up of Burma that I even became aware of their existence, for there are no signs of any such practice today. Looking up the long stairways of the Shwedagon pagoda in Rangoon, where smiling girls sell freshly cut flowers – gladioli, chrys-anthemums, tuber roses of every shade – and tiny paper umbrellas of white and gold which are bought as offerings and which are added to the general colour and magnificence on the pagoda platform, pagoda slaves seemed to me a complete anomaly. The tranquillity and serenity of Burmese pagodas are at odds with such images of oppression or servitude. High up on temple spires golden wind bells gently sound and around the bases of the pagodas gilded images of Buddha sit silently exuding calm. The Burmese will proudly declare that they are an extremely egalitarian race; their society has never been stifled by rigid divisions of caste or even by class structures. Apart from the monarchy there were no striking divisions of upper, middle and lower class until at least the nineteenth century, there was no aristocracy and there were no vassals. This, I understand, was largely due to land ownership rights: beyond the royal courts the land belonged to the people and could be claimed simply if it was cleared and put to agricultural use. Society was – and still is – largely rural, it centred on the village as the basic self-sufficient unit. Without a landed gentry there was no feudal system and therefore no structure which deemed that one person might be inherently superior to another. All the stranger, then, that within this framework of equal rights there should have been a division of outcasts, the lowest of the low set to look after the very symbol of what the Burmese hold most sacred.

George Scott, probably the most sympathetic observer and writer about Burma during British colonial rule, provides a wry explanation. Writing in about 1880 under the Burmese pseudonym Shway Yoe, he comments on pagoda slaves:

> The reason no doubt lies in the conviction of the existence of original sin. It is desirable to have the pagodas attended to. A very small acquaintance with human nature induces the belief that this will not be done if individual effort is trusted to do the work. Therefore prisoners of war and others whom it is not convenient to put to death are dedicated to the service.

In Scott's day there were still many pagoda slaves at Pagan. In all probability these would have been the shunned descendants of King Manuha. Apparently, under British rule many of them were freed from compulsory service, and today the pagodas are tended by well respected trustees.

With the Mon king and his people under the heel of the

Burmans, Anawrahta's Empire flourished. During his thirty-three years on the throne, he governed with wisdom and established the Burmans as the dominant race in the area. He died rather unpleasantly in 1077, having been gored by a wild buffalo, and was succeeded by men of far lesser ability.

It was during the rule of Anawrahta's second son, King Kyanzittha, that the great pagoda-building activities at Pagan began to mark the acceptance and the importance of Buddhism as a central part of Burmese life. The Ananda pagoda, which rises up from the plains in a series of fine white terraces (the shape and the style showing a distinctly Indian influence), the Nagayon temple and the Abeyadana pagoda were all built between 1084 and 1112 and are perhaps Kyanzittha's greatest monuments. His successors continued to build and to glorify Pagan but, lacking the foresight and the qualities of statesmanship of their forebear Anawrahta, the kingdom gradually began to falter and by the thirteenth century it had become very unstable.

It was at about this time that Kublai Khan and his Tartars were prowling around Asia in a predatory fashion. They had taken over Yunnan, now part of China, in the north and demanded tribute from the neighbouring kingdoms. When the Burman King Narathipate refused to acknowledge their claims, the Tartars invaded and, somewhat to their surprise, the Burman army found themselves swiftly defeated. Almost simultaneously the Shan attacked from the east and succeeded in bringing a large area of the rice plains around Kyaukse, near the foothills of the Shan States, under their control.

The Mon, meanwhile, staged an internal uprising and managed to regain their independence, seizing some of the sourthern part of the country around the Irrawaddy Delta. Pagan collapsed, the unity of Burma splintered and for about the next two hundred years the country dissolved into a confusion of warlike petty states.

The Tartars did not remain in Burma for long. But when they withdrew, the conspiracies and aggressive intrusions of the Shan prevented any re-establishment of the Pagan kingdom. The town of Ava, on the banks of the Irrawaddy north of Pagan, became a controlling point of the rice plains around Kyaukse and consequently acquired great political and economic significance, the surrounding area becoming known as Upper Burma. Many Burmans, however, found conditions so wearing and unstable that they fled from the warfare around Ava, congregating in an area to the south.

During this time the Mon, who had been subjected to Burman rule for two and a half centuries, succeeded in reforming their own kingdom in the Delta. In 1365 they set up a new capital at Pegu. Once again they developed a cultured and religious centre. They established control over an area that became known as Lower Burma and built seaports along the coast, developing links with the first known European traders to reach Burma.

I first went to Pegu during the rainy season when the roads become uncomfortably pot-holed and vegetation creeps over anything that remains stationary for long, emphasizing the sticky swampy nature of the Delta. Pegu lost its strategic importance as a port some time in the eighteenth century when the River Pegu changed its course, and it is now a somewhat forgotten place. But the enormous golden Shwemawdaw pagoda that dominates the town helps to serve as a reminder of all the former glory and importance of the place. We stopped to have a picnic lunch just outside the town and sat in a little hut, taking shelter from a relentless downpour. Directly opposite us, looming through the rain and the undergrowth, was a huge and extraordinary construction of statues about ninety feet high. Four great Buddhas sat back to back in a square round a central pillar, looking out at the plains around them. Like most Burmese temples, the Kyaik Pun statues have an interesting background of fact and fable: built in about 1476 by the Mon King Dammazedi, there were also said to be four sisters involved in the construction of the Buddhas. According to popular myth it was decreed that if any of them should marry, one of the statues would crumble; perhaps it was in another lifetime that one of the sisters did marry, for centuries later, in 1930, the Buddha on the west side collapsed after a massive earthquake shook the area. The unexpectedness of this enormous monument, the strange light created by the effect of the rain and the lushness of the intruding undergrowth combined to leave a deep impression of the lingering cultural richness of the place.

It was particularly under this same King Dammazedi, who tool control of Lower Burma in 1472, that the Mon developed an orderly and fairly peaceful kingdom. To the north, however, the Burmans and the Shan remained in a state of warring factionalism.

Those Burmans who fled from the constant disturbances at Ava gradually established a centre further south at the small town of Toungoo. A long way east of the Irrawaddy River, which provided the main routes of communication between Upper and Lower Burma, Toungoo was a relatively safe and secluded place. It was from here that the Burmans gathered strength and eventually established a new monarchy.

By the sixteenth century the Toungoo monarchs had started to intrude into other areas. Military manoeuvres reached a peak under King Tabinshweti who moved south, defeating the Mon and transferring the entire Burman capital to Pegu. Tabinshweti then rather overreached himself by attacking the Thais, with disastrous results, and his kingdom began to disintegrate. He was succeeded by his brother-in-law Bayinnaung, a man of vigour and determination, who regained control of the south and then moved north to defeat the Shan and conquer Ava.

Bayinnaung was a king very much along the lines of Anawrahta: fierce and aggressive, he was also culturally acquisitive, devout and far-sighted. He established feudal authority over many of the Shan States and also moved into other areas occupied by Thai, or Siamese, Shan. I was particularly impressed by an episode recounted in G.E. Harvey's *History of Burma*. (Harvey served in Burma under the British Indian Civil Service, and compiled a series of Burmese histories; his records of the kingdom of Burma up until the first of the Anglo-Burmese Wars in 1824 are a neat blend of legend and fact.) Apparently when Bayinnaung heard that the Siamese King of Ayutthia possessed no less than seven white elephants he decided that for the greater glory of himself and his people he must acquire at least one of these creatures. Although he already had four white elephants it was felt to be unfitting that the King of Burma should lag so far behind the King of Ayutthia. He duly sent envoys to the court of Ayutthia but when his requests met with refusal he simply called up his troops, routed Ayutthia and carried off four of the much prized elephants. He also took away the king and some of the princes and arranged to receive payment of an annual tribute of thirty war elephants. The king's son was left to rule as a Burmese vassal, surrounded by a garrison of about 3,000 of Bayinnaung's men. Wavering control over Ayutthia continued for the rest of Bayinnaung's reign and he died in 1581, allegedly leaving ninety-seven children. His successors kept a faltering hold over the kingdom and in the seventeenth century once again shifted the capital way inland up the Irrawaddy River to Ava.

Moving the capital from Pegu near the coast to Ava some 300 miles away had significant repercussions. Ava, very much in the heart of the kingdom, made sense strategically as a capital from which the outlying areas could be controlled. But set far from the coast, the Burman kings to a large extent lost touch with the world beyond and developed an introspective and arrogant belief in their own superiority, maintaining that their capital was truly at the very centre of the universe.

It is difficult to get to Ava today. Surrounded by rivers and with a channel now cut through from the small Myitnge River to the Irrawaddy, Ava is effectively an island. It is a quiet, sleepy place where few clues remain of its past importance or its courtly life. This is largely because the Burmese kings tended to use bricks and masonry only for religious buildings; courtly constructions were wooden and perished with time. With few tangible remains it is difficult to picture life in the Burmese courts, a frustrating limitation. Ava, however, became the centre of an extensive kingdom and the subsequent history of Burma saw the country once again unified but also projected into an international world that it neither knew nor understood.

While Ava was being established as the Burman base in the north, the Mon in the meantime gathered force and once again set up a kingdom in the south, reclaiming Pegu as their capital. By the 1750s they became sufficiently strong to attack Ava, and they subsequently defeated the Burman king and effectively destroyed the whole of the Burmese Toungoo dynasty. Things at that stage looked bleak for the Burmans. But about a year later there emerged, as if out of nowhere, the most extraordinarily powerful individual, who within seven years of intensive fighting conquered and reunited most of the country, establishing what was to be the last of the Burman dynasties.

Alaungpaya was the *Myothugyi*, or headman, of Shwebo, which lies to the north of Ava. It was then a smallish village of about 300 houses, governed locally by the headman, a position which was not regal but was nevertheless hereditary. Alaungpaya first came to prominence when he refused to acknowledge allegiance to the conquering Mon. A short time later he got together an army, moved south, and by dint of a large degree of military dexterity succeeded in dislodging the Mon. By January 1754 he had reclaimed Upper Burma for the Burmans and announced himself the new king. The Mon withdrew to Lower Burma, hotly pursued by Alaungpaya and his troops who gradually took control of the area, reaching the small town of Dagon in the Delta in 1755. It was optimistically renamed Yangon (Rangoon) or 'end of strife' and it was there that Alaungpaya first encountered, and misunderstood, some of the British and French traders who had ventured into the area.

Alaungpaya's reign was short, fierce and dynamic. Between 1754 and 1760 he conquered the Mon, invaded the

Shan States and moved in on Siam. Rather fittingly he died in combat in May 1760 while attacking Ayutthia. Within a brief period of brilliant military achievement he restored the morale of the Burmans and imposed a degree of national unity that had receded in the mists of time with the demise of the Pagan Empire back in the thirteenth century.

It was at this juncture that the commercial and political significance of European traders began to emerge. Inevitably it was the Portuguese who had first made their mark in Burma. Back in the fifteenth century they had established a trading settlement in Martaban which lies about thirty miles south of the ancient Mon capital of Thaton. They made treaties with the Mon but fell foul of the Burmans when, under Tabinshweti, the Mon were conquered in 1541. However, they managed to retain a hold over Martaban and the Portuguese trading post continued to operate until 1613 when it was finally routed by a resurgence of invading Burmans. The most flamboyant character during this period was a Portuguese national called Philip de Brito who deserves a quick mention because of his extraordinary achievements. He came to the area merely as a cabin boy and managed to set up a trading post at Syriam, a busy port in the Delta a little below the town that was to become the great trading centre of Rangoon. After a fairly short time he placed the port under Portuguese sovereignty but a little later actually declared himself king and held sway in the area for about thirteen years. He was finally ousted by the Burmans in 1613 and met a gruesome end: he was tortured and impaled and reputedly took three long days to die.

But the more lasting effects of European activity came later, particularly with the arrival of French and British commercial ventures. By the eighteenth century a number of European trading posts had been established along the coast around the Delta, and in the quest for greater profit and control over trading routes these foreigners began to angle against each other, backing the Mon or negotiating with the invading Burmans.

When Alaungpaya tore down the Delta to attack the Mon he found three British ships that had put in for repairs at Dagon, or Rangoon. With an eye to seizing their arms and ammunition, he sent his men aboard to requisition their supplies. The British, declaring themselves neutral, were appalled at what they considered a breach of international law. But although Alaungpaya had little understanding of such things, never having encountered the concept of foreign relations before, he was shrewd enough to recognize how much better off he would be with the British on his side. So he let them be, and the British then sloped off to cooperate with the Mon who were already in league with the French.

It was an uncomfortable situation for the foreigners. Alaungpaya subsequently wooed back the British, who at this point were doubtless rather confused as to which side it was prudent to support. In return for cannon and other weapons they were granted the right to trade, without being taxed, from the island of Negrais and a treaty was duly drawn up to that effect. The French in the meantime remained in Mon territory at Syriam and suffered heavy casualties as a consequence: when the Mon were totally defeated by Alaungpaya's army, the remaining French were deported, beheaded or forced to serve as captives in the Burman army.

Ultimately the British did no better. In October 1759 the residents on Negrais were unexpectedly ambushed by the Burmese army. The action was entirely unprovoked. On the grounds that the British had been aiding and abetting the enemy, eight British traders from the East India Company and about 100 of their Indian subordinates were massacred. After Alaungpaya's death a year later the British were allowed to resume their operations but the original treaty of Negrais was overlooked and officially forgotten, much to British indignation. The British East India Company was now taxed on its trade and was not allowed to return to Negrais. With some foresight it therefore opted to settle around Rangoon.

Alaungpaya's successors continued to expand their Burman Empire. The Mon were completely crushed, many of the Shan sawbwas were made to pay tributes and there were constant raids into Siam. But in the latter part of the 1760s Chinese from Yunnan invaded Burma with a great show of strength. Helped by the French captives taken at Syriam, the Burmese succeeded in driving these aggressive neighbours back and gained great moral, if not material, victory, which encouraged them to believe in their invincibility.

Burma was now a large Empire, and one whose directives had developed little from the aspirations of the Toungoo kings in the fifteenth century, despite the negotiations with foreign businessmen and diplomats from the West. The rulers built pagodas, acquired wives from the chiefs of neighbouring principalities and waged war to capture white elephants. Frequently the kings would also marry their half sisters. Insanity resulting from years of inbreeding became a regal problem.

Although the royal family remained securely in control, hereditary procedures were badly defined. There was no clear line of succession and much intrigue developed between brothers, sons and grandsons, with bloody results. There were eleven kings of the Alaungpaya dynasty; the title passed confusingly from father to son to brother to cousin then back to the previous generation before skipping sharply down two generations to grandsons and their progeny. Each king, with all due glitter and ceremony, had many wives and a great many children so that the ensuing competition for power was very fierce. Wholesale massacre of kinsmen became an unpleasant habit: reputedly, in the late eighteenth century, King Bodawpaya polished off many contenders for the crown. His great-grandson, King Pagan (who was slightly mad), did likewise in about 1846. He apparently ordered as many as 6,000 executions, some of which were witnessed by the European ambassadors who had reached the courts. They were suitably appalled.

These Europeans had their eyes firmly fixed on Burma's

wealth of teak forests, the hard and durable timber being required for the great shipbuilding activities of the time. They were also very keen to get commercial access to China through the trading routes to Yunnan. Such local factors were not, however, the motivating reasons for the first of the Anglo-Burmese Wars.

Under King Bodawpaya the Burmese had moved into Arakan, a princely state with an extensive coast to the west of the Burmese Empire. This invasion projected Burma into further diplomatic wrangles with foreign powers, for Arakan had a common border with British India. Border skirmishes and incidents, when Arakanese refugees were fiercely pursued into Indian territory by Burmese troops, were a constant source of irritation to the British in Bengal. Finally, in 1824, matters reached a peak and war was declared. The Burmese, who had been over-confident of their military prowess, were defeated after two years of warfare. Agreements were then reached under the Treaty of Yandabo, whereby Britain took over two disparate parts of the Burmese Empire: Arakan on the west coast and Tenasserim on the east coast.

The humiliated Burmese king retreated back to his capital where he proceeded to suffer from fits of insanity. He was deposed by his brother who then refused to consider himself bound by a treaty that had been signed under a previous king. The Treaty of Yandabo had stipulated that the Burmese court should accept a British Resident. Envoys were duly despatched, but they had a tough time and eventually withdrew, unable to contend with the subterfuge, the intrigue and the insults they met with at the court.

Plunging through history books, I was struck by the hopeless misunderstanding that characterized the relationship between the Burmese and the British. The Burmese thought the British envoys were merely a collection of greedy merchants out to rob Burma of all its riches. The Burmese kings, moreover, could not understand why they were never allowed to communicate directly with the kings of England, which they felt was fitting for their status.

Instead they were forced to debase themselves by dealing at a much lower level with the Viceroy of India. The British, on the other hand, thought the Burmese were arrogant, crude and barbaric. Both sides had a point. In *The Stricken Peacock*, the Burmese author Maung Htin Aung analyses Anglo-Burmese relations during this period and draws attention to a remark made by a Burmese minister to a British envoy at the time of the Yandabo Treaty:

> Your and our customs are so completely opposite in so many ways. You write on white paper, we on black paper. You stand up, we sit down; you uncover your heads, we our feet in token of respect.

Lack of understanding – and probably the desire for greater commercial gain – led to the second Anglo-Burmese War in 1852. The Burmese did not stand a chance against the full force of the British and were fairly quickly defeated. After painful negotiations the whole of Lower Burma was placed under British sovereignty. This meant that the Burmese Empire shrank to the territory of Upper Burma, leaving the entire coast controlled by the British, whose power also extended all the way up the Delta.

Back at the royal court the defeated king was once again deposed and his brother Mindon, an enlightened and devout man, came to the throne. The capital had shifted from Ava to Amarapura a few miles away, a move undertaken during King Bodawpaya's reign, apparently for astrological reasons. According to a popular story, which in all probability is largely true, King Mindon and his people now associated Amarapura with the double dose of defeat they had suffered at the hands of the British. The matter was discussed with the court astrologers who concluded that Amarapura was unlucky because it was not quite at the centre of the universe, previous calculations having been slightly incorrect. The true centre of the universe, they now realized, lay about five miles away down the Irrawaddy River at a place called Mandalay. So Mindon, anxious to make a new and auspicious start, packed up his palace – lock, stock and concubine – and moved the whole lot a few miles down the river, accompanied by about 150,000 of his people.

There is some dispute as to the manner in which Mindon constructed his new palace. According to ancient Burmese tradition, a number of people, particularly pregnant women, were buried alive at the founding of a new city; several under the various gates and at least one at each corner of the fortressed walls. Historians differ in their opinions as to the founding of Mandalay; some say Mindon, as a good Burman king, followed all these ancient rites, others claim that, as the model of a modern, peaceful king, Mindon dispensed with such barbaric customs.

The palace was vast. It had to be since it housed at least fifty wives and over a hundred royal children as well as the great throne rooms, the pavilion for the Lord White Elephant, the gardens and the finely built quarters for the king's ministers. It was a splendid city within a city, gleaming with golden spires, sharp white buildings and blood-red battlements. The foreigners – merchants, traders and diplomats – who came to Mandalay, lived in some discomfort outside the palace moat. When they were permitted to come to the royal court they were normally allowed in through the western gate which was chiefly reserved for corpses and funeral processions.

During the Second World War the palace was destroyed and today only the great red walls remain. The Burmese army have now requisitioned this fortress as their headquarters for the area, so ironically it is still difficult for foreigners to gain access to it. But I have always felt that Mandalay remains very much the heart of Burma, far more so than the present capital, Rangoon, which is, after all, principally a British-built city. There are very few cars in Mandalay but it bustles with bicycles, trishaws, horse carts and motor scooters. For a fairly extensive city it still has a rural feel; only a few buildings rise above tree level; the rest are hidden behind screens of greenery so that it is difficult to get your bearings.

The pagodas, though, stand out in the skyline and remain in their full splendour. King Mindon, as an extremely devout Buddhist, created a city that would also serve as a religious centre. In about 1857 he saw to the construction of the Kuthodaw pagoda which was modelled on An-awrahta's Shwezigon pagoda in Pagan. Some years later he organized the Fifth Great Synod of Buddhism in an attempt to draw together the Buddhist peoples of Indo-China and Ceylon. About 2,500 pungyis, or monks, attended for dis-cussions concerning Buddhist texts and the Buddhist creed. The Buddhist scriptures, the Tripitaka, were then chiselled in holy script on to slabs of marble. They were housed individually in little white pagodas that stand in rows around the base of the Kuthodaw pagoda. It is an enormous book laid out on a total of 729 huge tablets which is still much revered today.

Despite King Mindon's attempts to modernize Burma and to reach some understanding with the Europeans, foreign relations continued to be strained. Initial hopes that the British would withdraw from Lower Burma, and in particular from the religiously significant capital of Pegu, met with no results and many pungyis there migrated north to remain under the patronage of their king. By 1862, however, the Burmese kingdom had begun to recover from the humiliation of defeat. Mindon started bringing Burma into the modern world, introducing a telegraph system and building a series of new roads. A commercial treaty was even signed with the British and the king agreed to the presence of a British Resident at Mandalay.

The terms of the treaty seemed fair enough. Burmese traders were granted rights and privileges in British Burma and British merchants were to receive similar treatment in the Burmese kingdom. Special tax concessions were made on Chinese goods coming through Burma for British traders or on overseas goods transported through British Burma for the Burmese. However, the British complained bitterly at the stance of the king who allowed free markets in his country but kept total control over all imports and exports, thereby retaining a monopoly. The Burmese, on the other hand, viewed the British traders with deep suspicion and often accused them of being British agents sent to their country as spies.

At Mandalay the British Resident found himself subject to a medieval court with elaborate and strict rules of protocol. Umbrellas were particularly important and an attendant was always employed to carry one over the head of an official. The size and colour varied according to rank; huge golden umbrellas were reserved for members of the royal family and special ministers, the king himself had a series of nine white umbrellas (nine being an exceedingly auspicious number). Spitoons and betel nut boxes were also strictly demarcated and graded as to the metal used, the size and the weight. But for a foreigner, perhaps the most bizarre feature of the court was the status granted to the white elephant.

These creatures are rarely actually white in colour, but a series of tests will prove their suitability for the generic title: ordinary and inferior elephants have four toe-nails on their hind feet, white elephants have five; ordinary elephants will turn a dark blackish colour when being washed, white elephants take on a hue of red when water is poured over them. The last white elephant at the court of Mandalay was said to have been a bad-tempered beast. This was put down to childhood trauma: as a young elephant he was thought to have been extremely put out when the special revenue granted as his statutory right was appropriated to pay off the British after the first Anglo-Burmese War. At court the Sinbyudaw, or Lord White Elephant, was second only to the king and had white umbrellas held over him wherever he went. He was washed, perfumed and entertained daily by troups of courtly dancers and singers. When younger he was suckled each morning by rows of women eager for the honour of having their milk drawn directly from their breasts by the great creature himself.

The British Residents considered many of these courtly practices barbaric in the extreme and there was one particular point which was rather foolishly allowed to develop into a diplomatic rift. In Burma, even today, shoes are removed as a sign of respect when entering a house or visiting a pagoda. The Residents, along with everybody else, were required to take off their shoes when being granted an audience with the king. A few years after the commercial treaty of 1862 was signed, the British Resident of the time began to complain about the indignity of this procedure. It sounds absurdly petty but it had dire consequences: the 'Great Shoe Question' became a full-scale debate and eventually the British government of India sent orders that the Resident should not comply with this practice. Rather than being humiliated by receiving visitors with their shoes still firmly laced to their feet, Mindon subsequently felt obliged to end all direct personal contact with the British envoys, who were then forced to conduct their business through lesser courtly intermediaries. It was an outcome which served only to heighten the misunderstandings between the British and the Burmese.

When King Mindon died in 1878 the British were not granted access to the new king because they persistently refused to follow courtly protocol. They thereby lost the opportunity of improving their status and their diplomatic relations. It would have been a wise move, for the new king was not as broadminded or as forward-thinking as his father.

King Thibaw was not the obvious choice as a successor to the title. The son of an inferior queen, there was even some doubt as to whether King Mindon was actually his father. He was weak, cowardly and shy, but he was also something of a scholar, having been destined at one stage to become a monk. At the time of King Mindon's death, courtly intrigues had become frenetic. In order to avoid bloodshed, and even civil war, Mindon had delayed announcing an heir apparent until the last possible moment. He had, however, overlooked the deviousness of one of his chief wives who was determined that Thibaw, husband and purportedly half-brother to her daughter, should become the next king. In this way she hoped to retain some power for herself. But she had reckoned without her daughter, Supayalat, who was an even more power-crazed and tyrannical individual. When Thibaw was duly instated as king, Supayalat swiftly became the most feared person at court and forced her husband to fall in with all her ruthless schemes. Supayalat even encouraged him to secure his position by carrying out another mass slaughter of his kinsmen. Amid a ghastly festival which drowned the cries of the victims, over eighty of Thibaw's half-brothers and sisters were killed. Some were buried alive and trampled over by the elephants of the court, others were strangled, their bodies dumped in red velvet sacks and taken out of the palace by the western gate.

> 'Er petticoat was yaller an' 'er little cap was
>   green
> An' 'er name was Supi-yaw-lat – jes' the same as
>   Theebaw's Queen.

In passing, Kipling mentions the notoriously cruel woman in 'Mandalay'. Kipling's travels around Burma were not, in fact, extensive and there is some doubt as to whether he actually reached Upper Burma, but his poem brought Mandalay to a wider world than the kings, isolated in their medieval court, could ever have conceived of. By the time Kipling wrote it, the country was well on the way to becoming one of the major rice-producing centres of the world and Mandalay and the whole of Upper Burma had been absorbed into British India.

Rivalry between the British and the French and the developments of world trading activities led to the fall of the last part of the Burmese Empire. The Suez Canal had been opened in 1869, boosting trade between West and East and sharpening the competition among the European merchants. The British had already begun to exploit the potential of Lower Burma, particularly in the rice-producing Delta and in the teak forests around Tenasserim. They now wanted to develop the full trading potential of Burma's wealth of natural resources, much of which lay in Upper Burma outside their territory. They were also still eager to establish better trading links through Burma with the Chinese province of Yunnan. The French, too, wanted the natural resources and the Chinese trade, and at that juncture they had better dealings with the court at Mandalay.

By 1879 British relations with the Burmese court had become so bad that the Resident withdrew completely. It seemed that the way was left open to the French and so the British looked for some pretext to reassert their control. In April 1885 a row developed between the Burmese government and the Bombay Burmah Trading Corporation, a British logging company with teak concessions in Upper Burma. The British company was accused of bribery and corruption, failing to pay their employees and extracting more timber than was permitted. At the same time the British Indian government suspected the Burmese of secretly negotiating with the French over arms deals and special trading rights. Tension mounted, the British issued demands and ultimatums and finally, on 14 November 1885, they invaded Upper Burma.

Under King Thibaw the power of the Burmese Empire had weakened and when the British arrived they met with very little resistance. Although there is some evidence to suggest that the British did not actually want to take full control of the area, they could find no alternative solution to the problem of Upper Burma. On 1 January 1886 the last part of the Burmese Empire was formally annexed and together with Lower Burma it became part of the British Indian Empire. Courtly life and the power of the kings ceased abruptly.

King Thibaw and Queen Supayalat were removed from the palace by bullock cart, taken to Rangoon and then shipped off to Bombay where they were treated with some courtesy. A palace was built for them and the Burmese court was resurrected in exile. The British apparently did their best to make life comfortable for the deposed king, but for the next twenty-nine years of his life he remained a miserable man. He had only ruled for seven years and when he lost his Empire he was still a young man in his twenties. After his death in 1915, Supayalat returned to Burma, but she was never allowed back to Mandalay. When she died the British, fearful of nationalist demonstrations, insisted that she should be buried in Rangoon. They used the pretext of an outburst of the bubonic plague up country to keep all the funeral ceremonies well controlled at the British-built capital, and they claimed that in time they would move Supayalat's body to Mandalay. But today her tomb still sits at the foot of the Shwedagon pagoda in Rangoon.

The bad-tempered Lord White Elephant was also removed from Mandalay. He was destined to spend the rest of his life at the zoo that the British had established in Rangoon. But he was then an elderly elephant and he died almost immediately on arrival. The prestige of white elephants, though, has not diminished. When I was last in Rangoon in the early part of 1990, I was shown the zoo and told with evident pride that it had once housed a white elephant. Unfortunately the creature had recently died and they had not yet found another to replace it.

Having taken responsibility for governing Upper Burma, the British then set about re-establishing law and order. Thibaw had been an insecure and ineffectual king, rarely setting foot outside the palace for fear that one of his surviving brothers would immediately seize power and usurp him. Control beyond the court had therefore diminished and by the time the British arrived much of the area was in a state of disorder. While the formal invasion of Upper Burma had been quick and fairly bloodless, the next four years were characterized by fierce fighting which the British obversely termed the 'pacification' of Upper Burma. As well as by dacoits and bandits, the situation was further complicated by a strong force of guerrilla resistance remaining loyal to the King. However weak the last of the monarchs had been, the Burmese were still fiercely and proudly nationalistic. Records show that within the first year of formal annexation about 2,000 British troops were invalided out and about 1,000 died. Most deaths, though, were from malaria, dysentery and other diseases.

The British had an easier time in the areas lying beyond the immediate control of the Burmese kings where there was a clearer pattern of organization under tribal chiefs and rulers. The Shan sawbwas had been nominally subject to the Burmese king but had remained largely independent, provided they paid their tributes and taxes. The amounts varied between states, depending on how close they were to the Burmese kingdom: nearer to Mandalay there was tight control over the export of *letpet*, or pickled tea, which is still a popular delicacy today, but to the far east the Shan State of Kentung sent tributes only of flowers and ornaments. Meanwhile the Kachin in the north and the Chin in the west had managed to remain relatively free from Burmese interference. The British gradually took control of these states but although they retained ultimate authority they largely left these areas to be governed autonomously.

Within Burma proper the British did not get off to a good start. They retained Rangoon, their base in the south, as the capital and by 1887 had set up a provincial government in the old palace at Mandalay. At first, however, they lacked credibility: they chose to house this new government in one of the seven-roofed buildings of the old court. In Burmese eyes only buildings with the auspicious number of nine roofs were suitable for supreme rulers, moreover the British government building was lower than King Thibaw's Lion Throne room, which still towered over the court. The British headquarters therefore failed dismally as a symbol of authority and the image of the British suffered as a result. Had they been more in tune with Burmese etiquette and Burmese ideals, the job of disarming the rebel groups and of bringing peace to the area would probably have been a great deal easier.

But by 1890 the British were firmly installed and had shown that they were not so bad after all. The country was at peace, the people enjoyed more freedom than had been allowed under the Burmese kings and economic conditions were showing a steady improvement. The British did not threaten the country with any rival religion but by removing the king they took away the patron of the Buddhist clergy. Although Buddhism continued to be a central feature of Burmese society, the power of the pungyis diminished when education was largely taken away from the monasteries and made secular. British law was imposed, causing some initial confusion, but the general structure of society remained relatively unaltered.

British officials in Burma were for the most part fairly sympathetic, but the country was controlled entirely through the British Indian government and for those outside it was regarded merely as a province of India. Ultimate power lay back in Britain and the authorities there failed to recognize that Burma had a completely separate identity. However, unlike the effects of British rule in India, society did not become permeated with British customs. The Burmese did not take to cricket (although football became very popular), local officials continued to wear their national dress and did not adopt European trousers and, although many people spoke English, Burmese remained the national language.

Today there are still some souvenirs of British rule in Burma. At the house where we used to live, a bust of King George V sat proudly outside the rain porch. He was bearded, dignified and middle-aged. However, like the British who had once lived and worked in Burma, he was not well suited to the climate. His nose had become detached from his face and at periodic intervals we would ceremoniously glue it back on. But even the best efforts of Superglue could not withstand the rigours of the monsoon and the nose would inevitably slip off again when the rains started. It all seemed appropriately symbolic of the very last vestiges of the British Empire fallen into decay. There is a happy ending, though, for when I last visited Rangoon I was pleased to see that George V had acquired a new marble nose that had been securely cemented in place.

Of course, for the Burmese, the monarchy in Britain bore little similarity to their own kings. British royalty was distant, alien and, on the whole, benign. The Burmese kings, on the other hand, had generally been fierce and despotic. Theirs had been a medieval world of glittering courts and totalitarian government. Perhaps this implies that the Burmese were a cowed and submissive lot, crushed by the absolute control of the kings and their armies. But I think the social pattern of the Burmese, with the lack of feudalism and the emphasis on village communities and on individuals, points to a rather different type of sovereignty. It seems, to my mind, to have been characterized by powerful leaders who disciplined and united an extensive kingdom. Today, the Burmese seem immensely proud of their history, their traditions, and their warlike kings. For the tribal minorities, though, it's a very different story; Burman domination was bitterly resented. Under the Burmese kings the Mon and Karen were perhaps the most severely repressed but for all the minority groups the Burmans were aggressive, cruel and acquisitive. Nothing has really changed, even now. They're still suppressed by the Burmans, and they're still fighting.

CHAPTER TWO

INHERITANCE

There's an odd sense of curiosity and *déjà vu* about going back, revisiting a place last seen through another perspective – a different context of time and expectation. Change brings resentment but also relief – the regret of time passing set against the satisfaction of seeing that life has actually moved on. It was with such mixed feelings that I went back to Rangoon after a gap of about twelve years. It had once been home and it was a place I had responded to with the heady subjectivity of a teenager. Returning, I was merely an observer, a visitor with another life and another outlook. When I went back in the dry season of 1990 I had expected to find Rangoon familiar but different. It would, I had thought, be the same finely preserved colonial city but even in Burma there would surely be changes to make me feel I did not belong any more. I was largely wrong. Rangoon was gleaming with a fresh coat of paint, there were a few new buildings, but beyond that nothing had really altered and I was plunged back into a world I thought I had left behind with my teenage years.

Despite the recent political unrest, Burma remains stuck in a time warp. Superficially this presents a delightful feeling of old-world charm. But underlying the old-fashioned values and customs is a deep sense of oppression. Rangoon revisited not only looked the same but it felt the same: below the surface lurked the same sense of menace, the same muttered conversations, the gossip and the rumours. Flying in from Bangkok is like taking a step back into another lifetime: it's a relief to leave behind the self-interest, the pollution and the commercial thrust of Thailand's rapidly developing industrialism, but that also means leaving behind opportunity, progress and personal freedom.

Friends took me to re-explore Rangoon and we drove around cheerfully wedged together in a small Toyota. Traffic is light and the few new cars on the roads are mostly Japanese. Due to hefty import restrictions the majority of vehicles hark back to another era, dating from at least the fifties or sixties, and are skilfully kept running by inventive mechanics who create spare parts out of anything that comes to hand: a new floor made out of beaten kerosene cans, a gearbox adapted and developed from a completely different model. My friends were relatively wealthy and the newish car, although small, was a symbol of their good fortune.

We drove past truckloads of soldiers to the outskirts of the city where a few grim satellite blocks have been built by the government to rehouse some of the many people being forcibly moved from shanty towns within Rangoon. We passed two new sports centres: an open-air football stadium built by the Japanese and, directly opposite, a vast indoor stadium built by the Chinese. I noted that they were both foreign contributions. 'They're really the only significant buildings to have gone up in your absence,' I was told. 'In your absence.' I rather liked that.

Downtown were several recently built cinema halls with lurid posters advertising Burmese films or romantic English language numbers I had never heard of before. A large poster for *The Story of Love* showed a swooning European lady; behind her were florid scenes suggesting passion and violence; a car chase, a lovers' meeting. It had a certain gaudy appeal but I felt it did not belong to the 1990s that existed beyond Burma.

The rest of Rangoon, though, has remained much the way the British left it forty or so years ago. It is a truly colonial city constructed on a neat grid system with gracious tree-lined avenues and large, fine examples of Victorian colonial architecture. Among all this, the golden pagodas that rise above the buildings look strangely set apart and serve as a reminder that this city is in fact in Burma. Even today there are no high-rise buildings and Rangoon is dominated by a wealth of Victorian-built offices; the old Secretariat, the High Court building with red and white stucco work, and Strand Road. Here neo-Palladian buildings look on to the busy wharves of the Rangoon River where life continues in a timeless pattern, unchanged since the days of the British; river traffic is still a vital means of transport within the country and I watched as passengers, bicycles and goods were crammed on to ferries going up country or across to the old trading settlement at Syriam.

On the last of the Pegu Yomas ranges the Shwedagon pagoda hovers magnificently above Rangoon. One of the most sacred of the religious buildings in Burma, it is difficult to determine exactly when the pagoda was first constructed. It has evolved through time and through legend and it continues to remain at the very heart of Burmese Buddhism and Burmese national pride. The main stupa, towering up a full 325 feet, is entirely covered in gold leaf which glistens, even from a far distance, in the sunlight. Around it are a vast number of Buddha images, smaller stupas and pavilions housing huge bells, pagoda donations and large offering bowls. A gentle throng of people and prayer creates a sublimely peaceful atmosphere that makes Rangoon, spread out below, seem absurdly like a bustling, thrusting commercial centre.

As an essential part of the Rangoon tour, my friends drove me to the pagoda. We unscrambled ourselves from the car and went up to the temple platform where people were quietly praying and making their pagoda offerings. A few soldiers stood around awkwardly, clutching their rifles and watching out for any anti-government activities.

'Please be careful when you walk round the pagoda, there are military intelligence officers watching and listening.'

'Why?' I registered a sense of outrage.

'I don't know, maybe they find it interesting.' Much

smiling and a little laughter. The Burmese are good-natured, easy-going people, translating, where they can, the iniquities of their lot into little jokes, smiling at absurd regulations laid down by the government. Laughter also hides their embarrassment from foreigners.

We paused to take a look at the view over the city. 'You'll see we have a lot of new parks, and you must have noticed how the whole place has really been cleaned up,' one of my friends remarked with a worn smile. 'That's progress for you,' he laughed very softly.

This, indeed, was the most discernable but superficial change to Rangoon. The place looked spruce with whitewash and new plants. After the mass demonstrations of 1988 the government had ordered the people of Rangoon to repaint their houses; it was a literal cover-up of the bloody outcome of the disturbances. The authorities continued to enforce these new regulations at the end of each monsoon. They had also put into operation a programme to clean up the city, clearing out the shanty towns, creating parks, planting flowers and shrubs and vigorously repainting everything – public buildings, road kerbs, railings. People always used to say that in the stickiness of the monsoon if you stood still too long the encroaching vegetation would start to creep over you. Now they said that the dry season had its hazards as well and that if you stood still long enough you would risk being bodily removed or painted along with everything else.

Superficially, Rangoon looked very different to the city I had known in the seventies. Then there had been a sense of faded glory. Once a sparkling, swinging city of colonialism, Rangoon had acquired a hungover shabbiness – the day after the party, as it were. The uninvited guests had departed but life had not progressed. Time had stood still and begun to disintegrate; empty buildings had remained abandoned to the monsoon and the creeping vegetation; paint had peeled from walls and battered cars were coaxed into life along roads that had been built for better days. Now the roads were repaired and widened (many said this was just for the army tanks), a few of the buildings had been renovated and a coat of paint restored Rangoon to some of its former foreign splendour. It would inevitably wash off in the monsoon, I was told, but in the meantime the government were trying to boost morale, create a sense of progress and encourage confidence in their administration before the elections to be held that May. I began to appreciate the wider connotations of 'whitewash'.

Lack of any true progress underlies the timeless nature of Burma, where history is tangled up with the present and events that happened years ago remain profoundly significant in life today. Beyond the stagnant echoes of the past, I wanted to get an impression of what life must have been like for the British in Rangoon, a life centred very much on their clubs, sport and social activities. So, before dropping me back at my hotel, my friends took me to the surviving hallmarks of the British occupation. We went to the old race course. It was quiet and rather forlorn. The grandstand must once have been an imposing building but it had become a dilapidated reminder of the prosperous past that still mournfully haunts Rangoon. In front of the pavilion rows of empty seats looked out over a dusty expanse that had once been a well-tended course. A splendid Burmese gentleman of some seniority told me he could remember coming to the races there when he was a boy. 'It was just like Ascot,' he said – an Ascot, though, of the twenties and thirties. The European ladies wore lavish hats and carried pretty parasols, and amid a hum of excitement and activity the governor would arrive in a smart coach with horses. It was not difficult to picture the former life and colour of this strangely deserted place, but why, I asked had it been left, neglected and unchanged, after all these years. 'Oh, it's still used today, as a riding club,' and I was shown a small group of ponies at the far end of the course, nibbling at the odd blade of dusty grass.

The race course remained active after the British left at the end of the forties. As an extension of a great zest for life, the Burmese had been inveterate gamblers and the races were enormously popular. But on 2 March 1962 the army took control of the country and two weeks later, in one of their first public statements, they announced that all horse racing would be banned within the year. The Rangoon Turf Club closed down and the jockeys' association was disbanded.

We drove on to the Kokine swimming pool. It is still an exclusive club, today patronized by wealthy Burmese. We walked through an archway abundantly covered with purple and white flowering bougainvillea, down to the old club house. It had a lingering sense of the past and the walls were still decorated with framed photographs, faded relics of British imperialism. A picture, dated 1924, showed a group of Englishmen in knitted swimming costumes, the winning team of that year's club competition. Another echoed the wider context of the British Empire and recorded a group of smiling British swimmers complete with moustaches, the 1932 Rangoon v. Calcutta team. These were the men of the Empire who worshipped the great outdoors. In an unwelcoming sweaty climate they worked hard and they played hard, superior beings in a country that was not their own. Their world had ended abruptly with the devastation of Second World War.

I returned to the Strand Hotel which is in itself a splendid example of crumbling colonialism. At the far end of a vast empty bar, a small man played sad strains of Chopin on an upright piano while huge ceiling fans stirred the air above us and waiters in white jackets materialized to offer drinks. It was a willing gesture, but there was little choice since foreign spirits are not legally sold in Burma. I sipped some watery Mandalay Beer and thought over the layers of life, past and present, that I had recalled and observed that day: the reconditioned Rangoon I had just seen; Rangoon as I had known it twelve years ago; and beyond that the city as a supreme legacy of the British and what they had made of Burma.

I think the British genuinely never wanted the responsibility of governing Burma; it was not really from any grand desire to expand the Empire that they moved into the country. Once acquired, Burma became rather neglected. It was an extension to India, a buffer state with rich pickings to be taken.

Burma was jolted into an international world by the British as they looked for profit and revolutionized the economy. This moved rapidly from subsistence level to flourishing, export-driven enterprise as British businesses developed the forestry, the mines, the transport and, most importantly, the agricultural possibilities of the fertile lowlands. Correspondingly the effects of the industrial revolution in Britain reached the East where British manufacturers found new markets for their mass-produced cheap cotton goods. In Burma, trade also developed inland as railways and roads were laid down and communications within the country improved. The bulk of the traffic, though, continued to operate along the waterways and centred on the Irrawaddy as the most navigable of Burma's thoroughfares.

In 1863, seven years after the second Anglo-Burmese War, a small British commercial venture bought up some of the British government steamers in Rangoon and began to compete with other river fleets for passengers and cargo travelling between the Delta and Mandalay. By 1868 the firm had expanded, renaming itself the Irrawaddy Flotilla Company. Although a private concern, the British government offered the company attractive subsidies to operate a regular weekly service up to Mandalay and back to Rangoon (hence the 'old Flotilla' and all those 'paddles chunkin'' in Kipling's 'Mandalay'). The firm continued to flourish and acquired large new steamers and 'flats' which were lashed alongside the steamers and acted as travelling bazaars. During the final Anglo-Burmese War and the subsequent 'pacification' of Burma, the Irrawaddy Flotilla Company in turn offered special assistance to the British government troops, providing express steamers and becoming an essential means of communication between Upper and Lower Burma. They subsequently profited from a vast increase in trade as the country opened up and by 1900 they had established a virtual monopoly over the inland waterways. The Irrawaddy Flotilla Company became a feature of British rule. On independence, though, the firm was nationalized and the great age of steam travel came to an end.

It had been an elegant way to travel, as many of the British traders and civil service officers have recorded. From the first-class deck there were fine views of river life, beyond which paddy fields or vast forests unfolded as the steamers chugged along. There were little cabins with mahogany bunks and an excellent service was provided by Indian butlers dressed in crisp white jackets. The deck passengers below had a more uncomfortable time. The largest of the steamers could carry about 2,000 people who were invariably accompanied by huge bundles of merchandise and live animals.

But the most characteristic feature of the steamers was the pervading smell emanating from the flats that were towed alongside. These were usually laden with cargoes of *ngapi*, or fish paste, which was, and is, the staple diet of Burma. 'A loathsome and evil-smelling moist preparation of fish pickled and pressed with coarse salt,' was how one British officer described it. I always found that beneath the smell it was a rather palatable dish. I was particularly fond of a luxury form of ngapi called *balachaung*, a reddish paste made with dried shrimps and a lot of crushed garlic. Our cook used to press jars of the stuff into my hands every time I left for England and this caused various winks and little chuckles when I went through customs: balachaung, being red, could easily conceal other small red objects thrust into it and had been a traditional and excellent means of smuggling out Burmese rubies. It was for this reason that travellers were not technically permitted to take balachaung out of the country. Presumably the customs officials reckoned I looked pretty innocent for my jars were never confiscated. I probably missed a trick there.

The ruby mines at Mogok, north of Mandalay, still produce some of the finest gems in the world. During the days of the British, native miners paid royalties to the government for the stones they extracted while European companies bought leases and mined in specific areas with more sophisticated machinery. Since the army took over, the gem trade has become State controlled under the Myanmar Gem Corporation. Every year a great auction is held in Rangoon where jade, pearls, rubies and sapphires are sold to an international collection of gem dealers, mostly from the USA, Hong Kong, Japan and, more recently, Thailand. One year I can remember being told how Ferdinand and Imelda Marcos swept in from the Philippines on an official visit that neatly coincided with the glittering sale of all this wealth. Although, like the Burmese kings of the nineteenth century, the government ostensibly controls the entire gem market, an enormous quantity of stones slip out of Burma 'via the back door', as the smuggling activities are euphemistically described.

Of all the mineral reserves in Burma, however, oil is the most commercially attractive. During the British administration the Burmah Oil Company became the most successful of the mining and mineral enterprises. It was a Scottish firm, registered in Edinburgh in 1886, the year of the final annexation of Upper Burma. At first their products were principally kerosene and paraffin wax. An enormous demand for oil came from India where kerosene was used in domestic oil lamps. Within Burma there was a steady need for a vast number of candles that were lit at shrines and used in homes. As time progressed and the motor engine developed, gasoline became a valuable commodity and was added to the company's product lines. The firm had refineries in Rangoon and developed major oilfields up country at Yenangyaung and Chauk on the banks of the Irrawaddy; the wells being leased from the British government or from private owners who had developed interests there. Townships grew up, American drillers were recruited and an oil culture developed. It was at first a rough life with a great many brawls and gunfights, particularly among the American drillers who brought with them an air of the Wild West and were often asked to 'park' their guns outside certain offices and clubs before being allowed to enter.

Oil rapidly became one of Burma's major exports. In 1900 forty million gallons of crude oil were produced, by 1907 this had increased to over 230 million gallons. But the oilfields were one of the major casualties of the Second World War when they were all but destroyed, burnt down by British troops retreating from the Japanese. When the war ended the oil companies returned to the charred remains of their oilfields and resumed operations, working with the Burmese government after independence. Most companies survived there until the mid-sixties when, in the aftermath of the 1962 military takeover, foreign businesses were expropriated by the new government.

Steel Brothers, the largest of the British trading ventures in Burma, also had oil interests. Back in England, I looked up one of their former engineers who had worked in Burma during the thirties and remembered the place with amusement and affection. He showed me photographs of Steel Brothers' oilfields at Lanywa which lay directly across the river from Chauk. Huge steel pylons towered above the oil wells which stretched over acres of flat plains land. Among this forest of metal several small hand-dug wells remained. These were owned and worked by local Burmese who continued to operate them along traditional lines. They would descend into their pits to a depth of about 100 feet, armed with buckets and ropes for hauling up the oil. They wore heavy masks that looked like early examples of deep-sea diving apparatus with tubes attached through which a steady supply of air was pumped down from the surface by hand. At the end of their oil-gathering activities the men would emerge like alien creatures from the depths of the earth, their skin covered in gleaming black oil.

Steel Brothers had a great many operations in Burma, almost covering the entire range of the country's wealth of natural resources: oil, tin, timber, cement, rubber and, most important of all, rice. Their first rice mill was built in 1871, the start of an operation that was to make Steel Brothers one of the major rice millers and shippers in the world. The

Company established mills at the principal ports of Moulmein, Rangoon, Bassein and Akyab and at the outbreak of the Second World War these were handling nearly half the total ouptut of Burma's paddy fields. With their diverse range of interests, Steels had ventures throughout the country: in the ports, in the rice-producing lowlands, in the Magwe district of the Irrawaddy where the oil was found, and up north in the jungle land of the forest-covered hills. The company's operations came to an end shortly after 1962 but there are still some lingering marks of their presence. In Rangoon young bachelors arriving to work for Steel Brothers would be put up at establishments known as 'chummeries', a term that must have encouraged some of the high-spirited antics that became a feature of these places. On Signal Pagoda Road one of the chummeries still stands, but today it is used for a very different purpose. It has become a military intelligence office.

East of the Irrawaddy and the oilfields of central Burma are forest-covered hills rich in teak and other hardwoods. During the British occupation the roughest life of the expatriates must have been that allotted to forestry workers who spent months in malaria-infested jungle camps extracting timber and fighting disease. Burmese hardwoods became particularly valuable as the age of the railways developed and the timber was cut down for sleepers in railway tracks. Teak itself continued to be used principally for shipbuilding, the oily wood being highly prized for its resistance to termites. Like the Burmese kings who had once controlled the forests, the British government owned all the teak trees in Burma and the Shan States. No teak tree could be felled without due authority. Companies bought leases from the forestry department and had to observe strict measures of conservation. Forestry officers would oversee the initial stages of felling procedures and check that the trees were large enough to be extracted. Felling operations were lengthy: the trees would be 'girdled' – the foresters cutting into the bark and sapwood – so that the sap rising from the roots would bleed out and the timber would become sufficiently dried and seasoned before being taken down, a process that took about three years. It was important that the timber should be floatable for most of the movement of logs was by raft transport down Burma's many rivers. Once the mature trees had been taken from a given area it was then closed to further forestry activities for the next thirty years and saplings were planted to replace those trees that had been felled.

The forestry companies owned herds of elephants which hauled the teak from the jungle to the rivers. Just before the Second World War Burma was known to have a working population of over 5,000 of these strong, slow moving animals. It is a method still used today. In a country where few jungle tracks survive the onslaught of the rains each year, elephant power has not been entirely replaced by the internal combustion engine.

The climate for all this burgeoning private enterprise was created by the British government of Burma. From a remote centre of authority in London, which in turn channelled its government through India, they practised a policy of *laissez-faire*, open-door free trade. In the meantime the British administrators in Burma controlled law and order, education, taxes and land rights. The country was split into divisions under the control of a commissioner; beneath him were the deputy commissioners of individual districts and under them were subdivisional officers and then the village headmen. Settlement officers would tour the country, by boat, train, horseback, bullock cart or elephant, to assess land and villages for taxes. Many found it tough-going in remote areas where the nearest British community might be a small-minded group of individuals intent on creating that peculiarly colonial existence of clubs and sports, a world apart from the country around them. But for a great number of British officials life was very rewarding, particularly up in the hills where they found themselves travelling through a rich tapestry of colourful tribes, wild animals (monkeys, leopards, tigers) and spectacular scenery – trailing with jungle plants, orchids and giant spider webs.

In the hot weather the women were sent away to escape the heat, and British society reassembled at the hill station of Maymyo, Burma's answer to Simla, about fifty miles east of Mandalay. A guest house there still serves roast beef and also strawberries (which are grown locally). I last travelled up to Maymyo in a 1940s American army jeep, a memento of the war and the only vehicle locally available for hire. The driver stopped first to buy some white chrysanthemums which were tied to the bonnet of the car, where they swiftly became covered in dust and wilted. These were to propitiate the local nats, or spirits, and to bring us good fortune; judging by the age of the jeep and the winding steepness of our climb I began to see why we needed luck. We passed bullock carts pulling heavy loads of harvested rice, dust showering out from under hoof. Traffic further up in the hills was, mercifully, very sparse and pretty slow; ancient buses were laden with people, their chickens and bicycles strapped to the roofs. We stopped several times to allow our exhausted vehicle to cool down and finally we reached the old hill station. For all its colonial origins the whole place seemed strangely like something out of a set for a Wild West movie: large timbered houses with gables were set back from the dusty road and little horse carts trotted around the town looking just like tiny stage-coaches.

At Maymyo there is, though, that distinctly British creation, the botanical garden. This is neatly laid out on the edge of a lake at one end of the town. The plants are still clearly labelled in Latin and curly Burmese script and, when the universities are in operation (at intermittent and spasmodic intervals, according to the political climate), botanical students from all over Burma are sent up to Maymyo to complete their studies.

The British in Burma were the *thakin*, or master, class, equivalent to the sahibs in India. Their officials were members of the Indian Civil Service (ICS), the Indian Army and the Indian Imperial Police. It always struck me as strange that this police force in Burma became a seedbed of literary endeavour. Hector Hugh Munro (otherwise known as Saki) was born in Burma in 1870, son of the

Inspector General of Police. As a young man, he in turn joined the force and served in Burma for about eighteen months. He never wrote about the country but his short stories, peppered with dry humour, reflect a lonely childhood in England under the thrall of fierce maiden aunts. More notably, Eric Blair was sent out to Burma in 1922. Aged nineteen, he had only just left Eton. He spent the next five years serving as an Imperial police officer in the hot and sticky swamps of the Delta. He never really came to terms with colonial life or with Burma, factors which are reflected in *Burmese Days* – written under his pseudonym, George Orwell.

If Burma had a disturbing and lasting effect on Orwell, he in turn left his mark on the country. Today there are strangely sinister echoes of his later works. The present-day bureaucracy and the cruel intimidation of the people are like some ghastly enactment of *1984*. Other more ludicrous aspects of life are almost direct reverberations from *Animal Farm*. After the political crisis in 1988, huge red signs mushroomed up throughout the country, scarring the landscape with government messages in clear white script that read in both Burmese and English, 'Only when there is discipline can there be progress', or 'Never hesitating, always ready to sacrifice blood and sweat, is the Tatmadaw' (the military), or even 'Down with minions of colonialism' – this, curiously, right outside the American Embassy.

It was the British 'minions of colonialism' who put together the last full census of Burma in 1931. Since independence the country has been so divided by warfare that a thorough report has been impossible to produce. One of the marked achievements of the British was that they managed to bring peace to an area where tribal battles and skirmishes had become almost endemic. I feel, though, that this was largely due to the fact that they operated along a 'divide and rule' basis. There were marked and very different levels of British control. The Burmans and the other peoples (like the Mon and the Karen) who had been directly governed by the last kings of Burma, fell under full British rule. The hill states beyond Burma proper, meanwhile, were allowed a large degree of self-government. These were known as the frontier areas: the Chin Hills, the Shan States and most of Kachin State. Even more loosely administered were Karenni State and the outlying regions of Kachin State. Two tribes remained more or less beyond control of the British: the Naga in the north-east of the country and the Wa in the northern Shan States. For many of the hill tribes British rule had distinct benefits in that they were no longer threatened by Burman domination.

The 1931 census records showed that, inevitably, the vast majority of the population was employed in the production of raw materials. About 160,000 people were considered literate in English (the test being to write a letter, read it and answer it), nine English books having been published during 1930 as against ninety-three Burmese books. There were then 14.6 million people in Burma. There were over nine million Burmans, one million Shan and one million Karen. There were also over one million Indians.

The flood of these Indians into Burma was the most controversial and certainly the most resented aspect of British rule. But for the British administration they were an essential workforce in the expanding economy. Thousands would arrive by steamer from Madras, Calcutta and Chittagong: human cargoes of cheap labour. With no rigid social structure, life in Burma had considerable attractions for many Indians, particularly the low-caste labourers who could escape from some of the more degrading aspects of their miserable social status. Burma offered better and wider-ranging opportunities than many of the other countries of the British Empire such as Nigeria, Kenya, and particularly Ceylon and Malaya where work centred largely around the rubber and tea estates and afforded a very poor lifestyle and scant wages.

Public rows provide a degree of sensation and leave a wake of revealing detail. In May 1917 the Deck Passenger scandal broke. Reading through the records, I felt it provided a fine example of how Britain allowed Indian immigrant workers to become the bedrock of Burma's economic development. A full-scale inquiry was set up following allegations of gross hardship and ill treatment suffered by immigrant Indians travelling into Burma. Deck passengers from the ships of the British India Steam Navigation Company complained bitterly that they had met with inhuman disdain. Tickets were sold at exorbitant prices, well above the standard fare, but having fought to acquire these tickets passengers were subsequently treated like cattle. Thousands of travellers were forced to wait on the wharves for hours before being swiftly herded with sticks and canes on to the steamers. These had few facilities and barely enough space for the teeming masses who were driven on to them. Overcrowding became so great that in some cases the passengers were forced to sit in the life boats.

'The horrible scene I saw at the entrance makes one's heart rend to describe. I saw the durwans standing at the gate as a second god of death with sticks in their hands [and] driving and beating the passengers as if they were cattle,' wrote one Indian to J.P. Hardiman, chairman of the Deck Passengers Inquiry Committee.

The Rangoon Chamber of Commerce duly commented, 'The unrestricted inflow of labour into Burma is of the very highest importance. Burma has to depend very largely on India for the all-important labour supply with which to move her harvests . . .' In addition to the agricultural labourers, they continued, a vast number of skilled Indians worked as clerks in the Burma Railways, the Burmah Oil Company and the Irrawaddy Flotilla Company. A shortage of ships, owing to the effects of the First World War, was, the committee conceded, the main reason for overcrowding on the steamers. But they concluded their inquiry by recommending that the Indian immigrants should be treated with more respect. They advised that greater competition should be developed between steamships bringing travellers to Burma. In the aftermath of the war, they warned, there would be a vastly increased demand for Indian labour across the Empire. Burma should be mindful of the valuable contribution of the Indians.

It was easier for the British to deal with the Indians, who generally spoke better English than the Burmese and who, through longer association, were more widely understood as a race. Rangoon became an Indian city. Indian labourers took over the wharves and worked in the rice mills while those of a higher caste had government positions under British officers. The bulk of the Indian immigrants worked in the paddy fields of the Delta. These were poorly paid labourers who lived in squalid and insanitary conditions. The death rate was huge. The Burmese, who are an inherently clean and tidy people, could not exist under such circumstances and removed themselves from the towns, leaving further openings for the Indians to take over urban jobs.

It was typical of the Burmese to shrug their shoulders and look for a more pleasant way of life. Theirs was not a country of great need. They were used to an easy existence and had few demands; by and large they were content provided they had enough to eat and some spare cash for festivals and pagoda offerings – and perhaps a little gambling.

When the British had arrived in the Delta area in 1856 much of the land was jungle swamp. Elephants and tigers wandered through the heavy undergrowth which was infested with insects and was rife with malaria. Anticipating potential profit from this lush and sticky area, the British started an operation of land clearance, reclaiming the jungle and turning it into richly productive rice fields. With the construction of rice mills and the arrival of consumer goods from the West, people were initially drawn to this sparsely populated area from the dry and less fertile lands of Upper Burma. Despite the fact that this was the heartland of the Mon, traditionally an enemy territory, Burmese peasants arrived in great number and settled in the area. In 1860 there were about 50,000 acres under paddy. By 1875 over 130,000 acres of the Delta region had been transformed into productive agricultural land.

It was at this juncture that the British began to ship in

substantial numbers of Indian labourers. With them came
the *chettiars*, the money-lending classes from Madras. They
had a significant effect on the finances of the labourers.
Land clearance was a time-consuming and expensive operation and credit began to play an increasingly important part
in the balance of day-to-day life. With little understanding
of the export-driven, and essentially capitalist, economy of
the British, the Burmese made carefree use of this ready
supply of cash. Many of the British considered them to be
flagrantly spendthrift, a criticism which is not entirely jus-
tified. They borrowed with a charming and happy-go-lucky
attitude, and much of their extra money was spent on
religious donations, *pwes*, or festivals, and village feasts.
Debt crises consequently spiralled and the Indians were
increasingly resented.

In the meantime the rice production increased and became
the backbone to Burma's flourishing economy. Rice was
milled and sold to Europe, the USA and principally India
where Burma became known as 'the rice bowl of Bengal'. In
the 1930s over three million tons of rice were exported, this
was in addition to the quantities of rice consumed by a people
dependent on the crop for their national diet.

But, inevitably, statistics are deceptive. In fact by the
thirties Burma's rice economy had started to falter, and many
of the agricultural labourers were in serious financial difficulty. External factors had a part to play in this. The export market to Europe diminished due to new competition from
the developing rice harvests of the USA, the Iberian Penin-
sula and Italy and at the same time the effects of the 1930s
depression reached Burma. But matters closer to home were
also significant. There had been little progress in terms
of industrial development and the land continued to be worked
by a fairly primitive method of cultivation. Manufacturing industry also remained undeveloped and the prosperity of the
country continued to rest simply with the unearthing of natural resources – of which there were, and still are, plenty.

In 1921 a Director of Industries was appointed, but presumably this was not a great success for a year later the post

was abolished and the modest position of Superintendent of Cottage Industries created to replace it. Potential conflict of interests with India probably undermined some of Burma's industrial possibilities. The textile industry, which was given a boost in India, remained largely ignored in Burma. Weaving had been a national skill of the Burmans, particularly around Mandalay where colourful textured silks had been produced for courtly functions and ceremonial occasions. The industry all but died as cotton goods arrived from the West and little attempt was made to develop the flagging Burmese tradition. There are still a few silk weaving centres in Mandalay, but it's a costly business and even now lacks technology. Three or four people will be employed to work behind large looms painstakingly threading through the myriads of bright silks by hand. It will take weeks to produce just one lungyi length of material.

British rule in Burma is, of course, marked by omissions as well as achievements in the economic sphere as elsewhere. While manufacturing was largely overlooked, so too was the organization of a national Burmese army. This was a factor which was to gain importance in the development of independent Burma and the subsequent power struggles. Lack of an army meant lack of a power base so that the country was effectively an impotent state. Control remained with foreign powers as the British brought in the Indian army for external defence and internal security. It was an issue that puzzled me, particularly in the light of the Second World War; why was Burma denied the possibility of self-defence? When the British retreated in 1942 the country was left powerless against the onslaught of the invading Japanese.

I remember discussing the matter once with a Shan friend; 'The British must have had good reasons for not forming a Burmese army, and I am sure they were quite valid,' he remarked. The Shan, who had enjoyed a good relationship with the British, sympathized with the apparent distrust shown to the Burmans. But was it really because the British did not trust the Burmans that a proper army was never developed? Perhaps it was just more convenient, and cheaper, to use the Indian Army already in existence to control an area that was, after all, regarded by the British as an extension of India. Beyond that, though, was the whole question of the social make-up of Burma. The Indians, with their caste divisions, had a distinct warrior class (the Chatris, the Dogras and others) from whom the Indian Army was formed. As a fundamentally Buddhist country, there was no such caste structure and no such class in Burma. The history of Burma is, of course, punctuated by wars and skirmishes between different ethnic groups and there had been a proud military tradition under the kings of Burma. But after the final Anglo-Burmese War very few of these soldiers were willing to serve under the conquering foreigners and the Burmese army, as such, dispersed.

There were, however, a few Burmese recruits to the Indian Army. The Burma Sappers and Miners consisted mainly of Burmans from the plains and also a number of Karen. During the First World War this company was distinguished for their operations in Mesopotamia. There were also a number of battalions raised chiefly from the Karen and hill tribes. As the issue of Indian independence became an increasing reality, the British gradually started discharging all Burmans from the Indian Army and by the 1930s only the battalions of Karen and hill tribes remained.

Resentment of British rule and of the preference enjoyed by the Indian community reached a peak in 1930. Anti-Indian riots broke out in Rangoon, leaving about a hundred dead and a thousand injured. The disturbances were swiftly quelled but they left a simmering sense of unease. Towards the end of the year a separate movement developed in the Tharawaddy district, about fifty miles north of Rangoon; a peasant's revolt started to gather force. This was led by an individual who, with a bevy of five wives, announced himself the new King of Burma and set out to free his followers from the yoke of the British. Saya San and his army of rebels became a distinctly formidable force. The movement spread and by 1931 there were several thousand Burmese troops fighting against the British Indian Army.

Theirs, though, was a medieval army. The soldiers relied on charms and amulets to protect them from the bullets of the British, a weakness that finally led to their defeat the following August. Saya San was captured, tried and hanged.

Although the uprising had been played out by credulous and superstitious rebels who showed little understanding of modern politics, the trial of Saya San threw into prominence two figures who were to become increasingly important in the unfolding nationalist movement and the bid for independence. Saya San was defended by leaders of two of the emerging Burmese political parties: Dr Ba Maw of the Sinyetha party and U Saw of the Myochit, or Nationalist party. Doubtless the trial provided them both with a convenient political platform.

The issue of independence had begun to develop after the First World War. The Young Men's Buddhist Association (YMBA) was the first springboard for political agitation, particularly as the First World War came to an end. At that stage India, whose army had made a valuable contribution to the war effort, was being granted a greater degree of self-government. Burma, which lay on the fringes of India and had been denied any sort of national army, was not considered sufficiently developed to cope with similar procedures. The YMBA subsequently sent two delegations to Britain in 1919 and 1920 to urge for greater scope for national responsibility within Burma. Ultimately they were successful and in 1923 the first popularly elected Legislative Council was created. Such power as it had was limited to Burma proper, the area directly controlled by the British. The outlying hill states of the Shan, Kachin, Karenni and Chin continued to be loosely governed by the British, an arrangement that suited the hill tribes who were anxious to avoid coming under the control of the Burmans.

In 1937 Burma officially became a separate state from India. There had been some ambivalence about this; although the Burmese had resented the Indian workforce within their country, they nevertheless recognized that their independence movement was closely tied in with India's own negotiations for independence from the British. They feared that through separation they might lose ground and be regarded as too politically underdeveloped for significant reforms. Despite their concerns, however, a new constitution was introduced allowing for a considerable degree of self-government and with a full and widely elected cabinet to advise the British Governor of Burma – who reserved the right to ignore them.

Several political parties were established and in the absence of any national Burmese army at least two of these parties began, disturbingly, to form private armies. The factionalism and confusion of Burmese politics was well under way, and it has wearily continued ever since. In December 1936 the first and only elections to be held under the British took place. Dr Ba Maw became prime minister and held office until 1938 when he was overthrown by a coalition of opposing parties. After much wrangling and manipulation U Saw subsequently ousted the following prime minister, U Pu, and came to power at the end of 1940 against a backdrop of the widening World War. He didn't last long. On a visit to Europe and the USA the British discovered that U Saw was making secret negotiations with the Japanese, offering help in the event of an invasion. They arrested him and slapped him into prison in Uganda where he remained in detention until the war was over. His replacement, Sir Paw Tun, held an uneasy position as prime minister and remained in power until the Japanese invaded the country between 1941 and 1942.

Evacuation from Burma started in October 1941. Earlier that year it had seemed inconceivable that the country would be attacked by the Japanese. With no full resident army and no air force Burma was hopelessly unprepared for a major invasion. Ultimately the British had very little option but to pack their bags and leave, taking with them thousands of Indians and Anglo-Indians. It must have been a strange and deeply dispiriting experience for the Burmese who had to watch powerlessly as the British thakins, once regarded as a forceful ruling body, simply departed leaving them to the mercy of the Japanese.

There are appalling stories of the hundreds of thousands of civilians who had to walk out of Burma through the jungles and hills over the border into India. The casualties were immense; thousands died from disease or from horrific acts of gross inhumanity in the scramble to get out and away from the Japanese. As the Delta area fell, the British Burma government removed themselves to the hill station of Maymyo and from there they evacuated to the Indian hill station of Simla. They spent the rest of the war as a government in exile, drawing up copious plans for the future administration of Burma. There are over forty large boxes of these plans now sitting in the archives of the public record office in London. It is tempting to find their proceedings rather absurd; while the Burmese were suffering under the Japanese and British and Indian troops were fighting along the border, protecting India from Japanese invasion and building up sufficient force to repel the Japanese from Burma, there was a group of civil servants plotting the future of a foreign country they no longer controlled. But Sir Reginald Dorman-Smith, who had been the Governor of Burma, felt strongly that Britain had let Burma down and he wanted to draw up feasible proposals for resurrecting the tattered remains of the country before handing the Burmese their independence. An event he now thought would be impossible for at least ten years.

His feelings were well grounded. As the army had withdrawn, Burma was left in chaos. The 'scorched earth' policy of the British wreaked total devastation on the country as retreating troops burnt down everything of value. Oilfields, farmlands, vehicles, boats, even houses were destroyed so that they would not fall into the hands of the Japanese. The country went up in smoke and was left charred and badly damaged.

Under the Japanese Burma was declared independent and Dr Ba Maw was set up as head of state. Karenni State and most of the Shan States were included as part of this new nation but even at the outset there were wavering degrees of support for the Japanese overlords. While various politicians and independence fighters gained government positions under the Japanese, others were sceptical. Many Burmans kept a very low profile during the period of the war and the hill tribes by and large remained rigidly opposed to Japanese occupation. The Karen, who had formed some part of the Indian Army, stayed particularly loyal to the British and set up underground resistance movements. Howerver, it soon became clear that such independence as the Burmese had been granted was merely a sham. Theirs was a puppet government with the strings firmly pulled by the Japanese. Throughout the country, Burmese met with Japanese arrogance and cruelty. It was a military occupation by a foreign power that considered itself infinitely superior; the Burmese suffered a distinct loss of dignity as they were made to assist the Japanese who very often would merely turn round and, literally, slap them in the face. Having hoped and believed that the Japanese were a liberating force come to assist their fellow Asians, bitter disillusionment set in. By August 1944 a nationwide resistance movement had started, calling itself the Anti-Fascist Organization. The AFO were recognized by the British Force 136 which had been set up to promote resistance movements in enemy-occupied territory, and were already operating with the Karen.

The Japanese were finally driven out of Burma in 1945 as the British 14th Army, aided and abetted by the Burmese, fought its way down the country from India, reaching Rangoon by May that year. As the Japanese departed, they too left a trail of destruction and Burma emerged from the war a bombed, wrecked and deeply shattered country.

But if the British had assumed that they could move back into Burma and simply resume their operations with the aim of granting independence at some stage in the future, they had reckoned without the full force of national sentiment. During the war independence leaders had emerged who were of a very different calibre to the politicians serving beforehand under the British. These men would no longer tolerate British interference. With some misgivings on the part of the British, negotiations for full independence duly began.

The Second World War effectively marked the end of British rule in Burma. They had treated the country as a poor relation to India, but it had not been an oppressive or violent occupation. There had been a number of considerable achievements: peace had been maintained between the different ethnic groups, the potential of the land had been realized and Burma had been brought out of isolation into a prosperous world of international trade. The British had found themselves in a land of plenty and had made ready use of Burma's own inheritance: the fertile land, the gems, the oil, the tin and the teak. In turn I think they had fully intended to leave the country in a prosperous state. But the war intervened, heightening nationalist feelings and crippling the country.

Owing to the speed with which independence was granted, the Burmese inherited very little from the British. Because the British had insisted on bringing in Indians as civil servants and administrators, for generations the Burmese themselves had been allowed little say and little training in how to run their own country. When India was granted independence shortly before Burma, there had been a strong tradition of nationals running the administration. Burma had no such tradition and when the time came few were properly equipped to take over the reins of power. For me, this was by far Britain's greatest disservice to Burma. When the British sailed away, the Burmese were left with a country burnt down by the war, a poorly developed political and civil service infrastructure and a massive ethnic problem that the British had been able to forestall through their separate levels of administration. Perhaps the saddest aspect of Burma's independence was the legacy the British left to the loyal Karen who retained a strong British military tradition but whose bid for a separate state remained overlooked. It was to be one of the first major problems facing the newly independent Burmese government.

CHAPTER THREE

INDEPENDENCE

My first encounter with things Burmese happened in Delhi. I always felt this had a slightly absurd neatness – a tiny echo from the greater scheme of things, of how the British involvement with Burma had been channelled through India. It was in the mid-sixties. My parents had been living in Delhi for a time and had become friendly with the Burmese ambassador. The family was duly invited to lunch.

My mother explained beforehand that the Burmese ambassador was a woman, a very important lady and the widow of Aung San, Burma's great independence hero. Her name was Daw Khin Kyi. I was a fairly small child at the time and I remember being rather confused by all this information; the name above all was strange and intriguing.

Delhi, characterized by much heat and disorder, seemed to evaporate as we walked into the Burmese Residence. The living room was divided by elegant lacquer screens and was cool and very exotic with finely worked silverware on coffee tables. India outside was dirty and earthy in comparison to the neat and delicate sophistication of Daw Khin Kyi and her house. She wore lungyi and engyi and her hair was pulled back into a tight bun on the top of her head where it was ornamented with an ivory comb, a gold pin and a single flower.

Her daughter appeared and was introduced simply as

Suu, although I later established that her full Burmese name was Aung San Suu Kyi. She must have been about sixteen or seventeen at the time, extremely graceful, astute and well informed. She joined the general conversation about Indian politics; Shastri, the prime minister, had died suddenly and unexpectedly. Elections had been held and Indira Gandhi, then in her late forties, had just become India's first woman prime minister. It was a position that had once been filled by her father, Jawaharlal Nehru, the first parliamentary leader of independent India. The second generation of what was to be a Nehru dynasty had come to power. As the daughter of another Asian independence leader, it must have been an interesting time for Aung San Suu Kyi.

All these matters were quite beyond the comprehension of a small child and I stared painfully about the room. But Daw Khin Kyi was a woman of great resourcefulness and imagination. Rather than leaving me fidgeting, trying hard not to be to be bored, she produced the perfect plaything: a glass bowl was brought in filled with ruby chips and water. While Indira Gandhi and her future prospects were being discussed, I spent a happy time paddling the Burmese rubies around in the water with my fingers and running them through my hands, watching how the redness changed in different lights. At the end of our visit Daw Khin Kyi, with true Burmese generosity, asked if I would like to keep the rubies. We left without them so I suppose the gift was politely declined.

It was only when we went to live there ten years later that I began to understand the significance of Daw Khin Kyi to Burma, both as a person in her own right and as a national figure, the widow of the country's martyred hero and the mother of the nation. By that point she had retired from public life and lived in a large compound with her sisters on the banks of Inya Lake in Rangoon. Nominally she had elected to remain in seclusion but she discreetly received many visitors and was always full of good gossip about the latest political intrigues which she despatched

with much wit and humour. Our own visits would always
follow a tidy pattern. On arriving at her large and rather
crumbling house we would be taken on a trip round the
garden to admire the newest plants: orchids, roses, even a
coffee bush that had been planted by her small grandson on
a visit from England. The garden also provided convenient
scope to be able to talk openly. Indoors, even in Daw Khin
Kyi's house, there was always the danger of being overheard
by the wrong people with the risk of unhappy results for
our Burmese friends. Most delicate conversations in Burma
would always take place out of doors. After the garden
expedition we would talk in her sitting room which had a
faintly Victorian air to it; there were hard, upholstered
chairs with anti-macassars and large sepia-tinted photographs were framed on the walls – Daw Khin Kyi and Aung
San on their wedding day, Aung San in military uniform.
Then we would be offered something to eat in the dining
room. Normally Daw Khin Kyi would produce a favourite
delicacy of black sticky rice with coconut milk and melted
juggary (or palm sugar). After that it would be time to go
and we would be dismissed with an affectionate Burmese
kiss – not a quick peck on the cheek but a gentle little sniff
from a nose rubbed on each side of the face.

Daw Khin Kyi was a very keen gardener. I often felt it
was an extension of her spirit of generosity and her propensity to nurture life. She had originally been trained as a
nurse. During the Second World War she had worked at
the Rangoon General Hospital and had helped to evacuate
patients to Calcutta ahead of the Japanese invasion. She
subsequently returned to Japanese-occupied Burma and
continued her work as a nurse. It was in 1942 that she met
and married one of the patients in her hospital. He was the
young *Bogyoke,* or General, Aung San, already the most
charismatic and prominent of Burma's independence
leaders.

I find it exceedingly difficult to get a clear picture of
Aung San. The reality of the man is now so shrouded in
reverence that he has become an almost mythical figure.

His picture still hangs proudly in schools, homes and public buildings and his face still smiles up from Burmese bank-notes. In a country that had seen no national leader since the British shipped out King Thibaw in the aftermath of the last Anglo-Burmese War, during the 1940s Aung San became just the hero Burma wanted and needed.

By all accounts he was a striking and rather moody person. He was very thin and, according to one of his colleagues, looked almost undernourished. On a first meeting he seemed stern and cold. He could be awkward, anti-social and brutally frank, but he was also clear-sighted, determined and positively loquacious when he got going on political matters. 'Depending on the mood, he could talk a listener to a stage of weariness or maintain an unapproach-able silence,' wrote his university friend U Mya Sein. 'He would grit his teeth when thinking, and his well-formed lip would protrude a little. His laughter was hearty, loud and uninhibited.'

Aung San was born on 13 February 1915 in Natmauk, a small town in the Magwe district of Central Burma. He went to the National High School at Yenangyaung, which at that time must have been bustling with British and American oil drillers. From there he proceeded to Rangoon University where he studied for an arts degree, reading English literature, modern history and political science. It was at Rangoon University that he became involved in politics and in the student movement for independence. Rather than any of the political parties that gained legislative power under the British, it was this student group that ultimately led the country to independence.

Burma did not have any universities until after the First World War. The richer Burmese had gone abroad to India or to Britain for higher education. Rangoon College had been affiliated to Calcutta University and it was not until 1920 that it was elevated to full university status. By the time Aung San arrived in the 1930s it had become a focal point for young nationalist thought. He became president of the student union and editor of the student magazine

Oway. Among his fellow activists was an older student who had returned to university to study law after a stint as a school teacher. Ko, or 'elder brother', Nu joined Aung San in deliberately provocative activities against the British university authorities. While Ko Nu made openly critical speeches, Aung San published articles that were considered by the authorities almost libellous in their vitriol. Both students were consequently suspended from the university. But they had the full force of the student union behind them and over 700 students went on strike; hundreds marked a peaceful protest by camping out on the platform of the Shwedagon pagoda in Rangoon. It all had the desired effect and in the end the university authorities had no option but to reinstate the student rebels. Political agitation among student groups has continued to be a powerful weapon ever since.

By now both student activists had decided to go seriously in to politics and on leaving university Ko Nu and Aung San joined the Dobhama Asi-Ayone (the All Burma Party). Members of this party were recruited largely from ex-university students and to establish a sense of nationalist dignity they called themselves thakins, or masters – the term of deference normally used to address the ruling British. The Thakin party was highly unpopular with the British and also with many older Burmese politicians who tended to regard these younger graduates as hot-headed militants. U Saw was even known to send in his private army to break up their political rallies. Dr Ba Maw, however, chose to form an alliance with the party after his political defeat in 1940 and the Freedom Bloc was founded. This was an organization centred on general opposition to any involvement in fighting for the British during their war with Germany.

Aung San's prestige grew and he became a forceful member of the Thakin party. His subsequent push for independence is a dramatic story of subterfuge, betrayal and firm loyalty to the cause. In 1940 he was sent to a session of the Indian National Congress where he met both

Mahatma Gandhi and Nehru. On his return the Freedom Bloc had fallen into serious difficulties. After denouncing the war efforts of the Allies, Dr Ba Maw and Thakin Nu, along with many others, were arrested by the British and locked up in prison. A warrant was also made out for Aung San's arrest. Radical protests by students throughout the country forced the government to withdraw their warrant but in the meantime Aung San slipped out of Burma and headed for China where he hoped to establish contact with communist sympathizers and find assistance for Burma's independence struggle. He was then twenty-five years old.

In the meantime, Japanese agents had been moving around in Burma looking for collaborators who would assist them in the event of an invasion. They caught up with Aung San in Japanese-occupied China and took him to Tokyo where they worked out various agreements. Aung San was rigidly determined to secure Burma's independence and I think he wanted to believe that the Japanese, as fellow Asians, were sympathetic to his cause and would obligingly drive the British out of Burma, ridding the country of imperial rule. The Japanese were suspicious of Aung San's communist leanings but were ready to use him as a lever to gain Burmese support.

Disguised as a Chinese seaman, complete with false teeth, Aung San was then smuggled back into Burma. There he got together a team of thirty young men who were taken by ship to Japan where they received six months' military training under Japanese commanders. The idea was that they would return with the invading Japanese and set up a Burmese army to fight alongside the Japanese troops. At that point many of Aung San's young colleagues were being held under detention by the British and therefore were not able to take off for Japan. (Thakin Nu in any case would not have been a party to any military activities since he was a devout Buddhist.) Consequently Aung San had to spread the net fairly wide to recruit tough and able young men. They were known as the Thirty Comrades and have acquired an almost legendary place in Burmese history.

Among the Thirty was a clerk of Chinese extraction called Shu Maung. He had originally gone to Rangoon University to study medicine but had failed to complete the course and had subsequently found a job working at the city post office. He had become involved on the sidelines of political activity through his uncle who was a member of the Thakin party. It probably did not seem possible then, but Burma's recent history has been dominated by this same Shu Maung whose military and political career actively started when he was recruited as one of the Thirty.

In December 1941 the Thirty Comrades, having completed their military training, assembled in Bangkok prior to the full onslaught of the Japanese invasion into Burma. It was here that they officially founded the Burma Independence Army and pledged allegiance to their cause and to each other by pooling their blood in a cup and drinking from it. They each gave themselves an auspicious and appropriately grandiloquent name: Aung San became Bo Teza, Powerful General, while Shu Maung became Bo Ne Win, General Brilliant as the Sun. He has retained that name ever since.

In Thailand the Comrades built up a small army of Burmese who had fled from the country to join them. As they invaded Burma with the Japanese their numbers swelled, but they were a fairly raw, headstrong and untidy rabble. Many village headmen who had worked with the British were executed and the treatment the Burmese troops dished out to the Karen was particularly brutal. It left significantly bitter feelings. By July 1942 various groups within the Burma Army had become virtually uncontrollable and the Japanese ordered the whole army to be disbanded. Aung San, exhausted and dispirited, was admitted to the hospital where he met Daw Khin Kyi.

Doubts about the Japanese had started fairly early on during the invasion. It was particularly after they took Moulmein in the south of the country that incidents of Japanese bullying and disdain of the Burmese troops caused grave concern. Aung San advised forbearance and self-restraint. According to his colleagues of the time, his principal intention was to build up a strong Burmese army and to organize the people. He was firmly convinced that the future of the country lay with a powerful national army. After the Burma Independence Army was disbanded the Japanese set up a new administration and they allowed a smaller and more disciplined army to be reformed with the job largely of maintaining internal security. When nominal independence was granted in August 1943, Aung San became Minister of Defence with Ne Win as Chief of Staff of the new Burma National Army.

But already they were holding revolutionary meetings, setting up the resistance movement, the Anti-Fascist League, and planning for organized guerrilla warfare. It became increasingly apparent that the Japanese were not after all going to win the war and so the revolutionary leaders secretly made overtures to the British. They quite sensibly wanted to side with the winning team. Although this all smacks of betrayal and counter-betrayal, I think some sympathy can rest with the Burmese. The independence leaders were single-minded in their efforts to reclaim a Burma for the Burmese; as members of a fairly introspective and isolated country, the wider implications of the World War did not really impinge on their movement.

The way Burma was to achieve independence, the agreements reached and breached at that point and the divisions that were emerging even as the war ended were to have a significant effect on the shape of the future.

When Mandalay fell to Indian troops on 20 March 1945, this was a signal for the Burma National Army to take some decisive action. Although a week later Burmese troops left Rangoon with full Japanese military honours, they soon melted away into the jungle and started attacking Japanese troops. They continued their offensives while the British 14th Army moved down the country, led by General Slim.

As the British regained control of Burma there remained the awkward question of what to do with the Burma National Army and, even more of a problem, what to do

with Aung San. Was he a traitor or a hero? On a first
meeting with General Slim, Aung San claimed that his
troops and his provisional government were allies of the
British. Slim rejected this; under British law Aung San was
indeed a traitor. But the influence of the Burma National
Army and the popular support for Aung San was so strong
that the British moved with caution to avoid widespread
revolt by the Burmese people. Lord Mountbatten, then
Supreme Commander of the Allied Forces in Southeast
Asia, duly sent directives:

> On NO account will Aung San be placed under arrest.
> Aung San is to be informed that his assistance is ap-
> preciated, that any past offences against HMG must NOT
> be forgotten, that he may be required to stand trial in
> due course, and that any service to the Allied cause,
> however, both in the past and in the immediate future,
> will be taken into account.

It is interesting to speculate what might have happened if
Mountbatten had not been in charge at this juncture.
Government opinion in London and in India, where the
previous British Burma administration were still sitting it
out, was totally at odds with Mountbatten. Sir Reginald
Dorman-Smith had not yet resumed his role as Governor of
Burma and was still pushing out piles of proposals far away
in Simla. He clearly felt that Aung San should be dealt with
very firmly. Many of the British had hoped that Aung San
would be treated as a war criminal. In the event he was
never even brought to court. Mountbatten backed him and
saw him as the one man who could unite the factionalism of
Burma and lead the people to the independence they so
clearly wanted.

'Aung San should have been strung up as a traitor,' I was
told back in England by one former British resident who
had worked in Burma, fought in Burma and returned there
after the war. He felt very let down by Mountbatten.
Other, younger, British officials who first arrived in Burma
only after the war was over, were more detached and could

find some sense in preserving the status of the national leader. In any case they saw that the Burmese would no longer accept British rule and that it just remained for the British administration to sort the country out as best they could and then to leave the Burmese to it.

British military administration of Burma continued for about four months. The army Civil Affairs Service during this period was headed by General Hubert Rance. He had the uneasy task of overseeing the disbanding of the Burma National Army and the absorption of some of the soldiers into a new regular army. Aung San was pressured into agreeing to this move although he resented the fact that his army was being broken up. Shortly afterwards some 3,500 of his soldiers quietly regrouped themselves and became known as the People's Volunteer Organization (PVO); they were effectively Aung San's own private army and became an increasing public menace.

Mountbatten had, in fact, offered Aung San the position of Deputy Inspector General in the new Burma Army. During an earlier session of meetings at the Southeast Asia Allied Headquarters in Ceylon, he had advised Aung San to decide clearly whether he wanted to be a military commander or a political leader – a Churchill or a Wellington, Mountbatten had said. I cannot see that Aung San bore much similarity to Churchill, but by September 1945 he had chosen to follow a political career and he wrote to Mountbatten declining the army offer. The distinction made at this point between political and military power strangely strikes at the very heart of Burma's future problems. It was a distinction that would become increasingly blurred by the army of the new independent nation.

British civil administration duly returned to Burma and Sir Reginald Dorman-Smith came back as Governor in October 1945. Dorman-Smith was not impressed by Aung San. He was on far better terms with U Saw, the disgraced politician who had been locked up for the duration of the war, ironically enough because of his dealings with the Japanese. U Saw was released and he returned to Burma buoyant and ambitious, determined to challenge Aung San's leadership.

British negotiations with Aung San's political organization did not progress very smoothly. To emphasize its wider bid for independence, the Anti-Fascist League was by now renamed the Anti-Fascist People's Freedom League (rather a mouthful and therefore reduced to its initials of AFPFL). It was by and large an alliance of the former resistance leaders and it had been very closely associated with the Burma National Army. The AFPFL refused to take part in elections for a new executive council under the British. They were especially perturbed by a British government statement that Burma's independence would not be granted for some time. This asserted that only at the end of 1948 would Burma be considered for the status of self-government within the British Commonwealth. The Shan and other hill tribes would remain under British control until they agreed to become associated with Burma proper. In the end none of this happened. The British were forced to reconsider, and in the midst of a growing crisis, Dorman-Smith became increasingly ill, resigned and went back to England.

Sir Henry Knight, the last of the Indian Civil Service governors, became a temporary successor to Dorman-Smith. On arrival he was immediately confronted with enormous problems: there was still considerable unrest in the outlying areas of the country, the Karen were continuing to lobby for a separate state and on top of it all there was a threat of a total breakdown of internal services. The police in particular were becoming increasingly dissatisfied with their lot. The devastation caused by the war also added to the nightmarish difficulties. Knight must have been more than a little relieved when a permanent governor was appointed and, on the advice of Lord Mountbatten, General Rance was chosen to return to Burma and ease the way to independence.

When Hubert Rance arrived back in Burma in September 1946 the country was virtually paralysed by strikes: civil servants, railway and oilfield workers, students and, most importantly, the police all stopped work. Although certainly the police were on strike to demand more pay, the matter developed into an issue of political significance. The situation improved considerably when the governor began negotiating with Aung San. By the end of the month a new Executive Council, which included representatives of the minority peoples, had been set up under Aung San. Shortly afterwards the strike ended. Aung San and a Burmese delegation were then invited to London to meet Clement Attlee and discuss the next steps towards full independence.

At this stage it becomes imperative to unravel the complexities of the Burmese political situation. The AFPFL were, broadly, a socialist alliance largely drawn from the Thakin party. They were led by Aung San who, although sympathetic to the Left, was not a communist. But there had been a distinct and powerful communist group also emerging from the Thakin party. During the war they became part of the Anti-Fascist Organization. When the British resumed control of Burma, some of the communists refused to accept another imperial government and formed a splinter group, adopting the name of Red Flag Communists. They were led by Thakin Soe and dissociated themselves from the AFPFL, becoming underground revolutionaries. The other communists who initially continued to cooperate with Aung San, took on the title of White Flag Communists and were led, slightly confusingly, by Aung San's brother-in-law, Thakin Than Tun. In addition to all this was, of course, U Saw's Myochit party which continued to operate independently of the AFPFL, watching out for any chance to seize control.

Matters became still more complicated when the White Flag Communist Than Tun started to challenge Aung San for leadership of the AFPFL. Ultimately all the White Flag Communists were ousted from the alliance. They continued to operate openly and had a fair degreee of popular support. Than Tun hovered on the sidelines waiting for Aung San to make a false move with the British so that his party could form an alternative government and lead the country to independence.

But quite beyond the realms of political parties was the age-old problem of the ethnic divisions within the country. While the Burmans were dividing into rival groups angling for power, there remained the entirely separate issue of the minority groups and how they could possibly be integrated. The hill people, the Shan, Chin, Karenni and Kachin, were very reluctant to come under Burman rule. There were also the other ethnic groups living in the area the British had designated as Burma proper; these were the Mon, the Arakanese, the Karen and other smaller tribes. There was particularly bad blood between the Karen and the Burmans.

The Karen largely lived in scattered villages within what was considered Burman territory, but they were a very different race. Many of them were Christians. Undoubtedly this must have contributed to their understanding with the British and the fact that it was the Karen, above all, who had been recruited into the Indian Army. They probably made better soldiers than the essentially passive Buddhist Burmans. There is a very strong Karen Baptist tradition even today. During a recent visit to an area now held by the Karen National Union Army, I felt one small incident highlighted the enormous cultural and religious difference between the Burmans and the Karen.

The long-standing struggles with the Burmans have left many Karen communities isolated and cut off from any big towns. Many Karen children are brought up to survive in rough jungle land, but against all odds a few schools have been established for them. I was staying in a Karen area when one evening I heard faint strains of rather joyful music coming from one of the classrooms in a school near by. I went along to see what was happening.

> Walking when you're tired
> Running when you're weary

Fly like an eagle
When Jesus is your strength.

Little voices piped up from children sitting in their form room singing from the heart. I stood watching them and was joined by a couple of students who were teaching at the school. They were Burmans from the Delta who had come to the Karen territory in the aftermath of the 1988 demonstrations. As the children continued singing enthusiastically, these Buddhist students looked on, bewildered by what they clearly considered very curious antics.

When Aung San and the Burmese delegation went to London in January 1947 to negotiate for full independence there was no representative from any of the minority peoples. Agreements were reached that independence would be granted within a year, that quite substantial reparations would be made for war damage and that negotiations should be made with the hill peoples as to how they could be united with Burma proper. Unlike the hill people, the Karen had never been governed separately by the British and they remained an awkward issue.

While the Burmans were busily negotiating for independence, the minority peoples, who had enjoyed a more amicable relationship with the British, anxiously observed the proceedings. In order to draw up an agreement with the Burmans, the Shan sawbwas hosted a series of conferences for all the minority peoples at Panglaung in the Shan States. The first meetings were held in 1946. Further sessions took place in February 1947, attended by Aung San. The upshot of it all was that the Shan, Chin, Karenni and Kachin would become fully associated with Burma but would retain a degree of autonomy over internal administration. The Shan and the Karenni also reserved the right to secede from the Union of Burma after the first ten years of independence.

There remained a big question as to whether this new Union of Burma would become part of the British Commonwealth. The British had hoped and expected this would happen. But the Burmese shrank from any further association with the imperial power and the question was tossed about and debated at some length. Ultimately Aung San and the AFPFL were wary of the communists (the White Flag ones) who were hanging around in the background ready to jump on any opportunity that might be interpreted as a sell-out to the British. By remaining part of the Commonwealth the AFPFL feared that the people would think they had not managed to obtain complete independence for Burma. The sticking point had been over the issue of the King of England remaining as ultimate head of state; the Burmese had not been prepared to accept dominion status. In fact the same problem later arose over Indian independence. At that juncture the British recanted; they were reluctant to sever all links with India and so they permitted a full sovereign state to remain within the Commonwealth. But it was by then too late to reconsider Burma's position; independence had already been granted and the country had slipped away from any further direct association with the British.

Apparently Aung San himself had not been unwilling for Burma to remain within the Commonwealth and certainly this was what the governor, Hubert Rance, had wanted. Despite obvious differences in outlook, the two men developed a fairly high regard for each other; Rance was something of an avuncular figure to Aung San, still a young man in his early thirties. Lady Rance, the Governor's wife, told me of the last time she had seen the young leader. She had been ill and had returned home from hospital to convalesce. Aung San came to pay his respects and brought with him a magnificent bunch of gladioli from Daw Khin Kyi's garden. With the Governor, he sat awkwardly beside Lady Rance's bed and nervously cracked his knuckles. Then he looked shyly up at Sir Hubert and told him how he had heard that preparations for Princess Elizabeth's wedding were well under way in England. His wife, he said, would particularly like to go to the royal wedding; would it be possible as the future head of state . . . 'Ah, but

Aung San,' the Governor had teased, 'only heads of state of Commonwealth countries will be invited.'

Commonwealth or not, Aung San would never have been able to go to the wedding. He died the next day. It was Saturday 19 July 1947, and Aung San had called a meeting of his council in the half-empty Secretariat. Shortly after the session began, three young men dressed as soldiers and armed with Sten guns burst into the room and opened fire. The job done, they left as swiftly as they had arrived. Five of the council were killed outright, Aung San and another council member were badly injured and died shortly afterwards.

I spoke to a British official who happened to be holding another meeting in the next room at the time. Hearing the commotion, he had rushed in to find dead bodies slumped round a table, their feet pathetically still tucked under their chairs with their sandals half kicked off in the midst of their discussions. A few survivors had totally escaped the gun blast, others were injured and were taken immediately to hospital.

Aung San became the greatest martyr of Burmese history. Forever young, forever the hero figure, he never lived long enough to see any of his plans turn sour or to be publicly criticized for any compromising political moves. He died when he was only thirty-two and his achievements are really quite staggering. Despite the original intentions of the British, he brought the country to an independence dictated very much on his own terms. But it was also an independence he obtained by moving deftly through the minefield of Burmese politics and by acquiring the trust of the minority groups with whom he was able to negotiate. He had actually said at one point that after independence he wanted to retire from political life, having developed a distaste for the endless manoeuvrings and power struggles. He left a widow and three children: two boys, one of whom was later drowned when still a child, and a daughter, Aung San Suu Kyi, who was then only two years old.

What might have happened if Aung San had lived is a

haunting issue. Undoubtedly he was trusted and respected by the people of Burma and by many of the minority groups. He was also the founder of Burma's National Army. That army has now repressed the Burmese people and many tribal minorities for more than a quarter of a century. Had Aung San lived (and remained in control), it seems to me unlikely that he would have allowed the military to get so muddled up in politics; he had, after all, deliberately left the army to become a political leader. There are so many variables that it seems almost pointless to conjecture how Aung San might have held Burma together and what the position of the army would have been had he lived. However, Aung San's untimely death left the country without a national leader capable of manipulating the balance of power; Aung San had represented the wishes of the people while retaining the support and respect of the army.

Who killed Aung San? It is a question that still seems to leave a sneaking doubt in the minds of some Burmese. But for the Burmese law courts and for the British it was a very clear case, and there appears to be plenty of evidence to support it. About a month earlier there had been reports that a number of guns, together with ammunition, had gone missing from the Base Ordnance Depot in Rangoon. (There is a hint of possible connivance on the part of a misguided British officer here.) Aung San himself had been worried that these arms would be distributed for a revolt up country. Suspicion centred on the opposition leader U Saw and he was watched very closely. There had been subsequent plans to round up about 200 of his people and place them under protective custody on Sunday 20 July. News of this must have leaked out, for the assassination happened just the day before. It was later established that U Saw had personally seen off the assassins' jeep from his own house on the morning of 19 July. When they returned triumphant, he congratulated them. The masterplan had been to create a state of anarchy by finishing off Aung San and his council and then, in the confusion, to seize power by force. U Saw was arrested, tried and later executed.

The assassination left the country very tense. Anti-British feeling flared up as the people at first suspected the foreigners of foul play. With many of the foremost politicians of the country dead, Hubert Rance had to act quickly to avert the collapse of everything they had built up. He called on Thakin Nu, the erstwhile colleague and friend of Aung San, to take over immediately and set up a replacement council.

Thakin Nu had played his own part in the wartime struggle. He had served in Dr Ba Maw's government under the Japanese but it had been at his own house that the Anti-Fascist Organization had been founded in 1944. He had also become an increasingly devout Buddhist. At the end of the war he retired to meditate and write; he had wanted to become the George Bernard Shaw of Burma. It was Aung San who called him back into politics. At the time of the assassination Thakin Nu had been serving in the government of Burma but he had not been a member of Aung San's council and therefore he had not attended the fateful meeting.

Accompanied by members of his new council, U Nu visited London in October 1947 to draw up the final independence treaty. The date by which the British government would leave Burma was set as 4 January 1948 and it was agreed that British businesses could and should continue to operate in the country unless fairly and squarely bought out by the Burmese. It is questionable as to whether independence would have been pushed through quite so quickly under another British government, particularly given the fact that so many of the original independence leaders had been killed. Certainly Churchill had earlier criticized Attlee's Labour government for their unseemly haste in getting rid of Burma. But given the appalling experiences of the war, it is unlikely that the Burmese would have tolerated foreign rule for much longer.

It was U Nu's intention to create a state based on a mix of Western socialist ideology and Buddhist philosophy. In a speech to his Constituent Assembly on 24 September 1947,

U Nu declared Burma would be 'a leftist country in which the people working together . . . strive to convert the natural resources and produce of the land into consumer commodities to which everybody will be entitled each to his need.' But beneath the apparent influence of Western ideology, the new nation was founded very much on the Burmese Buddhist tradition of equal rights and equal status. U Nu also remained strongly guided by Burmese belief systems and Burmese astrology.

Even before the British left, U Nu sometimes felt he needed to dissolve the new council for auspicious reasons. Having observed these rites, U Nu and his council would then simply ask to be reinstated by the Governor. 'Sir Hubert became rather used to our Burmese rituals and would obligingly turn up when we asked him,' one of the former members of the council remembered with affectionate humour. 'Sometimes he would even come directly from playing a game of tennis and would still be wearing his shorts as he solemnly swore us all in again.'

It was not surprising, therefore, that the precise time for independence to be officially granted was set by Burmese astrologers. Four o'clock in the morning was deemed to be the most auspicious moment. So in the small hours of 4 January 1948 the Union Jack was duly lowered from the flagmast of Government House and the new Union of Burma flag replaced it. The British officials sailed away and Burma was left a fully independent nation.

It was actually quite an achievement. The British left with a great deal of goodwill on both sides. Given the potential problems over ethnic dissent and the bloodbath that occurred due to similar issues over independence in India, it seems remarkable that Burma's independence was achieved without blood-letting or loss of life (the assassination of Aung San's council notwithstanding). All that, though, was soon to come, and has relentlessly continued right through to the present day.

The new government was almost immediately thrown into a state of confusion by political factionalism which rapidly developed into armed insurrection. The first problem was the communists. The Red Flag Communists continued as an underground revolutionary organization; meanwhile the White Flag Communists (now renamed the Burma Communist Party) began their offensives against the government just a few months after independence. Then there was the question of the PVO, which had been Aung San's private army. Attempts had been made, even at one stage by Aung San himself, to disband this army but on independence they still remained a threatening force and with their leader assassinated they slipped beyond the control of the government. In the early stages of 1948 they had grown into a strong force of about 100,000. Subsequently the PVO also split and by July 1948 the majority group, known as the White Band PVO, had taken up arms against the government.

The inability to agree or compromise seems to be an inherent weakness of the Burmans, a self-destructive element of an otherwise long-suffering and tolerant Buddhist people. It has often been said that the Burmans are the Irish of Asia. It's not a bad analogy. There's an appealing and relaxed attitude to life, a laid-back charm, but there's also a deep sense of obstinacy. Within the first few years of independence there were fierce disagreements even between members of the government. Meanwhile the opposition splintered into smaller and completely separate groups which showed little desire to come to terms with the government and no inclination to unite as a single force. Bands of communists and PVO activists roamed the country terrorizing the people or calling on their support. At the same time they launched attacks on the Burmese government troops. But even among the government troops there were mutinies and defections as members of the military police and some battalions of the army also rose up against the government.

Within the first year of independence, U Nu's government had to contend with something in the region of nine separate groups, all in armed insurrection. It is extremely difficult to get a clear perspective on the situation, and doubtless this reflects the confusion within the country itself. Quite apart from the dissent among the Burman political forces, there was a growing struggle against the government by various of the minority peoples. Some of the ethnic groups that had not been party to the Panglaung Agreement of February 1947, went into open revolt.

On independence, Muslims from the north of Arakan had already taken to arms, and in the meantime the Mon and the Karen also formed their own armies (both of which still exist today). The Karen presented the biggest threat to the stability of the government.

'Please, have you met Saw Ba U Gyi's son in England?' I was asked by a young Karen boy when I visited his school. I felt the world was very large and I was very ignorant. I confessed that I needed an explanation. Saw Ba U Gyi, I was told, was the founder of the Karen National Union – the KNU. He was married to an English woman and his children would now be middle-aged and living in England. I was shown his picture which is printed each year on the KNU calendar and was told that he had been killed in action in 1950 when fighting against Burmese government troops.

'When did you hear about the Karen revolution?' the small boy persisted. 'Do many people know about the Karen?' he asked. I tried not to deflate his enthusiasm. It was difficult to explain that even after forty years of warfare, the rest of the world has remained largely oblivious of the KNU and their cause.

Could the British help the Karen, the boy asked. In attempting to explain that Britain was no longer a significant world power I found myself telling him about the European Community and the possibility of some sort of future economic and political unity among member states. 'Ah, perhaps the Karen join this Community,' he suggested. 'Then we'd be truly free of the Burmans.'

Right from the start the KNU had refused to recognize Independence Day in Burma and had declared that 5 May was their own independence day. Fighting broke out shortly afterwards and became particularly brutal. Provoked by the KNU troops, the Burmese army burnt down entire Karen villages, raped the women and even massacred people in their churches. It set in motion a horrific pattern that remains unbroken today. The British left the Karen with little but a legacy of warfare and a military tradition. By the early part of 1949 the Karen troops had taken a considerable amount of Burmese government territory and at one point they even reached the outskirts of Rangoon. But towards the end of the year the Burmese government army succeeded in driving the Karen forces back and re-establishing some sort of control over the country.

There's always the temptation to apportion blame. Was the Karen problem really the fault of the British, who side-stepped the issue of this minority group and sailed away leaving enormous problems behind them? But on the other hand the bitter animosity between the Karen and the Burmans dates back long before the arrival of the British whose administration of Burma merely put a temporary lid over the simmering unease. The KNU originally took up arms to fight for total separation from Burma, an independent Karenistan, for want of a better term (after all, the British were creating an independent Pakistan in India and so such things were not beyond the bounds of reason). However, as time wore on they increasingly found themselves fighting merely for survival and their ideals became modified. Today they fight for a separate state within a federal union of Burma.

Quite apart from the loss of life and the bitterness resulting directly from the struggles, the Karen insurrection had a significant effect on the future government of Burma. The Burmese military forces, which had been reorganized by the British just after the war, had been to a large extent led by the Karen. In fact the commander-in-chief of the army and the police had been the Karen General Smith-Dun. When the warfare between the Burmese government troops and the KNU became particularly fierce, these Karen leaders had felt that they were unable to fight against their own people and they had resigned. The way was left open to Ne Win, formerly one of Aung San's Thirty Comrades, and he duly took control. The army became very much his own and he built up an extraordinary loyalty and allegiance among the troops. As General Ne Win rose so the downfall of Burma's first democratic constitution started.

In spite of the appalling confusion, the bands of armed insurgents and the spasmodic warfare, U Nu's government managed to survive and by 1951 they had regained control of much of the country. Insurgency continued, and still persists today, but the government remained in power. The first general election was held in the summer of 1951 and with little parliamentary opposition the AFPFL was returned with an overwhelming majority.

There remained a further difficulty over armed activity, this time on the Chinese border. When Chiang Kai-shek's regime in China had floundered at the end of 1949, most of the Kuomintang troops had withdrawn to the island of Formosa (now Taiwan) but a number of them had slipped across into Burma. Operating principally from the northern Shan State of Kentung, at first these troops (known as the KMT in Burma) continued to fight the Chinese Communist Red Army across the border. But they intruded further and further into Burmese territory, probably funding themselves on smuggling activities centred on opium poppies which grow prolifically in the region. The Burmese army, reinforced by international political pressure, succeeded in driving many of these troops back, but the KMT continued to prowl around the region creating a sense of menace and unease.

With all the problems, the armed revolutionaries and the ethnic dissent, it seems remarkable that within the first decade of independence the Burmese government managed to lay down foundations for what might have been a prosperous nation – given time to recover from the ravages of the Second World War. The Korean War in the early fifties indirectly created a greater world demand for rice and

Burma's exports rose quite substantially. Meanwhile delegations from the United Nations were invited to advise on the development of the national economy and the social welfare of Burma. While nominally remaining an isolationist, non-aligned country, U Nu was very conscious of Burma's international status. He developed a good relationship with Pandit Nehru in spite of awkward issues arising over the claims of former Indian residents of Burma who were demanding hefty compensation for sequestered land. He made official visits to China, Vietnam and Cambodia and attended the Bogor and Bandung conferences in Indonesia.

Between 1954 and 1956 Burma hosted the Sixth World Buddhist Council (the last international Buddhist synod having been held in Mandalay during the reign of King Mindon). It was perhaps U Nu's greatest, and certainly his fondest, achievement. The Kaba Aye Zedi, or World Peace Pagoda, in Rangoon still marks the occasion. It was attended by thousands of Buddhists from all over the world but its significance was possibly stronger within Burma where it revived Buddhism as a central point of the new nation.

U Nu and the AFPFL were again returned to government after the general election of 1956. But, given the uncompromising nature of the Burmans, a serious ideological split was already emerging within the party. By October 1958 the rift had deepened irredeemably and the party divided into two groups, the Stable AFPFL and the Clean AFPFL, names which are apt to sound a little strange in English translation. Against a backdrop of confusion and some increasing lawlessness, U Nu was urged to relinquish his position and the army were asked to take temporary control of the country pending another general election. Between October 1958 and February 1960 General Ne Win, as head of the armed forces, formed a 'caretaker government' and undoubtedly acquired a strong taste for power.

History uncannily repeats itself. When I visited Burma in 1990, I could not help feeling that the military government's cleaning-up campaign bore a remarkable similarity to the

very measures taken by the army in 1958. When General
Ne Win first took temporary control of the country in 1958
he instituted a massive cleaning operation, repainting buildings, rebuilding roads and shifting whole communities from
shanty towns and slum dwellings to areas beyond the cities.
By many accounts it was a much-needed move. With all the
major difficulties the government had faced, various facets
of everyday life had been overlooked. Rangoon particularly
had become squalid; there were slum areas, public buildings
had been neglected and the general infrastructure of the
city was in a state of disrepair. There were many at that
stage who welcomed the measures taken by the army.

Under Ne Win, the military pledged to restore law and
order and to create conditions whereby a full and free
democratic election could take place. Army officers took
control of the administration and were given positions in
government departments and public industries. Initially six
months were considered sufficient to restore order but,
having taken responsibility, the army demanded more time
to be able to realize their objectives. In the event they
remained in power for a full fifteen months. But by the end
of February 1960 they had relinquished control, a general
election had duly taken place and U Nu, leading the 'Clean'
AFPFL, returned to government with a landslide victory,

Two years later, however, the army once again took over.
This time it was a full military *coup*, and it was for real. In
the early hours of 2 March 1962 army tanks rumbled
through Rangoon. U Nu and his government ministers
were arrested and later that day General Ne Win announced
that a revolutionary council had taken charge of Burma.
The army were in full control and have rigorously retained
that position ever since.

Ne Win contended that Burma needed strong, firm leadership in order to safeguard the unity of the country. On the
face of it he was right. Since independence, political and
ethnic factionalism had left Burma in a state of considerable
confusion. The British had pulled out of the area before
being able to bring together the different peoples of the

region and to lay the foundations for what would become a single, united country – an ideal, in fact, that has never really been achieved. Ethnic dissent provided a reason for the military takeover. The electorate had only fourteen years of free choice before being plunged into a system of totalitarian government. To a large extent it was simply a return to the authoritarian control that had existed under the former kings of Burma.

PART TWO

CHAPTER FOUR

MILITARY

By the 1970s the military were firmly lodged in place as the ruling class and Burma had become a frightened, reticent country. My own direct experience of the place dates from that time. For foreigners based in Rangoon, it was a strange place to live. An initial nostalgic impression of a haunting colonial heritage preserved amid golden pagodas soon gave way to a sense of stagnation and repression. Beneath the easy-going charm of the Burmese was a latent throb of unrest. There were whispered stories of people missing or suddenly thrown into prison. There was endless speculation about new restrictive measures to be taken by the military. Rumours abounded. It was often difficult to establish what, if anything, was actually happening. As foreigners we could only remain on the sidelines, sensing the intrigues and the fear.

Occasionally we escaped from it all. Foreigners had their own restrictions and our movements were severely limited. However, we were often given permission to visit an area in the State of Arakan where we found a temporary release. We would drive to the airport, fight our way on to a precarious domestic flight and, half an hour after leaving the city, we would be far away beside the sea.

Fringed with coconut groves and palm trees, long sandy shores curved for mile after mile along the extensive Arakan coast. It was a glorious cliché; an unspoilt, unexploited tropical paradise. There were stretches of coral of unimaginable and gorgeous shades of red and blue, where tiny vibrantly coloured fish darted around and larger, more ponderous types nosed through soft banks of waving fronds. There were shells with fantastic shapes and patterns. There were clear bays where the clean blue sea sparkled and rose up in waves that pummelled the golden beaches. There were no tourists. Those were balmy, sun-drenched days when every dry season we would get away from the tension in Rangoon to lose ourselves in the timeless quiet of Burma's half-deserted seashores.

We rented a little house just above the beach at Ngapali. It was really a small shack with no electricity and an open kitchen area outside around the back. It had a thatched roof which was in a permanent state of disrepair, punctured by falling coconuts from the surrounding trees. Every evening we would sit listening to the gentle percussion of the sea and we would watch the sun sink down, leaving the sky glowing with fading shades of orange and pink. Sometimes there would be a few other people in the area, mainly foreigners resident in Burma (and there were only a few at the best of times), but occasionally some of the richer Burmese would take a holiday there. President Ne Win himself had a large house at the far end of our stretch of beach; it was reputedly a handsome place.

It was at Ngapali that we met the Colonel. I cannot remember his name, if indeed I ever knew it, but he had taken the rather grander shack beside ours and after a few days we developed a nodding acquaintance with each other. Then, unexpectedly, we were invited to meet him. 'The Colonel wishes to see you,' we were told, and we were left in no doubt that this was a great honour and a command we could not ignore. It was unusual for foreigners to have any personal dealings with the army. The military were set apart, an overclass that viewed the outside world, and each other, with great suspicion. In Rangoon, permission had to be granted before any army or government members could come to our house. When they did come they were never alone. Officials would arrive in a bunch, nervously watching over each other and keeping a check on what was said or revealed. It was only in the rarest of circumstances that we could visit their homes.

I think the Colonel was merely curious about us. His seaside holiday gave him an almost illicit opportunity to meet these strange people from the free and democratic West. There were just two of us who duly strolled one morning through the coconut grove round to his beach shack. We found the Colonel sitting in his porch surveying the scene around him with the satisfaction of one who felt he deserved his privileges. He did not get up to greet us but grunted and indicated that we should sit down in two chairs that were brought out to us. Dressed only in a lungyi, he was not wearing a shirt and his bare belly descended in fat rolls and flopped over the checks of his skirt. Had we been in Burma long, he asked abruptly. Did we like his country? Our conversation followed a safe pattern of blunt questions and bland answers. Suddenly he clapped his hands, a battery-driven razor was brought to him and to our slight astonishment he started shaving. We sat in silence until he had finished this performance, which we realized had been put on entirely for our benefit.

'My wife,' he said, and waved a hand at the woman who had fetched his razor. She was dressed in a pale pink engyi and a flowery green and pink lungyi which was neatly and tightly tucked in around her waist. She smiled submissively. We nodded politely back and returned the smile. Then an Identikit woman appeared in duplicate pink and green. She was clutching a small child by the hand. 'My wife,' the Colonel said, and again waved a hand. Again we smiled and nodded politely, attempting to conceal a certain amount of confusion. Was it possible that this man had two wives? 'My wives are sisters,' said the Colonel, as if by way of explanation. I never did find out whether this bigamous arrangement meant that the Colonel was one of the very few Muslims in the army or whether, as a Buddhist, he continued to follow outmoded and outlandish marriage practices. Certainly in Burma it was extremely unusual to come across any man with more than the one wife. It all seemed to highlight the Colonel's appalling male chauvinism which was, again, unusual for the characteristically egalitarian Burmese.

Did we like milk, we were asked. Yes, we did. Three glasses of hot boiled milk were produced, one for the Colonel and one for each of us. The wives and child stood quietly on one side, excluded from this treat. 'You can tell it's pure, real milk,' the Colonel proudly told us, 'because of the skin forming on the top.' Boiled milk with a slimy membrane of skin on the surface was something I found particularly unpalatable, especially in the midst of the tropical heat, but in a country where real milk was a rare commodity I tried to appreciate the generosity on the part of the Colonel. I also suspected, more realistically, that this was another show to impress us, to let us see that as a senior army officer he was in a privileged position.

We talked a little more about Burma, about the places we had visited and about Rangoon. We even (stoically British) talked about the weather. Then we thanked the Colonel for his hospitality, he nodded fatly, and we left. He did not get up to say goodbye but he brusquely ordered one of the identical pink and green ladies to accompany us back through the coconut grove.

The arrogance and the lack of courtesy was entirely out of keeping with the gentle good manners of the Burmese. Our talk had, of course, remained entirely superficial but the visit left me with a deep impression of the sublime superiority of the army. Although I have subsequently met other, less brash, Burmese army officers, the Colonel remains fixed in my mind as the epitome of a chauvinistic, privileged class – the military élite.

When I met the Colonel, more than twelve years had passed since the army seized control of the country. During that time Burma had been transformed from a free nation into a country where the people had become increasingly oppressed, living in fear of the military as the army tightened their grip to a stranglehold on all aspects of life.

The military *coup* of 1962 had been almost bloodless. The only casualty had been an eleven-year-old boy, the son of Sao Shwe Thaike, the President of Burma. As the army tanks rolled through Rangoon that morning, the young boy got up on to the roof of his father's house. Presumably it had been an act of youthful curiosity. In a nervous reaction soldiers shot him down. Apparently the army expressed some regret over this incident; they had hoped the takeover would be a peaceful event. The boy's death, however, marked an inauspicious start to the new regime. Early the same morning of 2 March 1962, truckloads of soldiers surrounded the houses of all the government ministers. They were woken, informed that the army were now in control of the country and then they were taken away, locked up as political prisoners. Some remained in prison for as long as six years. They were six wasted years in which wives died or were forcibly deported and children grew up without their fathers. The former president, Sao Shwe Thaike, died behind bars in circumstances that remain largely unexplained. Meanwhile the country was set on a new course that was to lead Burma into stagnant isolation and economic decline.

Along with the government leaders of Burma, all the former Shan sawbwas were also rounded up and taken into custody. The former sawbwa of Kentung had been a patient at the Rangoon General Hospital at the time; soldiers took him straight from his hospital bed to jail. It was the Shan, the military claimed, who had disturbed the equilibrium of the country and had given the army no alternative but to seize control. Under the Panglaung Agreement of 1947 the Shan had reserved the right to secede from the Union of Burma ten years after independence. I have been firmly assured that in 1962 the Shan, collectively, had no intention of realizing their claim, but General Ne Win alleged at the time that Shan leaders were secretly negotiating with the government for a separation that would cause untold damage and disruption to the security and unity of the State. It was undoubtedly an excuse rather than a reason for the military *coup*.

In any case, the Shan sawbwas had relinquished all their rights back in 1959. Within the socialist ideology of the new nation, the princely existence of the sawbwas had been considered anachronistic. Medieval courtly life had duly come to an end as papers were painstakingly drawn up and the sawbwas were pensioned off and replaced by civilian administrators. One of the former sawbwas told me:

> Within the new Union of Burma, we remained a federation of states. It was a very workable system. The Shan States were well organized and fairly prosperous. I don't think the Burmans themselves cared very much for this, they have a history of totalitarian government and they've never really understood the idea of federalism.

Burma in the early 1960s was still feeling its way through the aftermath of colonialism and the devastating effects of the Second World War. Since 1948 the civilian government had been juggling with economic, ethnic and political issues to retain control of a country whose enormous potential, in terms of natural resources, remained relatively undeveloped. It was still a land of promise. But in the light of General Ne Win's takeover, some fairly black pictures have been drawn of Burma's first decade of independence. It has been described retrospectively as a chaotic period of political power struggles and civil wars, a time of anarchy and internal division. Yet when I talked to foreign businessmen, who had continued to live and work in Burma during the fifties and early sixties, a rather different view emerged. They maintained that despite the initial problems immediately after independence, the country did not dissolve into total confusion. It was, they said, perfectly possible to continue their operations. Burma had remained a pleasant, easy place to live. 'In all probability the civilian government would have muddled amiably through their problems,' I was told.

What, then, was the real justification for the military *coup* of 1962? Power struggles within the leading party led to the collapse of U Nu's government in 1958. When the army consequently stepped in to take temporary control, they showed they were capable of controlling the country and of establishing a clear sense of law and order. It proved to be a useful dress rehearsal. After the army stepped down and U Nu's party was re-elected in 1960, the political in-fighting continued and in the meantime insurgency among the ethnic minority groups became an increasing threat. Although the activities of the Karen rebel army had been curbed since about 1951, the situation remained explosive and continued to menace the government. Other rebel groups also took up arms; by 1961 a few of the Shan had gone into open revolt while to the north, beyond the Shan States, militant Kachin had set up the Kachin Independence Army (the KIA). In 1962, the internal political and ethnic unrest gave the army some grounds for their takeover, although many saw the military *coup* merely as Ne Win's personal bid for power.

With hindsight it is difficult to gauge what the initial reaction of the Burmese people must have been. Views and opinions have become coloured over time. Today few Burmese who are willing to discuss the matter with foreigners would ever admit they had actually welcomed the military takeover. Interestingly, international opinion at the time was clearly supportive of Ne Win; in Britain, a leader in *The Times* of 3 March 1962 commented:

> The army took over ... to end factional disputes and the corrupting influence of an unprincipled struggle for power ... General Ne Win ... will ... have to justify his action, though that may not be difficult when so many Burmese have suffered from the tyranny of political bosses. He will have to expound his policies. From what is known of him they are likely to be sensible and moderate.

Today this seems an odd view. Despite the enormous problems they had confronted, U Nu's government had not been a tyrannical regime. In fact, far from it; U Nu himself had been eager to promote Buddhism as the gentle guiding force of the country. The army, on the other hand, was something of an unknown quantity. Although Ne Win's previous fifteen months in power had shown him to be a strong and efficient ruler, subsequent events were to prove *The Times* inordinately optimistic in supposing that his policies would be either sensible or moderate.

The first sign of repressive action came about two weeks after the *coup*. As I have mentioned, horse racing was banned. With a curious sense of priorities, beauty contests shortly went the same way. These had been a legacy of foreign rule. The military had taken power to bring order to Burma but they also quickly proved themselves anxious to rid the country of foreign influence and foreign exploitation. It was Burma for the Burmese. A process of rapid nationalization began as banks, shops and private companies became State controlled and all foreign businesses were expropriated. The position for foreigners in Burma became extremely uncomfortable. Most of these people were Indians who had come over to Burma during the days of the British and had lived there for generations. Many of them were forced to leave, while the private enterprises they had owned fell into the hands of the new regime. Others stayed on and suffered the consequences. It became extremely difficult for anyone of foreign extraction to get a job. Indians, Burmese of Indian descent and even Anglo-Burmese were left largely unemployable. The official attitude to foreigners and to the outside world subsequently developed into almost paranoid xenophobia.

On taking control of the country, the military set up a Revolutionary Council. Headed by General Ne Win, this was a group of seventeen military officers who claimed absolute power and total authority over the people. On 30 April 1962, they published a declaration of their policy. Entitled 'The Burmese Way to Socialism', it was effectively an interpretation of Marxist socialism within the context of traditional Burmese thought. Parliamentary democracy was rejected as being unsuitable for Burma and the Revolutionary Council declared an intention to start a process of socialist democratic education and training. From a Western point of view, I find it difficult to understand this particular interpretation of socialism; in the light of subsequent events I still find it puzzling today. State control gradually extended over most aspects of life; there were People's Shops and People's law courts, and agricultural activities became largely subject to the dictates of the new government. This State control effectively meant army control and military officers were placed in all top administrative positions. Former army colonels became chiefs of all industry, agriculture, pearl collection and fisheries, forestry and even mining. They ranked well above those who had specific training in these fields (the agricultural scientists, engineers, minerologists and others) and, significantly, they had total control. It undoubtedly had a crippling effect on the economy.

The official formation of the Burmese Socialist Programme Party – the BSPP – was announced with the publication of their formal constitution on 4 July 1962. The party was really a support team for the Revolutionary Council and subsequently all other political parties were abolished (in any case, most of the opposition leaders were by then residing in Burmese prisons). This was followed by another publication, 'The System of Man and his Correlation to the Environment', which came out in January 1963. It reflected the very curious philosphy of the BSPP, an eccentric mixture of Marxist, humanist and Buddhist thought which seems idiosyncratic almost to the point of incomprehension.

I feel that my own difficulty in understanding the military government's policies and philosphy must to some extent be due to their rejection of Western ideals and the reversion to what they considered traditional Burmese political thought. There are, though, many civilian Burmese who remain equally confused. But while I was merely an observer, the system introduced by the military was one the people of Burma have had to live with for more than twenty-six years.

The government's stance against foreigners and foreign interference turned Burma in on itself. The country was plunged back into a state of isolation not dissimilar to that of the Burmese kings who had remained proudly aloof from the outside world until the arrival of the British. It was argued (with some degree of justification) that in Burma's own experience colonial rule had resulted merely in exploitation. Foreigners had grabbed at all the riches of the land and had left the Burmese themselves with very little. Introspection became the hallmark of Ne Win's administration.

I've often felt that Burma has become rather like the 'sensitive' plant, which grows abundantly (like all other vege-tation) in the Delta. If you brush the delicate, pointed leaves they curl up, recoiling from the touch of an external force. Wandering down to the sailing club in Rangoon, I used to pause by bushes of sensitive plants. It was always a bit of a game to see if, by quickly touching all the leaves, an entire bush could be made to curl in on itself before a few brave leaves would unfurl to face the world once again.

Burma is only now unfurling itself but the self-imposed retirement from the world has had some obvious advan-tages: Burmese culture has been very strongly retained. Ne Win's socialism embraced a nationalist fervour that pro-tected the country from some of the more crass develop-ments of the modern world. Western, and indeed Japanese, culture was never perceived as being in any way superior. Burma has been allowed to preserve intrinsically Burmese qualities of life. Initial impressions are of a country whose cultural integrity remains complete, whose national values have not been degraded. The people still wear their national dress, the pagodas remain tranquil places of worship rather than tourist sites, the cities have not been turned into jungles of concrete and high-rise buildings.

Ne Win's isolationist policy also kept the country free from the massive upheavals that have shaken Southeast Asia. The ravages of war in Vietnam and Cambodia have not touched Burma. The people have not suffered from external conflict and any resulting famine or disease. Burma has remained tucked away in the backwaters of international politics, contending only with itself. When Ne Win came to power in 1962, he outlined his foreign policy: he would, he said, steer a peaceful, neutral course in world affairs. At the outset this seemed little different from the pronouncements made on independence by U Nu. Burma had subsequently joined the Non-Aligned Movement along with India and Pakistan. But Ne Win's bid for total non-alignment proved so extreme (so pure, some of the more indulgent might argue) that Burma actually left the Non-Aligned Movement in 1979 to go it alone.

Isolation underlies the lack of development within the country. Elephants haul teak in the jungle, buffaloes work the land; these traditional, old-fashioned methods tend to conjure up images in my mind of a lush, romantic country; sepia-tinted impressions of a place where time has charmingly come to a standstill. It is tempting to think of Burma as a living museum, a sort of theme park of folklore, with jewelled temples, quaint buffalo carts and men in skirts. The reality is somewhat different. Locked away from the outside world, the country is trapped in a sinister time warp where progress has been rejected in the name of cultural integrity.

The central figure of latter-day Burmese folklore is Aung San, the quixotic symbol of Burma's independence and Burma's hopes. He remains at once the hero of modern Burma, the founder of the Burmese army and the nation's great freedom fighter. Aung San the outspoken student, Aung San the wartime leader of the Thirty Comrades, Aung San the forthright politician: these images have produced conflicting interpretations of his legacy. For the military, Aung San was the champion of the army. Ne Win himself has shrewdly preserved the memory and the legend of the nation's hero, subtly attempting to position himself and the army as the inheritors of all that Aung San had struggled to achieve. But for generations of students and disabused civilians Aung San was the architect of a free nation, a leader who fought only for the ideals of his country.

The students were the first to mark a protest against the military takeover. In July 1962, five months after the army *coup*, students at Rangoon University began a series of peaceful demonstrations. On 7 July things started to get very nasty: soldiers fired into crowds at the university campus. Official reports claimed that only a few students were killed, but in reality it is thought that the death rate reached the hundreds. The next day the student union building was blown up by the army. The massive explosion was a dramatic show of the strength and power of the military. The student movement was crushed; open opposition to the new regime became a foolhardly activity while underground dissent grew increasingly fraught with danger.

In the 1930s it had been a student movement that had launched Aung San as an independence leader. It was the student union that had supported him and had shown their strength by peaceful protest. Today, the story of Burma's struggle for independence is a national epic while the destruction of the student union building fourteen years after independence is the first part of a long tale of repression. By striking at the very beginnings of the Aung San legend the army started an endless series of contradictions; they remained unquestionably loyal to the memory of Aung San as the founder of the army, but they had blatantly destroyed a symbol of his fight for Burma's freedom.

Ne Win claimed that the student demonstrations of 1962 were led by activists from other political factions, principally the Communist party. These people, it was implied, were the enemies of the State and this provided the justification for the army violence. In September that year, as the monsoon ended and the country once again became easier to cross, the army started a major campaign against those other enemies of the State – the rebel armies.

The Red Flag Communists, the Communist Party of Burma (BCP), the rebel Kachin, Shan, Mon and Karen all had active, armed guerrilla groups. There were also various smaller armies from some of the other ethnic minorities – the Arakanese, the Chin and the Karenni. Since independence the Burmese army had been fighting the growing number of these groups to maintain the country's internal security. In 1962, when the military ousted the democratically elected government, they were able to bring a greater part of the country under their control and this in turn increased their authority and the legitimacy of their rule. By 1963 amnesties were offered and a series of peace talks were held starting in July that year. There was some temporary success with the Karen National Union but by November most negotiations had broken down and the rebel groups reverted to their insurgent activities. The BCP were increasingly supported by the Chinese and consequently the Burmese army had to move with caution to avoid provoking a large-scale offensive (and, possibly, even an invasion) on the part of this powerful neighbour. But in any case, internal conflict gave the army a reason for remaining in power. Burma was not at war with any other country and, it could logically be argued, the army needed an enemy (even several enemies) to justify the continued military occupation of their own country.

General Ne Win's army protected the State. This was the message that came across loudly and clearly when we lived in Rangoon during the seventies. However, who, exactly, the State was being protected against remained a blurred issue. There was (and still is) a confusing quantity of separate rebel armies, but within the government-controlled part of Burma the military authorities managed to refine this into a general and pervading impression of threat. There were few specifics and very little was reported about actual rebel activity. It was a smart move on the part of the government. They created and sustained the sense of a faceless enemy with whom, through lack of detail or information, the people could have little sympathy. Intermittently news would come through of advances on the part of government troops, but insurgency remained the broad and undefined term for all groups in armed opposition. We would occasionally hear that someone's nephew or cousin had 'gone off to join the insurgents' and very often the news would be left at that. Perhaps it was because we were outsiders, or perhaps it was because the relatives were fearful of army reprisals, but there always seemed to be scant information about which precise insurgents and what they were actually fighting to achieve.

The government's power hinged on the control they established over communications. There is still little, if any, communication between the insurgent groups and the people within Burma proper and there is hardly any contact with the outside world. Within the government-controlled area, Burma is an awkward country to travel through; there are few good roads, cars and lorries are ancient and, in a country that once produced millions of barrels of oil, petrol is scarce. Travel along the seaboard or by river, rail and air is carefully monitored by the army, and, in any case, within the transport sector all top positions are held by former army officers. Personal movement is therefore difficult and limited. The media, meanwhile, is totally controlled by the government. There is no free Press. Newspapers in both Burmese and English read like some parody of a government handout, while the real issues of the day remain largely unreported.

The voice of the free world, bringing international news and reports of events within Burma, crackles through on the Voice of America and the BBC World Service. For many Burmese people these radio transmissions are their life blood. But in order to broadcast reports about Burma, all real news is hazardously obtained and sneaked out of the country. A ban against foreign journalists has periodically been lifted, only to be reimposed again with more vigour.

While nothing much seemed to happen in Burma and the country continued to show a dismal lack of any progress or development, it was always deeply frustrating to feel that information was constantly being withheld and that the people were being conned into a state of uneasy submission. There have, though, been periodic moves to create the illusion of change. This has been achieved largely through empty gestures and through nominally reshaping and re-forming the government. In January 1974 a new constitution was adopted. The Revolutionary Council was formally replaced by the one legal political party in Burma, the BSPP. It was the military in another garb. For what it was worth, the Union of Burma was renamed the Socialist Republic of the Union of Burma. But the changes were merely niceties. New names did not signify a new start and life continued in much the same pattern.

The chairman of the Burmese Socialist Programme Party became the new President of the country. He was the former head of the army, General Ne Win. In order to produce a semblance of civilian rule, many army officers had officially retired from military service only to pop up again in the reshaped government. Ne Win shed the prefix 'General', presenting himself in mufti with the Burmese honorific 'U', or Mr, but few have ever dissociated him with the military, and certainly he continued to command an extraordinary allegiance from the armed forces – they remained his own troops.

Ne Win became a military dictator, the most feared man in Burma whose power and control was more extensive than that of the Burmese kings a century before him. Conversely, his public image is still characterized by paranoia. Even before the military *coup* he displayed an almost unnatural fear of assassination; in his office he always kept a revolver beside the blotter on his desk; whenever he visited the golf club he was invariably accompanied by a battalion of his men while other soldiers were posted along the route, lurking in peoples' gardens with their guns trained on the houses. A quiet game of golf became a military exercise. In the course of time Ne Win has almost disappeared from public view, heightening speculation about his private life and his wealth. His paranoia has reverberated back on the people; few will dare to mention his name even in whispers. In the seventies he was referred to elliptically as 'The President', 'The Chairman' or, with shocking familiarity, 'The Old Man'. Today he is nominally no longer head of state but people will still drop their voices to talk about 'Number One'. Such intimidation is catching; even in England I found myself studiously avoiding having to mention him directly by name.

It was widely known that Ne Win enjoyed the good life. He was a keen gambler and, despite the ban he imposed on horse racing in Burma, his subsequent visits to Ascot have been frequent and extravagant. He used to come over to England and Switzerland fairly regularly for medical checks and he has established loyal friendships in both countries. Despite the fact that he never completed his own medical training, he retains a deep interest in the subject – this undoubtedly underlies the highly respected status of the medical profession within Burma today.

The authoritarian control of the military has obvious echoes of the totalitarian rule of the Burmese kings. Ne Win himself has shown an obsessive interest in Burma's past and Burma's culture. On becoming head of state, one of his first international negotiations centred on a symbolic aspect of Burmese history. When the British had moved into Mandalay back in 1886, not only did they remove King Thibaw but they also seized many of the Burmese crown jewels. The Mandalay Regalia subsequently became part of the collection of Indian art at the Victoria and Albert Museum in London. In 1964, as a gesture of good-will to the new head of State, the British agreed to return most of these treasures to Burma. There were 167 cere-monial items (courtly jewellery, salvers, urns, images of sacred birds) mostly of pure soft gold-encrusted with huge pigeon-blood rubies, jade and other precious stones from Burma. In November that year Ne Win came over to London where Lord Mountbatten, with all due ceremony, handed him the first of the treasures. It was not the most valuable piece in the collection, but it was certainly the most symbolic. Ne Win carried back to Burma a wooden sword sheath covered in (slightly grubby) cream velvet and decorated with gold and rubies. It was valued then at just £15 but in terms of its historical significance it was priceless. The sheath had belonged to Alaungpaya, the founder of the last dynasty of the Burmese kings.

By July 1965 most of the treasures had been returned to Burma, and they now sit in glass cases at the National

Museum in Rangoon. It's a gloomy building, rather badly lit, but the kingly treasures are all there: King Thibaw's great Lion Throne, gilded and jewelled swords, knives and royal robes in various states of decay. When I was last in Rangoon I had to pay US $5 dollars (hard currency) to take a look at them. I asked my guide why many of the precious stones seemed to be missing from the treasures (there were blank holes once filled by jewels and I even noticed that the back of a golden urn had been shaved off). After an embarrassed silence I was told they had all been stolen.

Like the Burmese kings before him, Ne Win has had a number of wives, but not all at once. It is widely reported that he has been married seven times. When the military *coup* took place Ne Win was married to Daw Khin May Than, reputedly his third wife. Along with many Burmese of the same generation, she had also adopted an Anglicized name and was principally known as Katie or Kitty. She had been a nurse and had worked at the Rangoon General Hospital during the Japanese occupation of Burma. Trained by the British, she had developed a fairly high regard for Western culture and capitalist comfort and this was said to have been the cause of a great many violent arguments with Ne Win. At one point she was even thrown out of the State House because of her untenable extravagance. Ne Win himself was hardly frugal so these expenses must have been formidable. However, since Ne Win was known to be extremely fond of Katie, she was later allowed to return.

Katie and Ne Win had four children: three girls and a boy. The eldest daughter, Sanda, became a particular favourite of her father. Although she was trained as a doctor, it seemed that by 1989 she was being schooled and presented as the second generation of a Ne Win dynasty. But, like her father, she has subsequently disappeared from public view; an American businessman who was allowed a rare opportunity to visit Ne Win in 1989, noted that Sanda Win had inherited her father's paranoia and even kept a revolver by her plate during dinner.

I find the looming, shadowy figure of Ne Win one of the more recent puzzles of Burma. There are many who hold that he is the ogre of the present-day country, that he sought power entirely for his own ends and that he is personally responsible for the subsequent misery. However, there are some who maintain that he genuinely wanted the best for Burma, that he originally seized control to avert a national disaster and to hold together his disintegrating country. Those who have known him well will insist that his love of the country has been very real; he was, they say, a man slightly out of his depth, convinced that Burma's problems would best be solved by adhering to a strict socialist doctrine. He relied heavily on his wife Katie, and when she died it seems that Ne Win's personal life went slightly awry. His control over the army, however, remained absolute and, for all the criticisms that can be levelled against him, Ne Win has proved to be one of the world's great survivors.

When Katie died in 1974 she was deeply mourned by Ne Win despite the violent swings of their marriage. Her successor was a distant relation, Daw Ni Ni Myint, who was a very different calibre of person and worked as an academic at the history department of Rangoon University. Daw Ni Ni Myint herself was extremely critical of some of Ne Win's actions, notably the savage demolition of the Student Union building back in 1962. She is known to have braved Ne Win's fury by remarking that the destruction of a symbol of Burma's independence would only cause Ne Win to go down in history with a tarnished reputation. There were subsequent moves to rewrite this episode and dissociate Ne Win himself from the incident.

Daw Ni Ni Myint's marriage did not last long. It was rumoured during this time that Ne Win's frequent visits to Europe included trips to Italy where he was becoming very friendly with a woman of Burmese descent who had been married to an Italian. Ne Win subsequently divorced Daw Ni Ni Myint and June Rose Bellamy arrived in Burma from Italy. We were living in Rangoon at the time, and the stories became particularly colourful.

June Rose Bellamy was distantly related to King Thibaw. Her mother was a Princess Ma Lat, the granddaughter of one of King Thibaw's uncles (who was murdered by an ambitious brother). Princess Ma Lat had married the Australian race course manager at Maymyo and their daughter had grown up partly with a Western outlook and partly with a deep sense of her regal heritage. She was called June Rose but she also kept her royal Burmese name Yadana Natmai. She had lived a cosmopolitan life and was able to claim a variety of nationalities. While remaining Burmese she also had an Italian passport and she retained a right to British citizenship through her father (who had opted to hold a British rather than Australian passport). But when she subsequently married Ne Win, Rangoon became alive with speculation that the President was seeking to associate himself directly with the royal lineage of Burma.

It was not a happy marriage. June Rose was as wilful as her husband. In 1977 she was forced to relinquish her British passport when she accompanied Ne Win on a state visit to China and Nepal. By all accounts her behaviour was less than exemplary and Ne Win was publicly embarrassed. When they returned to Burma, their private rows became brutal. Rangoon buzzed with gossip.

It was rumoured that Ne Win accused June Rose of degrading and insulting Burma's international image through her appalling conduct. The arguments became violent and at one point, so the story goes, Ne Win threw a heavy ashtray at his wife which bruised her face. The next day a mysterious woman wearing a dark hat and veil was seen at the airport on her way out of Burma. June Rose did not return and Ne Win subsequently remarried Daw Ni Ni Myint.

It is thought that there is one further addition to Ne Win's catalogue of wives. During the public unrest in 1988 Ne Win, who is deeply superstitious, consulted the astrologers. They apparently recommended that he should make another, formal marriage. Ne Win's latest wife is believed to be a young woman in her twenties. But it is generally held that the arrangement has remained purely ceremonial and is of no domestic significance. Daw Ni Ni Myint is also still Ne Win's wife and has become the head of the history department of Rangoon University – where in 1990 they were busily rewriting Burmese history.

Quite apart from Ne Win's many marriages, Rangoon reverberated with scandals about his Swiss bank accounts, new legislation entirely based on Ne Win's superstition and arbitrary arrests of Ne Win's close associates. His violent moods were a subject of constant public alarm.

I was once a party to one of Ne Win's bizarre displays of public outrage. It was Christmas 1975. Burma had been under martial law since public riots broke out in 1974 but towards the end of the following year conditions were gradually eased and the curfew was lifted. The Inya Lake Hotel in Rangoon decided to take advantage of these clement business conditions and set about organizing a party for Christmas Eve. It was the first public party for some time. Tickets were on sale to the general public and were eagerly bought by anyone who wanted to be considered the cosmopolitan élite of Rangoon.

Inya Lake is a sizeable stretch of water in the middle of Rangoon. It's a prestigious area; along the banks of the lake, combating the mosquitos, are the US Embassy, the Russian Embassy Residence, the Inya Lake Hotel and, on the opposite side of the water, the heavily guarded home of Ne Win himself. The Inya Lake Hotel was built by the Russians in the 1960s and has an appropriate feel of the Eastern Bloc with characterless slabs of concrete and dark stuffy rooms. In the seventies it offered little in the way of elegance or luxury, but it was serviceable and was recognized as being the most up-to-date hotel in town. It was rivalled only by The Strand Hotel, whose atmosphere of depressingly faded glory and whose rumoured supply of rats did little for its reputation among visiting businessmen.

The Inya Lake Hotel had prepared for an event Rangoon would remember for some time. The party was held out of doors on the banks of the lake under a starlit sky. It was lively and was filled with people of some importance, sons and daughters of army officials, businessmen and members of the foreign community. It was a decorative occasion; there was music, there was dancing, there was a live band.

Towards eleven o'clock I noticed that we had been suddenly and silently surrounded by men in khaki carrying loaded guns which were trained on the crowd. A murmur of 'The President' became audible and I naïvely thought that Ne Win himself had come to join the party, bringing along a few soldiers for good measure. The band continued playing for a while but people on the dance floor rapidly melted away as more men in khaki with guns and heavy boots swarmed in. Ne Win leapt up on to the bandstand and the music stopped abruptly.

In the heavy silence that followed I watched as the President wrenched the drumsticks from the hands of one of the musicians and thrust them through the skin of the drum. The noise was picked up on the band's microphones. It made a hideous sound.

The atmosphere bordered on mute hysteria as a crush of people struggled to get out, leaving a few of the braver Burmese and the bewildered foreigners at their seats. The President started shouting at a European who had begun to object. There was some commotion as the man's wife then stood up. She was wearing a fairly low-cut dress which was personally and publicly ripped down the front by Ne Win. Then she was thrown back into her seat while her husband was roughed up, much to the amazement of all the on-lookers. I believe the couple left Burma for good the next day.

As the soldiers moved in to break up what remained of the party, I found myself being swept up and taken home by some friends. I later caught up with my original companions of the evening who had decided to remain there as long as possible, curious to see what on earth would happen next. A soldier had approached their table and indicated that they should leave immediately. They stayed firmly seated, pointing out that there was still half a bottle of beer to be finished. The soldier picked up the beer bottle, broke it against the edge of the table and thrust the jagged edge at them, repeating that they should leave. They went, defeated and outraged that such a harmless party should have caused so much aggression.

It was a bit difficult to understand why the President of Burma had decided personally to break up an orderly public party. Beyond being irritated by the noise from the other side of the lake there seemed little cause for such an extraordinary show of temper. It was later thought that he had had a row that evening with one of his daughters. She had then disappeared and in a towering rage Ne Win had assumed that she was at the party.

The incident (vastly inflated by rumour) became the scandal of Rangoon for weeks afterwards. It was even reported in the Bangkok Press in Thailand. Overnight, members of the band became local heroes, and I was later told that some of them then decided to walk out of Burma into Thailand. They never came back. All Western music was banned thereafter and for years there were no more public parties. 'It was the night Christmas Eve became Boxing Day,' as one Burmese friend remarked.

The Inya Lake Hotel fiasco certainly gave me an idea of what life was really like for the people of Burma. Quite beyond Ne Win's bizarre display of ungovernable rage, I was most shocked by the total panic and fear I had witnessed as the terrified people had silently scrambled to get away from the President and his army.

As a foreigner, it was extremely difficult to establish exactly how this army is recruited, although, this of course is a crucial factor underlying Burmese life. All the questions I asked were carefully side-stepped. Who were the officer class? Were they all commissioned or were some NCOs? I found some answers in the diaries of the late Earl Mountbatten of Burma and was taken on a trip to Maymyo to see the Burmese Services Academy where the officers were trained. His comments at the time continue to be significant: 'Incidentally, it seems quite odd that with an army of over

120,000 . . . they have only one or two Brigadiers, and all the rest are Colonels . . . In fact the only General is Ne Win himself.'

Of course, there have since been other generals in the Burmese Army but the position of the colonels has continued to be notable. Yet, for all their rank and power, it seemed, when we lived in Burma, that few of their sons would themselves join the army. Perhaps it was just that they failed to make the grade; however, it was rumoured that many sons of colonels would be sent abroad to university – and often they did not return.

Given that most Burmese live in fear and dread of the military it seems unthinkable that anyone would want to join this team of repressive bullies. But there are distinct advantages in being a soldier: pay, privileges, a future for the family. Many of the soldiers I saw on my last trip appeared to be painfully young. They were adolescents of about sixteen, I was told, largely unsophisticated people from the countryside, untainted by too much education.

More feared and more powerful than the ordinary troops, however, is the military intelligence. While Aung San had been the founder of the Burmese army, the Military Intelligence Service (the MI) was Ne Win's special creation. Before 1958, military intelligence units had been set up to gather information about insurgent activities. They were, apparently, not particularly effective. Under Ne Win's caretaker government this section of the army was revamped and reorganized. Major Tin U, who had been trained in England and the USA, was appointed by Ne Win to expand and retrain the military intelligence forces. He became Ne Win's right-hand man. After the 1962 *coup d'état*, Tin U was responsible for teaching, and indoctrinating, all army troops in 'The Burmese Way to Socialism'. The MI became increasingly powerful and their operations gradually extended beyond merely gathering information to assist troops fighting the insurgent armies. In time, MI officers even gained positions in government ministries (already run by ex-army officers). They became a network of spies, a powerful secret police force monitoring the activities of ordinary people.

Burmese names are confusing. There are no traditional family or clan names; people will simply be given one, or a series of 'first' names. Consequently there are numerous repetitions and quantities of people have exactly the same name. In the army, there were two very powerful Tin Us: Tin U, the head of military intelligence, and Tin U, the defence minister. Both men commanded a great deal of respect and loyalty from their troops, both men became very close to Ne Win and both men suffered the same fate. They became too powerful. General Tin U, the defence minister, was discredited, tried and sent to prison in 1976. He was released in 1980 and kept a low profile until 1988 when he became actively involved in the democracy movement. Brigadier-General Tin U, the chief of military intelligence, was forced to resign, accused of corruption and thrown into prison in 1983. The military intelligence forces were then purged of other corrupting bodies (including, presumably, those who had been dangerously close to Tin U), and in 1984 Brigadier Khin Nyunt was appointed as the head of the Directorate of the Defence Services Intelligence, the reorganized military intelligence service. He subsequently became one of the most powerful men in Burma. It is widely suspected that he gained too much control; in October 1989 Brigadier-General Tin U was unexpectedly released from prison, many saw this as a move on the part of Ne Win to counter the growing strength of Khin Nyunt.

There's always been much speculation about who could possibly succeed Ne Win, particularly now that he is an old man in his eighties. It's a difficult question; it seemed, when Ne Win first came to power, that his close associate Brigadier Aung Gyi was the most likely candidate. However, just one year after the *coup*, Aung Gyi was dismissed; he had been openly critical of Ne Win's economic policies. He was subsequently posted to Australia and was not recalled until the late seventies. When Aung Gyi returned to Burma he was told to wait until he was called by Ne Win. He waited for years. In 1980 he was permitted to go

1. U Ne Win, leader of
the coup that overthrew
the democratically
elected government.

2. U Nu, former Prime
Minister deposed by
Ne Win, now leader of
the League for
Democracy and Peace.

3. Brigadier U San Yu,
President of Burma
1981–88

5. Ex-King Thibaw is
removed from his palace
at Mandalay to the
British ships (1886).

4. The storming of Zeedaw by the Royal Welch Fusiliers during the expedition to Upper Burma (1885–6).

6. Sir Hubert Rance, Governor, and Sao Shwe Thaik, President of the newly constituted Burmese Republic, take the salute at the Independence ceremonies (1948).

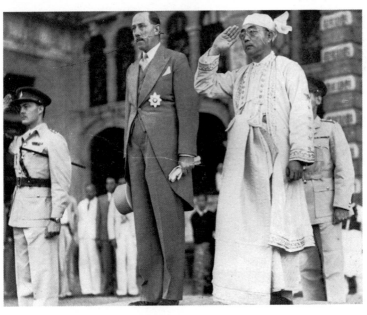

7. Giraffe-necked women of the Padaung tribe during a visit to London.

8. A Burmese girl shows off a traditional hairstyle.

9. Another one down. Burmese loggers felling teak.

10. Colonel Taw Hla, a Karen rebel leader, talks to Colonel Hla Maung of the Patriotic Liberation Army. A portrait of Saw Ba U Gyi, founder of the Karen National Union, hangs on the wall to the left. The picture of Jesus Christ reflects the Karen's Christian faith (1975).

11. & 12. Two scenes from the traditional Shin Pyu ceremony which marks a Burmese boy's spiritual coming of age. The initiate's feet must not touch the ground.

13. Aung San.

14. Daw Khin Kyi, wife of the legendary independence hero Aung San and mother of Aung San Suu Kyi.

15. Aung San Suu Kyi, leader of
the NLD, now under house arrest.

into business so he set up a number of profitable teashops
around Rangoon, and in the meantime he remained on the
sidelines, still waiting.

In 1981 there was another move to create the illusion of
change. Ne Win unexpectedly announced that he was resigning from the position of President. General San Yu was
appointed as the new President of the Socialist Republic of
Burma but he was considered by many to be merely Ne
Win's stooge. Ne Win himself continued to be the Chairman
of the BSPP and he continued to control the government
from a position of increasing seclusion.

When Ne Win and the military first took control of the
country, it might have been argued that this was just what
Burma needed: a firm, disciplined government capable of
uniting the country and controlling the political disputes.
However, the army found no solution to the problems of
insurgency and the demands of the rebel minority groups,
and while they managed to bring an end to political factionalism they achieved this by simply banning all opposition within the area under their control. A free nation was
turned into a police state. But after years of repressive
military rule I find it difficult to see what could feasibly
replace it; the army have controlled most aspects of Burmese
life and it is unlikely that any future free government would
manage without some degree of backing by the military.

Perhaps there has been some merit in Ne Win's brand of
Burmese military socialism in that the country has been
kept free from outside interference and from the struggles
that have devastated other parts of Asia. But cultural and
national integrity have been retained at some cost. Econom-
ically, the country has suffered. Burma, the easy-going land
of plenty, became a country of repression and poverty. The
people lived in fear of the military, who lived in fear of each
other and, in the meantime, day-to-day details like earning
and eating grew increasingly fraught with difficulty.

But it's surprising to learn how the people have survived
under the circumstances: Burma has developed its own,
curious enterprise culture.

CHAPTER FIVE

MONEY

It takes visitors a while, after arriving in Burma, to appreciate the eccentric features of the Burmese way of life, the legacy of Ne Win's 'Burmese Way to Socialism'. One traveller told me of her first impressions on landing at Rangoon Airport. She had taken a Thai International flight from Bangkok on which, as is customary, all the women had been given a single orchid. (With artistic Thai sophistication, the stems of the flowers are wrapped in small pieces of foil and bound on to little safety pins so that the orchids can be worn as decorative accessories.) Struggling through the general mayhem at Rangoon Airport, all the women from her flight were surrounded by gentle throngs of smiling Burmese children who giggled shyly and asked if they could have the flowers. The pretty young people asking for orchids made a delightful introduction to what seemed a charming country. It was only later that she realized the children had not wanted the flowers at all; they were an enterprising lot and had really been after the safety pins, which are very difficult to come by in Burma.

Such acumen has developed on a larger scale among the older Burmese. After the 1988 demonstrations, when the government issued an order that all houses should be repainted, the price of paint shot up. Since it was already an expensive luxury, someone, somewhere was making vast profits. At first the government distributed paint to the house owners and many seized the opportunity to make a little spare cash; by diluting the paint with water they were able to take the unwanted excess and sell it on the black market. The result was that in the monsoon all the paint washed off so that the cities reverted to their former shabbiness, but in the meantime many people had neatly profited from the exercise.

While the majority of Burmese people (and even their children) have had to acquire considerable expertise in overcoming their economic hardship, the government itself has stuck doggedly to its own brand of socialism and has proved inept at developing, or even retaining, the rich potential of the land. Rice was by far the most important element of the free trade developed during the days of the British. After the British left in 1948, attempts were made to nationalize the land and to bring the rice trade under the control of the State Agricultural Marketing Board. When Ne Win's Revolutionary Council came to power in 1962, the new government pursued a determination to nationalize everything. A State Trade Council was set up and the rice trade became a total government monopoly under the Trade Corporation No 1. The cultivation of rice, in the meantime, was ostensibly overseen by the Agricultural and Rural Development Corporation. It all sounds fine in theory but in practice it had miserable results. Farmers had to sell their rice to the government at prices that were fixed well below the rates the government was able to charge on export. Significantly, these prices also bore little relation to the subsequent cost of rice on the internal market. There was little incentive for farmers to grow much more than they needed for their own consumption. Rice production remained pitiably low and the general economy of the country dwindled.

Brigadier Aung Gyi had been critical of the economic policies drawn up shortly after the *coup*. He was subsequently removed from the Revolutionary Council and the nationalization programme came into operation with full force. During the first ten years of military rule, there was a concerted (if unsuccessful) effort to bring greater industrialism to Burma. This was largely funded by government sources, with a little foreign aid mainly from Japan. Correspondingly, imports of foreign consumer products were severely limited; from cars to paint and safety pins, it became almost impossible to buy goods from overseas on the open market.

However, despite the industrializing efforts of the government, rice production was still the key to the country's wellbeing and performance remained poor. Increases in rice harvests barely kept pace with the rapid rise in population. The export trade in the meantime plummeted dismally. According to government figures, in 1961 rice exports had reached a total volume of 1.6 million tons but by 1972 this figure had fallen to a dramatic low of just 262,000 tons. The government were forced to radically rethink their economic policies.

By the mid-seventies the emphasis on industrialization was toned down and there was an attempt to inject the agricultural and forestry sectors with new life. This made better sense, since Burma's potential wealth lies, readily available, in the land rather than in manufacturing and industry. The government also recognized that if the natural resources were to be developed some assistance would be required from the world beyond Burma. Foreign aid was encouraged and increased, and with it Burma's rigid isolation relaxed a little.

These new measures, though, were not enough to sustain a long-term programme of real improvement. Agricultural production showed some increase, exports rose slightly but the slow degree of apparent progress did not reflect the pace of change and development in the rest of the world. Shortages of food led to significant public demonstrations in 1967 and again in 1974. These rice riots were cruelly and abruptly quelled with a repressive show of strength by the military. Over the years Burma's economic problems stacked up and finally, in 1988, the government was forced to go cap in hand to the United Nations requesting the status of 'least-developed country' (LDC) so as to gain special grants. This has been a cause of grave embarrassment to the people of Burma. Not only are they proudly aware of their country's rich resources (and of the total mismanagement on the part of the government), but they also have a strong tradition of education and literacy. LDC status is granted if, among other qualifying factors, a country has a literacy rate of under 30 per cent. In Burma's case the figures had to be creatively juggled, for the true rate is impressive and over three quarters of the population are, in fact, literate. Meanwhile Burma has joined Ethiopia and Bangladesh to rank as one of the ten poorest countries in the world.

Burma's economic problems are partly the result of policies that the military government could not make work and partly because Ne Win's measures of isolation have cut the country off from international trade and progress. It reflects a paranoia about the outside world that has had disastrous long-term effects on the development of the country. Industry and agriculture have not kept pace with international developments; advances in technology and agricultural science remain a mystery. The country that was once the great rice-exporting centre of Asia now barely grows enough to feed itself. Given a vast increase in population (Burma now has an estimated forty million people), there is obviously a greater internal demand for rice, but Burma has also missed out on an agricultural revolution that transformed the outlook for many other Southeast Asian countries. A few 'iron buffaloes' were at one stage introduced to the paddy fields. These tractors were not enough to have a significant effect on the rice riches of Burma. The fields, in any case, were too small for the modern machinery and flesh-and-blood buffaloes still plough the land and provide much of the fertilizer.

By slinking out of world view and away from world affairs Burma has, so far, escaped the Coca Cola culture. It's perhaps a perverse comment on the nature of Burmese socialism, and certainly not a tragic one, but I am not entirely convinced that the Burmese people themselves have any abiding gratitude for this. Without question, most Burmese are deeply proud of their culture and their religion, yet they also have a sneaking suspicion that they might have missed out somewhere along the line.

Travelling through Burma in 1990 I had to wait at one point for a number of hours at a provincial railway station. It was hot, very hot. I finished my book and with nothing else on offer to read I wandered round the station in search of a thirst-quenching drink. An obliging child guided me to the hut that passed as a station restaurant. We sat down together and drank some tea and played around with my camera, a useful if rather nerve-wracking source of entertainment. Restaurants in Burma do not charge for plain tea; a small price is paid for coffee or tea with sickly condensed milk which is something of a luxury. I wanted to find a way of paying the proprietor and I looked around for something to buy. Locked in a glass case were a few cans of imported fizzy orange. Here was the solution; I could buy a can of orange that would also do nicely for my train journey. The proprietor, wreathed in smiles, found a key, opened the case and dusted down one of the cans. Then I began to understand the reason for his good spirits. A small can of fizzy orange cost a small fortune. On the official exchange rate I was paying at least ten times more than I would pay in Europe. The child jumped up and down and clapped his hands, deeply impressed by my apparent wealth and by the foreign goods. With what was probably a self-indulgent streak of munificence, I found myself sacrificing the newly bought supplies and I handed the can of orange to my small companion who scarpered away giggling with delight and clutching the treasure that had come his way – the nectar of the outside world.

The small can of orange, along with most other imported goods, had found its way into the country through the semi-illegal black market. During my trip, I noticed that little stalls up and down the country displayed a few dusty and aged reminders of the luxurious world beyond Burma:

Johnny Walker Black Label whisky, bottled or canned soft drinks from India or Thailand, even jars of coffee and Ovaltine (with appropriate and nostalgic images of maidens smiling straight out of the 1930s). Despite the official rejection of foreign capitalism, these were prestigious goods with a value far in excess of their original perceived worth. They were luxuries only the rich could afford.

Among the cans of orange and lemonade that were locked up and displayed as prize possessions, I had expected to see some evidence of Coca Cola; but there was no sign of that familiarly shaped bottle, no hint of that ubiquitous red and white. However, when I returned to Rangoon after my travels around the country, I heard rumours (always rumours) that the government were negotiating a special deal with Coca Cola. By 1990, in a panic to bring in foreign exchange and relieve the economic misery of the country, doors were at last being opened to foreign companies and Coca Cola, so I was told, were considering launching themselves into this vast, new and totally untapped market. But in the event it was Pepsi Cola who stole the march and later that year established a deal with the Burmese military government.

While government policies brought Burma into economic decline there was also a constant drain on the country's financial resources. War is an expensive activity and the Burmese army have needed substantial funds for arms, ammunition and soldiers to fight against the insurgent groups. About a third of the national budget has been spent annually on defence and internal security. Possibly the one real achievement of the military government has been the development of an extremely efficient fighting force.

The Burmese army has been funded by the nation, but conversely the rebel armies have needed considerable means to defend their territories and to carry out offensives against the Burmese troops. Over a quarter of the country lies under the control of the insurgent groups and many of these disparate areas are rich in natural resources. While the government has been denied access to all this potential wealth, many of the rebel groups have been able to make effective use of the land and of the resources that it offers.

The world's finest jade is found only in northern Burma. Jade is highly valued in oriental markets and the Chinese, in particular, have a special appreciation of Burmese jadeite. For centuries they have imported vast quantities from Kachin State in north Burma. (It is a curious reflection that all the exquisitely carved jade figures from China are, in fact, created from Burmese jadeite.) But the richest deposits of this jade lie largely in an area held by the Kachin Independence Army. Huge boulders of jade find their way into China and provide a basis for the Kachin Army's financial resources.

Further south, the opium poppy grows in the hills of the Shan States. This area, bordering Thailand and Laos, is part of the Golden Triangle where sticky black harvests of opium produce the raw material for much of the world's heroin. It is a very profitable crop. The states of Kentung and Hsenwi are notable for their productivity and have provided substantial funds for the activities of the Shan rebel groups and also for the Burma Communist Party who, until recently, were operating in the area. Much of the district is also controlled by independent opium warlords with whom the Burmese government is suspected of periodic collusion: during the 1960s Lo Hsing Han was known to have struck up various deals with the Burmese military. However, he later fell foul of the government who managed to arrest and subsequently try him on the grounds of insurgent activity (significantly, there seems to have been no charge of drug trading). However, Lo Hsing Han was later released and now continues to expand his trading operations.

More recently, Khun Sa has risen to international prominence as the head of one of the largest opium-trafficking operations in the world. His rise to public renown started in 1969 when he was arrested by the Burmese government. His men later retaliated and caused the government much embarrassment by kidnapping two Russian doctors who were working at the time in Taunggyi, the capital of the government-controlled part of the Shan States. It is widely held that negotiations must have taken place; shortly after the doctors were released, Khun Sa was freed. His subsequent relations with both the government and the rebel forces appear to waver according to profitability; supported by his own army of some 8,000 troops, he is a businessman (with fortunes based on a criminal product) rather than a freedom fighter. Khun Sa, however, has often maintained that he is a Shan nationalist and that ultimately he wants to drive the Burmese army out of his country. A lithe, commanding figure, he is said to be more of Chinese than Shan descent. During the last few years he appears to have developed a keen appetitie for publicity and has proved more than willing to speak to Western journalists on several occasions.

The Shan States are also rich in teak forests which run down the eastern side of the country reaching far into the Karen Independence Union territory along the Thai border. These have been a source of deep frustration to the Burmese government who, for years, were unable to lay their hands on the wealth of timber. Lately, however, the government has sold concessions to Thai logging companies who, having chopped down many of their own forests, are eager to obtain teak from other sources. It's a complicated arrangement. In the past the Thais might simply have bought timber discreetly from the Burmese insurgent groups, however, at the end of 1988 logging was banned in Thailand and the Thais were left with a big problem. They still needed vast quantities of hardwood to supply the needs of their own markets. A deal was struck with the Burmese government whereby Thai logging companies, operating with the official approval of the Burmese, negotiated with the rebel groups for permission to work within their territories. Meanwhile the Burmese authorities monitored the proceedings from Thai soil.

It has proved to be a useful exercise both for the Thai companies and the Burmese government, who badly need foreign exchange. Whole forests have rapidly disappeared and while the Thais have profited from Burma's ethnic and economic muddle, as foreigners they have shown little inclination to observe any measures of conservation within Burma. The forests are being devastated for short-term gain leaving a wake of ecological problems for the future.

The Karen territory has probably suffered the most from the Thai logging operations. When I visited the area in 1990, the landscape looked miserably scarred where extensive teak forests had been chopped down; amputated stumps on hillsides along the banks of the Salween River remained as a pathetic memento of the rich natural life that had recently been plundered for profit. Elephants plodded out of the receding jungle areas dragging huge severed trunks of teak that were deposited by the side of the water and were stacked in massive piles waiting to be taken into Thailand. Just across the river, the small Thai village of Mae Sam Laeb had been transformed into a bustling centre for the local logging operations. Incongruously large Thai trucks shuddered into the village where they were loaded up with the Burmese timber. Then they turned around to wind their way heavily back along jungle roads, taking the rich supplies of teak to be processed for export or for internal use within Thailand.

The Thai logging operations have also had significant side-effects for the Karen people: every year the Burmese jungle roads used to be washed away by the monsoon, making it difficult for the army to sustain any offensives during the rains. However, the Thai companies have built rather more substantial roads within Burma so that they can extract the timber all the year round. This makes it easier for the Burmese army to continue their military operations during the rainy season. Many Karen communities have also become increasingly vulnerable due to the lack of tree cover.

The Karen maintain that they have never been involved in the opium trade. They have profited from the Burmese government's trade restrictions and the complex web of smuggling activities that have developed as a consequence.

Funding for the Karens has come principally from taxes levied on black-market goods which are carried over the border from Thailand, through their territory and then smuggled into the government-controlled area of Burma. Correspondingly, Burmese goods have been smuggled back through the Karen territory and over the border to be traded in Thailand. Smuggling, though, is perhaps an inapposite term for the scale of all this trade. Before I became aware of the Burmese border activities, I naïvely thought of smuggling as a discreet operation whereby small packages of valuable goods were illegally transported by devious or unlikely means. In Burma, discretion undoubtedly plays a part in the smuggling activities but the sheer size and quantity of many of the smuggled goods beggars the imagination. Enormous logs of teak, huge bundles of bamboo and even herds of cattle regularly make the journey from Burma into Thailand. The merchants ply their trade at considerable risk. They, and their goods, have to run the gauntlet between the Burmese army and the rebel troops (although doubtless there are agreements and subtle payments of substantial sums to Burmese soldiers that help ease the flow of these goods in and out of Burma). If the porters are captured, however, they meet with ruthless treatment. The Burmese army has become notorious for the cruelty inflicted on prisoners and many are forced to serve the troops by carrying arms and ammunition to the front line of the fighting. Often they are used as human mine detectors and are sent on ahead of the advancing soldiers.

Black-market trading activities developed rapidly after the 1962 *coup* and by the late sixties Karen taxing posts were set up at strategic points along the border with Thailand. Many of these posts were subsequently developed into substantial military bases for the Karen troops. Rather than fighting through itinerant guerrilla groups, the Karen were able to set up military townships from which they controlled the outlying areas. But such an obvious show of strength has had distinct disadvantages as, over the years, the Burmese army has become increasingly powerful. 'I think we made a big mistake in setting up our large camps on the border,' one Karen leader told me. 'They have now provided the Burmese army with major targets to destroy.' By 1990, prior to the general elections that year, the Burmese army had undertaken a full-scale campaign to capture the Karen bases. Undoubtedly they were also anxious to gain control of the teak forests. By the end of February many of the Karen camps had fallen and in the meantime, entire Karen communities were flooding over the border into Thailand as refugees. The Karen troops were subsequently being forced to revert to guerrilla tactics.

By losing control of the smuggling activities from Thailand, it seems that the Karen are likely to suffer an enormous loss of revenue. I received no clear indication of how they would manage, but I was told that, in any case, Thailand was no longer the focus of smuggling activities; by the end of the eighties, black-market goods had also been pouring into the government-controlled area of Burma from other countries, principally India, China and Indonesia.

The black market itself has become a pivotal feature of Burmese life and Burmese ingenuity. Within Burma proper the official economy has failed to meet the requirements of the country, and conversely, illegal free-market enterprises have flourished. In the late eighties the government was forced to recognize the country's dependence on this free trade and the black market gained a blurred, semi-official recognition. It is difficult to judge these Burmese black-market activities as being immoral. How else can the people get their toothbrushes, radios, lipsticks (the Burmese women are particularly fond of cosmetics) and even medicines? In the depths of the rural areas, of course, consumer goods and many medical supplies are simply not available but in the towns and cities you can buy anything from condoms to canned peaches – all at vast cost.

When we lived in Burma in the seventies, the black market was an open (if still illegal) operation. In central Rangoon, Scot Market was the largest and most interesting shopping area. The central building dates straight back to the British era and, like much Victorian architecture of the same period, reflects the great age of the railways; it looks and feels rather like the concourse of a station. Inside are rows of little stalls selling Burmese goods. In the 1970s the black market operated in the area immediately surrounding the building and was a hive of activity and a revelation of the extent of black-market activities.

Acres of open ground were covered with unsheltered stands selling foreign goods. These had all been precariously smuggled into Burma. It was a lengthy and unpredictable pastime to explore this straggling market and note the staggering variety of items for sale. There were foodstuffs: tins of butter, packets of Scots porridge oats, even blocks of chocolate melting in the heat. There were drinks: lots of whisky, some gin and a little wine as well as cans of fizzy lemonade and orange. There were clothes, watches, plastic toys, shoes, pens, pencils, paper, books and sometimes magazines of some age. None of these items ever looked very new, in fact many of them appeared extremely grubby, and they were all sold at huge prices that reflected both market demand and the risky business of transporting these goods into Burma.

All this had vanished when I returned to Burma some years later. As a mark of the semi-official recognition of the black market, the area around Scot Market had been cleared and all the stands had been rehoused in a new building some distance away. It had been specially constructed for the purpose. 'We must take you to see the new black market,' Burmese friends said when they were driving me around Rangoon. 'It will give you an idea of the craziness of this country and will show you how some things have genuinely changed since you were last here.' They clearly felt it was as important for me to see the contemporary life of the black market as it had been for me to visit the Shwedagon pagoda and all the past glories of Burmese culture.

They were right, of course. Markets and shops show the heart of a country's wellbeing; what's available, what it all costs and how it is sold. It seemed bizarre that the government itself had paid for the construction of this new marketplace to house what had been an illegal trade, and in doing so they had almost openly acknowledged the failure of their economic policies. We paid one kyat to park outside the New St John's Market in Rangoon and went in. For Burma, there was a surprising sense of prosperity; the market was crammed with goods of all descriptions, many of them larger and far more expensive than anything that had been available in the seventies. Where did it all come from, I wanted to know. 'Most of it comes over the border from Thailand, India and also China, but some arrives by ship.' Were there many rich customs men, I asked. It was a facetious question and I received only a smile and a little laugh by way of an answer.

The clothes section was selling quantities of Indonesian batik. There were also numerous different styles of denim jacket; dark blue, light blue, with zips, without zips, these were the very latest fashion in Burma. Demand was high, and so was the price; I was told that a jacket cost about 2,000 kyat (about £200 on the official exchange rate). The medicine section had a vast range of items from all over the world; ginseng from Korea, pills from China, serum (probably out of date) in little bottles, bandages, plasters, lotions, even syringes and needles. But most surprising of all was the electronics section. This was a distinct development from anything I had seen in the seventies. There were fridges, televisions, cassette recorders and quantities of ghetto-blasters. A cluster of people had gathered around a television set that was showing an old John Wayne film in English. How much for a television, I asked. It was around 40,000 kyat (officially, about £4,000).

I returned with my friends to have some coffee at their house. A couple of children were sitting on plastic-covered chairs in the living room, glued to the television. The John Wayne film was still running. The children made as if to leave but we indicated that they should stay; the film was coming to an end. As the hero emerged through gun smoke to sweep up the heroine and embrace her with a chaste kiss, I wondered what impression these children had of the West or even of the world beyond Burma. National television showed a few Western films but these were invariably limited to black-and-white classics from the forties and fifties. Some of the richer people had video sets and I had noticed a number of small stalls around town selling pirated videos of Rambo films. I couldn't help feeling that the combination of John Wayne and Rambo would provide a strange view of Western culture. Beyond this, very few Western books find their way into Burma; government censors are severe and also paranoid, and any book traded through the black market is a potentially dangerous item – people found selling anti-government propaganda (whatever that means) usually meet a dismal fate.

When the film ended the children left, politely bowing their way past me and their elders with traditional Burmese respect. We sat sipping cups of coffee with condensed milk, discussing the lack of books and access to real news. The television, meanwhile, was broadcasting a lengthy government session; administrative army leaders from the provinces were reporting to the President. 'There's the man with real power,' my host interrupted as the cameras focussed on Brigadier Khin Nyunt, the head of military intelligence. Given the horrific stories of secret police brutality, he looked a surprisingly ordinary man. There seemed little about him to suggest the enormous power that he wielded. A bland, unmoving face was principally character-ized by a pair of glasses behind which the all-seeing eyes of Burma stared steadfastly around the room. I got the im-pression he was the sort of man you would not care to argue with, the type of dogmatic person who would hold unshake-able views and with no inclination to countenance alter-natives.

The interest of my Burmese friends diminished as the cameras shifted and more army leaders were presented on the screen. They were not important. 'No real information comes out of these tedious sessions,' I was told. 'They're just bureaucratic procedures, televised to give people the impression that they know what is happening.' Control rested with a small collection of people who took their decisions far from public view.

Burmese television, though, was something I had not encountered before. During the seventies the media (all of which were government run) had been limited to print and radio. Television was introduced towards the mid-eighties; it was both a new form of government propaganda and a dangerous information system to be closely controlled. The enormous cost of televisions in Burma means that only the richer people can afford to own a set; it was in the towns that I noticed televisions and some video recorders in houses. When not in use the screens were tidily covered with dishcloths, probably to keep out the dust, but I also felt it was a mark of Burmese delicacy.

Of course, the richest people in Burma are principally the military, the ruling class. Salaries are not exorbitantly high, but there are considerable benefits from special army privileges. Retired soldiers are able to buy cars and land at moderate cost, well below the rates civilians have to pay – if they are lucky enough to have an opportunity to make such purchases at all. These retired soldiers, in any case, often go on to take up government positions, with more access to special goods. There are also Western luxuries which regularly come their way; whisky and cigarettes in particular (which have become something of a status symbol within the country). But undoubtedly the biggest benefits come from all the unofficial dealings that take place in the potentially affluent areas of Burma; negotiations over opium, jade, rubies, pearls and, probably, teak go to line khaki pockets and provide the soldiers with substantial funds to buy the black-market goods that make their way into Burma. It's a cycle of contradiction and corruption that leaves the morals of the ruling class in an increasing state of decay.

The shady nature of the Burmese gem trade is perhaps the most intriguing and romantic aspect of the country's inherent wealth. During my last visit to Burma I met some

Nepalese gem miners in Mandalay. They told me how they regularly carried stones out of the country, walking over the borders to India, Bangladesh and Thailand, 'all without any visas,' they laughed, as if their regular smuggling activities should have a stamp of officialdom. I was puzzled by all this. Why were there Nepalese in Burma involved in an underground gem market? It would have been difficult and dangerous to find out more about the gem world from within Burma so I tracked down a Burmese gem-dealer in Thailand and went to visit him.

We sat in a hot, scruffy office where we talked above the high-pitched whirr of gem-cutting machines in the room behind; it was an uncomfortable background noise and sounded rather like a dentist's drill. Occasionally a cutter would pop out with a bunch of half-cut stones on the end of long metal sticks. The dealer would examine them critically and then carry on talking. I had recently arrived in Thailand from Burma and it was a relief to be able to speak openly.

The rich ruby area of Mogok, he told me, was originally part of the Shan state of Mongmit. During the time of the Burmese kings, one of the sawbwas of Mongmit had been duped, or forced, by the Burmese court at Mandalay into swapping this wealthy area for land near the Irrawaddy. These diplomatic manoeuvres meant that the ruby mines fell into the hands of the Burmans, although even today most of the people living and working in the Mogok area are Shan. When the British annexed Burma they took over the mines and British companies subsequently developed fairly extensive operations – in the 1920s particularly Burmese rubies would fetch a very handsome price in London. On independence Mogok once again fell into the hands of the Burmese and it is now part of the Shwebo administrative division. The Nepalese miners and smugglers, the dealer explained, were probably there as descendants of the Gurkhas who the British had brought with them, but he reckoned it was only in the past ten years that these people had become involved in the mining activities.

It is the clarity of Burmese stones, he went on, that give them such high quality. Many Burmese sapphires are finer than those from Kashmir while the rubies have a matchless purity and colour. Pigeon's Blood rubies were until recently considered the best and were the most expensive. The British market, particularly, prefers this darker colour. Elsewhere, however, preference has shifted to a softer shade, largely through the influence of the Japanese who have become big gem dealers. Hare's Blood rubies are now very popular. They are a sweeter red, he grew lyrical, with a whisk of pink; a strong but lighter colour.

We paused to look at some stones. The mines in Burma, he explained, are still exceedingly crude, although the miners themselves have considerable skill. Normally a pit is dug into the ground, about three times the length of the longest bamboo (I thought of tall sweeps of bamboo grass and reckoned that on average each pit would be at least sixty feet deep). The miners clamber down the pit on wobbly bamboo ladders and, like the oil miners, they are attached to a tube for air which is hand pumped from the top. There is usually a group of about five people to each pit; three will go down while two remain to organize things at the surface (and to keep a look out if they are mining illegally).

I wanted to know how much control there was over the mining operations. Before 1962, he told me, private mining was neither legal nor was it positively illegal. He made motions with his hands. People went out to find gems rather like they would go out to cut down bamboo, it was a feature of the area. After the 1962 military takeover, mining became a distinctly dangerous activity. Some mines are now directly controlled by the State, others are worked independently and all stones are technically sold to the government. Smuggling activities, though, are widespread. There are large mining mafias, the latest big chief being of Gurkha descent.

There was news, he said, that an enormous and very fine ruby had recently been found, about the size of the inner bud of a banana flower. The miners of this stone knew they were in an awkward position; a gem of such distinction would cause a stir on the open market and could land them in a great deal of trouble if smuggled out. So they decided to sell their find to the government. The real value would have been about 200 million kyat (£20 million). The miners received half that amount, which was still a handsome sum although I rather wondered how much more the government would have been able to make on the deal.

Our conversation went the way of all talk about Burma and we became immersed in a discussion about the general plight of the country and the political set-up. He told me how he had left Burma shortly after the military takeover but how he would willingly return given another government and another political climate. Like many Burmese expatriates he was a reluctant exile.

The great golden pagodas of Burma, shaped like huge and magnificent bells with long spires, are spangled at the very top with quantities of gems: rubies, sapphires, emeralds and diamonds. These are the produce of Burma's natural richness. I always listened with some scepticism to stories about the unseen wealth huddling way out of sight at the tops of the gleaming spires until I once had a rare opportunity to see at close quarters the *hti*, or crowning umbrella, of a fairly large pagoda.

I was staying in Pagan shortly after an earthquake had tragically destroyed many of the pagodas in the area. The large golden pagoda there, the Shwezigon, had been damaged, but not beyond repair, and while restoration work was being carried out the golden hti was removed and placed under army guard near the main entrance in a little hut that passed as a museum. I went to see it, and there indeed were the rubies, emeralds, diamonds and sapphires the size of marbles. They were dotted around all over the hti, set in the gold in a slightly haphazard fashion as if casually placed there without much regard for the sheer size and value of the stones.

How much Burma's gem trade contributes to the overall

economy is difficult to estimate when so much smuggling and so many dodgy government deals are rife. While the value of the stones depends largely on their limited supply it is also questionable as to how far it might be profitable to develop the gem-mining areas. I was told, however, that Thai mining companies were showing a keen interest in moving into the area and setting up joint operations with the Burmese government; in which case the future for the independent entrepreneur would be fairly bleak.

For most Burmese, though, gems are of little direct relevance; life revolves around the more banal realities of affording enough to eat. There was a particular sense of tension at the market in Taunggyi, the administrative centre of the Shan States, when I last visited the area. Markets are places where people gather and, in Burma, where they grow increasingly resentful about the price of food.

Taunggyi itself was bursting with soldiers; on the streets, outside the cinema and particularly in the marketplace. The market itself was a colourful web of activity; the hills people, in their braided ethnic dress, were selling tomatoes, cabbages, chillies, garlic and other locally grown vegetables which were neatly laid out on the ground. Directly opposite, on the other side of the road, was the black-market area showing signs of Taunggyi's convenient proximity both to China and Thailand. There were stalls selling Chinese blankets, Chinese cooking pots, pens and paper from Thailand and even a dusty medical section with drugs that looked dangerously out of date.

Just beyond the black market was a weary line of people forming a queue outside the People's Shop. It was not a shop in any sense that I could appreciate; it was more of a shack. One part of the shack was closed; it was the section ostensibly selling a limited number of legally imported foreign goods. These, when in stock, are sold at considerably cheaper prices than the same goods on the black market. However, temptation and desperation often undermine the work of the People's Shop assistants who will simply buy up all the stock and then swiftly sell it for substantially more on the black market. There is nothing discreet about this; directly outside the closed section of the People's Shop were all the goods that should have been for sale inside. They were going for double the price.

The people forming a queue were waiting for rice. This was the rice the farmers were required to sell to the government. 'It's terribly poor quality; most of the grains are broken,' I was told. 'If you want to buy decent rice, you have to go to the vegetable market opposite. It's good quality but it's expensive and it's illegally sold.' The farmers, so I gathered, supplied a set quota of rice to the government and in some cases were able to sell anything in excess for considerably more on the unofficial market.

All these Burmese markets left me bewildered; I was more than a little confused by all the different sections set so closely together. The black market sold foreign goods of a quasi-illegal nature, the People's Shop sold government controlled goods and the vegetable market sold local produce – although the rice there was not a legal, free-trade commodity. By Burmese standards, everything was expensive although illegally sold goods were more expensive than others. Meanwhile the soldiers wandering around with their guns were simply keeping an eye on law and order. They made no attempt to stop any of the unofficial trade, it was a vital part of Burmese life.

How much did rice cost, I asked. It was then 10 kyat (or £1) a *pyi*. This was a cripplingly high price to pay in a country that grows the crop as its staple diet. The *pyi* itself is an eccentric measurement that reflects both Burmese tastes and the highly idiosyncratic way of Burmese life. Rice is bought not by weight but by volume and is measured out in empty condensed-milk cans. There are eight condensed-milk cans of rice to the pyi. Underlying this, of course, is the enormous importance the Burmese attach to condensed milk; some of it is made and tinned in Burma, some is sneaked in over the borders. Since refined white sugar is extremely hard to come by, even in the cities, condensed milk has become an everyday delicacy for the people who generally have a great propensity for sweet things.

Real milk, meanwhile, is a rare and desirable luxury. The shortage of milk at one point gave scope for considerable ingenuity and enterprise. A scandal broke in Rangoon concerning a stall in the centre of the city that had been doing a brisk trade in selling fresh milk. Buyers of this sought-after delicacy were convinced it was real milk because it had been boiled (to kill germs) and had consequently acquired the mark of authenticity; there was a thin layer of white skin on the surface. It was only after the milk trader had earned a small fortune that the truth was finally uncovered. The milk was not fresh at all, but powdered and the skin had been merely an additional and superficial accessory. Quantities of white tissue had been bought on the black market and the trader had used thin strips of this flimsy substance to masquerade as skin, giving his bogus fresh milk the required finishing touch. For weeks it was impossible to find white tissues, or even white lavatory paper, on the black market; this was partly because the milk trader had exhausted so many supplies and partly because other stall keepers became nervous about the implications of selling such items.

It's a small and rather absurd story, but it shows the lengths to which the Burmese people will go to get around, and even profit by, the limitations of the system.

Shortages have given rise to ingenuity in other, more crucial, areas of life. While medicines are in limited supply and many are sold only on the black market, Burmese doctors have a tradition of excellence and dedication. Working with a debilitating lack of resources often stretches their powers of creativity. Lack of plastic was at one time a big problem but, in some cases, it could be swiftly overcome; hip replacements would be carried out using ivory. In a land of elephants, it was a convenient and probably better alternative to the material used in other parts of the world. But in itself, the use of ivory as opposed to plastic reflects a distorted sense of values that has developed as a direct result of the shortages. Ivory, meanwhile, is another of Burma's more dubious exports.

All these eccentric (and impressive) signs of enterprise, though, leave me wondering how Burma would prosper with a free market economy. The businesslike ways in which many people have managed to overcome their difficulties show a natural entrepreneurial flair. While there are severe shortages, trading has become a sort of free-for-all for anyone who can devise a way of getting round the restrictions.

The first and most obvious signs of this are apparent when first entering the country. For outsiders, immigration and customs procedures at Rangoon Airport are a tedious exercise of bureaucracy and a bewildering series of Burmese business deals. For the Burmese themselves, the airport offers a combination of officialdom and easy access to foreign goods. The position of a customs clerk is a lucrative one.

When I last arrived at Rangoon Airport there was a general sense of chaos and confusion. It was a normal working day. There was, though, one gratifying change since I had last been to Rangoon; in the past, the departure lounge and the arrivals hall had been one and the same. Now, they had been separated so that there was, at least, some clarity about who was coming and who was going. But for those newly arriving even this point must have been difficult to grasp. Rangoon Airport is one of the few in the world to have a duty-free section that sits prominently in the arrivals hall. It sells only whisky and cigarettes, just in case travellers have not had an opportunity to stock up beforehand. This is a tacit recognition of the fact that, for most Burmese, these items play a vital part in easing the way through customs. On my flight I had noticed that a number of Burmese people were bringing in televisions, radios and video recorders. There was a rapid transfer of whisky bottles and cigarette cartons at the customs desk before these people emerged triumphant with their valuable goods.

Perhaps rather foolishly, I did not have any cigarettes or whisky and I spent two painful hours making my way through the airport bureaucracy. Having retrieved my luggage from a pile dumped outside the airport building, I was sent away from the customs desk because I had failed to complete my currency declaration form correctly. This seemed an absurd nicety in the midst of all the bribery I was witnessing. The currency form, however, was an important piece of bureaucracy for controlling illegal deals over foreign exchange (despite the fact that there were devious ways around the system). On mastering the art of filling in this vital document I was shoved to the back of the queue where I had ample time to observe the extraordinary negotiations that were taking place around me. It was as if there was a mad, secret code among the Burmese that outsiders were initially unable to comprehend. Whisky and cigarettes were feverishly distributed without much circumspection. One customs official placidly hid a whole carton of Winston under the papers on his desk. Another, more junior clerk thrust two packets of Marlboro into a waste-paper basket; presumably he planned to retrieve them later. Meanwhile bottles of Johnny Walker were being openly presented by the guides of tourist groups. I had managed to get a visa to Burma as an independent traveller and at that point I began to regret it; I was clearly at a disadvantage in not being able to work the system.

Emerging out of all this confusion I was greeted by a government guide who had been sent to escort me to my hotel and to monitor some of my movements. I was beset by a contagious sense of Burmese paranoia and felt it would be unwise to confess that I had previously known the country well. We passed a lorry-load of people escorted by armed soldiers; 'Those are workers being taken home from their factory.' They appeared subdued and, to my mind, they did not seem much like ordinary factory hands; they looked more like prisoners. 'The authorities have organized a series of improvements for the city,' the government patter continued, 'and they are hoping to encourage many

more tourists like you to visit our country.' Thinking back
to my recent struggles at the airport, I wondered how the
government could possibly hope to attract vast numbers of
foreign visitors. Rich tourists would inevitably expect a
certain degree of luxury and sophistication; they would be
appalled by the chaos in the airport and they would be
uncomfortable in any hotel Burma had to offer. The facilities simply did not exist for any serious attempt to capture a
new market of this sort. Added to this was a considerable
element of danger over travel within Burma. Basic main-
tenance within the country had been so overlooked that
aircraft on internal flights were occasionally known to come
crashing down from the skies.

Despite their xenophobia, the government wanted the
tourists because they were desperate for foreign exchange.
Correspondingly the unofficial value of foreign currency
had reached dizzy heights: on the government exchange
rate one US dollar was equivalent to six kyat, but on the
black market the same amount was worth about ten times
more. A single US dollar could be exchanged for anything
from forty-five to sixty kyat depending on negotiations.
After a short time my government guide dropped the official
touristspeak and began a desperate and earnest bid for some
foreign currency. There were clearly considerable advan-
tages in having access to foreign visitors.

At the hotel various people were lingering around outside,
eager to seize an opportunity of having a few quiet words
with any of the tourists and, with luck, to negotiate for
some foreign money. Everywhere I went in Burma conversations with shop keepers, taxi drivers, even guides all ended
the same way: how much did I want for my US dollars?
Nobody wanted to rob the visitors, it was just that they
were seen as walking funds of foreign exchange with whom
good deals could be struck. Realistically there was little
point in having any Burmese currency since tourists had to
arrange all their travel and accommodation through the
tourist board, for which they were charged principally in
foreign currency. By exchanging money at unofficial rates

one merely acquired huge wads of used notes that seemed rather like Monopoly money; there was little they could actually buy and it was not possible to take them out of the country.

It was necessary, though, to have a few kyat and, for the purposes of the currency form, to exchange some money through official channels. I duly presented US $100 at the bank desk in the hotel and waited patiently while the clerk copiously filled out a selection of forms. Then I stared in disbelief at the currency I was handed. As ever, Aung San's face smiled up from all the notes but for a moment I stumbled stupidly over the amount I had been given; I had not anticipated having to exercise my nine times table, for the highest value notes were in denominations of nine. There were no 100 kyat or 50 kyat notes, instead the larger amounts were determined in bills of 90 kyat or 45 kyat while the lower units remained decimalized. It was the clerk's turn to be patient; 'We also had difficulty in adjusting to this new system,' he said with sympathetic understatement as he helped me count the notes.

Nine is, of course, a particularly auspicious number within Burma but while the curious denominations are partly based on Burmese superstition, there were also more sinister reasons behind the introduction of these new units. It all dates back to 1985 when a series of new banknotes were introduced to what was then a decimal system. This was an attempted measure to assist the ailing economy. But rather than subsequently devaluing the kyat the government then simply withdrew all 100 kyat bills from circulation. Overnight these notes became worthless. Only rich people have 100 kyat notes – the people were told – they are therefore not needed. Many lost a considerable fortune since it was possible only to change a total value of 5,000 kyat. But worse was to come.

Burmese people do not generally keep money in the State bank. Tedious bureaucracy, lengthy queues, sharp questions and obligatory donations to State causes do little to encourage the public to deposit any funds with the authorities. Even when we lived in Burma, it was fairly common practice for the richer people to invest heavily in jewels. Often ladies coming to dinner would arrive wearing some of the family fortunes; bracelets of sapphires or rubies, strings of pearl necklaces, even little engyi buttons of emerald or jade. Meanwhile everyone kept savings literally tucked under their mattresses or locked up discreetly in little boxes. It was dangerous to admit to retaining these private funds since awkward questions would be asked and much of the money would be confiscated. Many of these savings were wiped out when the 100 kyat note was first abolished.

Despite these measures the overall economy showed little signs of improvement. Then, in September 1987, totally without warning the government abolished the three banknotes of the highest denomination – 75 kyat, 35 kyat and 25 kyat. These were replaced by the 90 kyat and 45 kyat notes that, along with many Burmese, I was subsequently to find so confusing. The introduction of these denominations of nine was undoubtedly a desperate, superstitious attempt to bring good fortune to the country's miserable economic plight. But this time the corresponding abolition of commonly held banknotes was even more devastating. About 60 per cent of the currency in circulation became valueless. Friends told me that at the time they had only just sold a car (a real asset of enormous value in Burma). They were consequently left with over 50,000 worthless kyat. One of their neighbours, meanwhile, died of a heart attack having lost nearly everything. 'We didn't think things like that ever really happened,' they said miserably.

The government claimed that this was a further measure to control inflation and to curb black-market activities. In the event it did neither. The people lost any sense of confidence in their own currency and resorted instead to buying land and goods. The net result was that inflation merely spiralled and black-market operations became increasingly profitable. Nobody wanted to have kyat, and in the meantime any sort of foreign exchange (but preferably US dollars) became increasingly desirable – hence the desperate bid for foreign currency, both on the part of the ordinary people and the government, when I arrived in Burma just prior to the 1990 elections.

Ideology forms a background to unrest but rarely spurs revolution; empty stomachs do. The government's measures of demonatization and the crippling effect on the people led to a mass uprising that looked set to change the face of Burma and end more than twenty-six years of oppressive army rule.

CHAPTER SIX

DEMOCRACY:
The Unfinished Story

Even during the seventies Burma seemed like a time bomb waiting to explode. People smiled. They were gentle and charming. But given the underlying tension and the rumours of arrests and tortures it was often incomprehensible that they tolerated the iron-fisted mismanagement of their country. 'The time is not yet ripe,' Daw Khin Kyi always used to say whenever we asked why the Burmese people put up with such oppression and financial misery. 'But the time will come,' she would add with a Burmese sense of drama. I doubt, though, whether Daw Khin Kyi could have forseen that a decade later her own daughter would become the leading force of Burma's bid for change and freedom when the time duly came in 1988.

Aung San Suu Kyi had been only two years old when her father, Aung San, was assassinated along with six other members of his constituent cabinet on the eve of the independence he had struggled to achieve for Burma. She was brought up with her brothers in Rangoon where her mother worked within U Nu's government first as a member of Parliament and then as the country's first Minister for Social Welfare. In 1960 Daw Khin Kyi was appointed Burma's Ambassador to India and Aung San Suu Kyi, then sixteen, went with her and completed her school education in Delhi. Although she subsequently made frequent and regular visits to Burma, Aung San Suu Kyi went to university, worked and married overseas. She never lived in Burma again until a family crisis brought her back to Rangoon in April 1988.

Daw Khin Kyi had diabetes, a condition she managed to cope with fairly comfortably for a long time. 'God is good,' I can remember her chuckling when she first learnt about it. 'In this country it is difficult get sugar, and now the doctors tell me I shouldn't take sugar anyway.' Her good humour was irrepressible. However, the diabetes weakened her and made her susceptible to other complaints. In March 1988 she fell ill, a few weeks later she had a severe stroke and was rushed to hospital. Relatives sent for her daughter and Aung San Suu Kyi arrived from England. She spent three months living in the hospital tending her mother and then took her back home to University Avenue on Inya Lake in Rangoon where she could be nursed in comfort.

Daw Khin Kyi lingered for several months. She was only dimly aware of the mass movement that became a widespread revolution and of the bloodshed and violence with which it was put down. Her daughter, in the meantime, gradually found herself becoming a figurehead within what started as a leaderless revolt. From there she became the national heroine of the Burmese people for whom she represented a viable alternative to the tyranny of more than twenty-six years of military misrule.

The first grumblings of the uprising started in 1987. In July that year Aung Gyi, the former second-in-command of the army, wrote an open letter to Ne Win in which he criticized the government's economic policies and warned of future violence and unrest. The letter was widely circulated and quietly applauded by the public. Although there is no direct evidence to suggest that the government took subsequent action, a few stiff regulations were relaxed. However, a month later the second of the government's demonetization measures took place and with it people's modest fortunes and savings were wiped out. A small student demonstration in Rangoon was swiftly quelled but a mood of simmering anger prevailed.

In March the following year the tension finally snapped when a fight between students and locals at a teashop in Rangoon got out of hand. The students complained that they had been treated unfairly and as their protests escalated the army grew more and more nervous. During a student march across Rangoon, troops attacked and shot into the crowds leaving many dead. Soldiers then rounded up large numbers of student demonstrators who were taken away in overloaded vans. Horrific stories circulating around Rangoon described how many students died from suffocation in the intense heat of these tightly packed vans. The general public became increasingly enraged.

The arrested students were locked up in Insein prison just outside Rangoon where news leaked out of people severely beaten and tortured and of girls gang-raped by army and prison officials. It was against a background of mounting shock and anger that Daw Khin Kyi was rushed to hospital and subsequently tended by her daughter, Suu.

For several weeks the atmosphere remained extremely tense and at the beginning of June Aung Gyi sent another open letter to Ne Win, denouncing the incident when the army had opened fire on unarmed demonstrating students. Given this slight degree of moral support, the students plucked up the nerve to continue their demonstrations. They began calling for an end to single-party rule and a return to democracy. Skirmishes between soldiers and students ensued; students were killed, soldiers were killed and many schoolchildren joined in the demonstrations.

On 19 July, along with army leaders and government officials, Aung San Suu Kyi attended the annual Martyr's Day ceremony commemorating the assassination of Aung San and his cabinet in 1947. It was a day of national honour and importance. Suu went in place of her mother who was too ill to attend. It was her first official public appearance since she had been in Burma and the occasion was recorded on the front page of the government-run *Working People's Daily* alongside a much shorter piece condemning some of the student disturbances. July 1988 was the month when things really started to happen; when the national veil of tolerance finally began to rip as the people grew increasingly angry and violent despite the superficial concessions the government tried to make.

As an outside observer, I find the secret workings of Burmese military politics almost impossible to anticipate or understand. Even if you take the line that the military are just bullies anxious to win their own game, there will be unexpected actions and pronouncements that appear to defy all logical explanation. Suddenly, during a congress held at the end of July, Ne Win made a startling announcement; following all the bloodshed earlier in the year he declared he was resigning as chairman of the Burma Socialist Programme Party (BSPP), the ruling army organization. San Yu, the President of Burma (widely held to be merely Ne Win's acolyte), also resigned. In what seems to have been a remarkably liberal speech, Ne Win announced that the people should be given a chance to decide whether or not they wanted multi-party rule. He said that a referendum should be held.

It is difficult to work out whether there was an attempt here to listen to the voice of the people or whether this was merely a studied farce. At any rate, the idea of a referendum was quickly opposed and overruled by other congress representatives. Meanwhile, after a show of some misgiving, the resignations of Ne Win and San Yu were accepted. It seems this might have been a move to dissociate them both from violence and the killings that were already characterizing the year. Sein Lwin, a former army officer known to be brutally authoritarian, became the next President of Burma. In the meantime, many people suspected that Ne Win would continue to manipulate things from behind the scenes.

Increasing their cries for democracy, the students managed to organize for a national strike to be held on the auspicious day of 8 August 1988 (8.8.88). This must have been quite some undertaking, given that all open communication within Burma was entirely controlled by the army. But on the appointed day, massive demonstrations duly took place throughout the country and the students were joined by thousands of civilians. The streets of the cities were filled with peaceful protestors carrying before them large photographs of Aung San, the national hero and the great freedom fighter of Burma. That night in Rangoon the army opened fire on crowds of demonstrators. Hundreds were killed.

Protests up and down the country continued on a smaller scale for the next three days. When the army attacked, some of the crowds fought back with bricks, stones and sharpened bicycle spokes, or *jinglees*. The casualties mounted and the hospitals rapidly began to run out of bandages, blood and other supplies. In an incident later reported by the human rights group Amnesty International, three nurses at Rangoon General Hospital were shot and later died when soldiers fired at medical workers who had come out of the hospital to plead for an end to the killing.

'You would have thought the Earth should have trembled with the weight of all the dead bodies falling to the ground,' a friend said later. 'The worst thing was seeing all the dead people piled up in doorways each morning after the streets had been cleared.'

Finally, after four days and nights of bloodshed, Sein Lwin resigned. It was the first of what the people hoped would be a series of victories. They were euphoric. As more and more civilians joined the movement, work stopped even in government ministries. The people of Burma continued to demand a return to democracy.

Sein Lwin was replaced by Dr Maung Maung, a former judge and Ne Win's official biographer. He was a civilian president although quite clearly he had the full backing of the military. It was a gesture, but for the people it was not good enough. They continued to strike and were joined by more and more government bodies, even members of the air force came out to demonstrate. Realistically, it is difficult to see what the military government might have done at this point without giving up completely and leaving Burma in a state of total anarchy. Over the past twenty-six years they had taken the country into a political and administrative cul-de-sac. They had banned all opposition to their rule and they had placed army officers at all controlling points of civilian life; they had left the country with no infrastructure to cope with anything else. The concession of a would-be civilian government was about as far as the military could go; at that stage there were no opposition leaders to offer any alternative government. I suppose it might have been different if all the army had put down their weapons and joined the people, helping them to establish the democracy for which they were struggling. Sadly for Burma, this did not happen.

However, as August came to an end, prominent figures were starting to emerge and to head up the revolution that so far had been leaderless: U Nu, the former prime minister overthrown in Ne Win's military *coup*; Aung Gyi, the former brigadier and author of the open letters; Tin U, the former defence minister discredited by Ne Win; and almost magically out of nowhere, Aung San Suu Kyi, daughter of the great independence hero. These opposition figures called on President Maung Maung to end single-party rule in Burma and to allow a neutral, interim government to be formed while political parties could be set up and full democratic elections subsequently held.

On 25 August, a rally held beside the Shwedagon pagoda in Rangoon drew crowds of nearly half a million. Several public figures had gathered but the people principally came to hear Aung San Suu Kyi speak. 'Her appeal was really the same as that of a film star,' a friend later told me. 'People came out of curiosity to hear what Aung San's daughter had to say.' But what she said made a lot of sense; using words her father had used years before as both the founder of the Burmese army and the leader of Burma's independence movement, she told the crowds that the army should keep out of politics. There should be no discord, she said, the people should respect the army purely as a professional body. She spoke of the vital need for discipline, peace and unity in order to avoid anarchy and achieve the return to democracy the country so clearly wanted. She said that as Aung San's daughter she could no longer stand on the sidelines while the people of Burma came forward in what was effectively their second struggle for independence. The crowds responded with overwhelming applause and approval.

At this stage of the movement total anarchy had become a real danger. People demonstrated in the streets every day, the country had come to a virtual halt and there were severe shortages of food while ships in the docks remained unloaded and normal working life was at a standstill. In many areas the Buddhist monks organized special councils so as to retain law and order and within the cities communities were divided up into vigilance groups to guard against theft and looting. But in the meantime the army retaliated with attempts to create havoc; prisons were opened and convicted criminals let loose to plunder and terrorize the towns and cities. A source told me:

> They released everything they could to cause mass confusion: murderers, thieves, even the criminally insane. The only things they didn't let loose were the animals in the zoo and the political prisoners. However, amazingly enough, people remained very controlled and even managed to keep some of their communication systems going; it was remarkable that during the entire period telephones in Rangoon continued to work.

Feelings against the army grew increasingly vitriolic. At one point it was rumoured in Rangoon that soldiers and a few government supporters were poisoning water stands that had been specifically set up in the streets for demonstrators. In a number of widely reported incidents, several suspects were rounded up and publicly beheaded on street corners.

Meanwhile the opposition leaders continued to press their demands for an acceptable interim government and a subsequent return to full democracy. President Maung Maung responded by announcing proposals for holding an emergency meeting of the BSPP to discuss a referendum over single-party rule. But this, the opposition leaders said, was too little, too late. U Nu, then aged eighty-one, declared that as the last democratically elected ruler of Burma he was the legitimate leader of the country. He would, he said, set up a parallel government to take charge of the country. However, the other opposition leaders rejected this as an undemocratic move that was not in keeping with the wishes of the people.

It seems that the blight of Burmese factionalism existed even at a time of crisis. While the official government had very little support or credibility, there was no clear unity among the opposition. U Nu was widely thought to have links with insurgent groups in Burma's rebel-held areas. Set against this, both Aung Gyi and the former defence chief Tin U still commanded a great deal of respect from various sections of the army and there were hopes that perhaps the military might split or even concede. But in the event it was Aung San Suu Kyi, as a complete outsider, who became an increasingly important figure. The very fact that she had no previous involvement with Burmese power-play, and all the wrangling it entailed, was a positive advantage.

By the beginning of September there were conflicting reports about the situation; some said the movement would inevitably succeed and that multi-party elections would indeed be held, others said that General Saw Maung, the head of the army, was planning to step in and take control to avert an all out civil war. Ironically, it turned out that both schools of thought were right: on 10 September President Maung Maung conceded and announced that democratic elections would be held within three months. But just one week later the army deposed Maung Maung and declared that they had taken full responsibility for governing the country. They called it a military *coup*, although I find the semantics of this somewhat questionable; Maung Maung's government had effectively been a civilian façade for the crumbling military rule and Saw Maung simply removed that façade in order to reimpose the full command and authority of the army.

Enraged demonstrators took up arms and went back on to the streets to protest; it seemed scarcely believable that the nationwide movement had been abruptly checked. But the army crackdown was extreme. After days and nights of street violence, bloodshed and killing the revolution ended and by the beginning of October people started going back to work, crushed and defeated. The army admitted that about sixteen civilians were shot and about 500 'looters' were killed in clashes with troops attempting to bring back a degree of law and order. It is almost impossible to establish how many actually died although it is thought that thousands were killed, thousands were arrested and thousands subsequently fled into rebel-held jungle areas to escape the harsh reprisals of the army.

Saw Maung set up a State Law and Order Restoration Committee, referred to by its acronym SLORC (which sounds appropriately like one of the more ghastly aspects of an Orwell novel). It would, he said, act as an interim government until democratic elections could be held as promised by the previous Maung Maung administration. However, only when law and order had been restored and the country had properly returned to normality would conditions be right for free and fair elections. It sounded quite reasonable but the promise was sufficiently woolly to give Saw Maung and the SLORC plenty of room for manoeuvre. Many people doubted that elections would ever take place. Meanwhile it was announced that the 'Burmese Way to Socialism' (the entire ideology on which the government of the past quarter of a century had been based) was no longer appropriate for the country and that the Burma Socialist Programme Party would be disbanded and replaced by a new party, the National Unity Party, or NUP – the Burmese are fond of acronyms.

These were gestures but for most of the cowed and frightened people they signified no real change. Few doubted that Ne Win was still behind all the moves despite his apparent retirement earlier in July; he had not deserted the army and, of course, the army had not deserted him.

Saw Maung, I was told, was just another puppet figure and meanwhile the man with real authority was Brigadier Khin Nyunt, the head of the secret police. (There were even rumours that he had become particularly close to Ne Win's daughter Sanda Win.)

But while the revolution had been crushed, Burma still had an opposition force that had not been able to exist before. The leaders at first continued to demand a proper, neutral interim government so that the country could prepare for the general elections it had been promised. U Nu set up the Democracy Party and meanwhile the National League for Democracy (NLD) was formed with Aung Gyi as chairman, Tin U as vice-chairman and Aung San Suu Kyi as secretary. Two months later, however, Aung Gyi left to set up his own party after power struggles threatened to split the NLD.

In late December, while the people of Burma were still picking up the pieces of their shattered lives and the bloodstains in the cities were being whitewashed, Daw Khin Kyi died aged seventy-six. As a figure of national importance, she was given a full public funeral. It was the first time groups had been allowed to gather in the streets since the military clampdown and it was the only occasion when the army, the students and the politicians came peacefully together. Thousands of soldiers, students, government officials and civilians marched quietly through Rangoon in a show of respect. It was a fitting end to the gracious and generous life of a woman who had served and pioneered for Burma. Aung San Suu Kyi applauded the restraint and decorum saying that it showed how the people and the military were able to cooperate. She hoped it would bode well for the future.

After her mother's death, Aung San Suu Kyi remained in Burma. She had now fully committed herself to the struggle for democracy. Her family, meanwhile, were based in England. The ties with England had begun with her student days; Suu had completed her formal education at Oxford University. After leaving school in Delhi, she read

PPE at St Hugh's College, Oxford. She subsequently worked for the United Nations in New York, serving on the Advisory Committee on Administrative and Budgetary Questions at the UN Secretariat. In 1972 she married a British academic she had met through the family of her guardians in England. Michael Aris had been the private tutor to the royal family of Bhutan and was at that stage employed by the government of Bhutan. Suu went to live with him in the Himalayan kingdom and worked as a research officer in the Ministry of Foreign Affairs. Bhutan had just joined the United Nations and, in particular, Suu acted as an advisor on UN matters.

Her first child, Alexander (also given the Burmese name Myint San Aung), was born in 1973. The new family spent several months in Nepal that year where Michael Aris was leading a research project on ancient monastic manuscripts. The family subsequently settled in Oxford and Suu worked and studied for a time within the oriental department of the Bodleian Library, while her husband continued his academic career in Tibetan studies. In 1977 her second child, Kim (or Htein Lin), was born. Frequent, lengthy visits were made to Burma and the family continued to use Oxford as their base.

In 1985, while her husband continued his Tibetan studies in Simla, India, Suu became a visiting scholar at Kyoto University in Japan. She had already learnt Japanese while at Oxford and this enabled her to research into some of the historical connections between Japan and Burma (and, specifically, the Japanese aspect of her father's struggle for Burma's independence). She then joined her husband in Simla where she continued her studies into Burmese history and subsequently returned to England to start a postgraduate thesis at the School of Oriental and African Studies in London. At that point her mother fell ill and she rushed out to Burma where she then found herself rapidly propelled into political prominence.

Various British papers reported that an 'Oxford housewife' had suddenly emerged to lead the democracy movement in Burma. It sounded intriguingly incongruous and helped sustain a degree of international interest in Burma after the revolution had been crushed and foreign journalists had once again been kicked out of the country. However, anybody meeting Aung San Suu Kyi would rapidly rethink the allusions to such a role of English domesticity. Quite apart from the academic background and the extensive travel and research, Aung San Suu Kyi was neither English nor simply an Oxford housewife.

My own childish impressions when I first met Suu in India had been of a poised and striking person with a proud, deep sense of being both Burmese and Aung San's daughter. On subsequent occasions I was struck by her uprightness, her fierce sense of values and her almost frightening determination. But in the face of such formidable characteristics she would suddenly smile or say something humorous and the commanding personality would become endearingly human. The sort of person you would never forget, even after a single meeting, I always felt she carried an air of total authority and unquestionable integrity.

Of course, comparisons are bound to come into play, especially when a prominent figure appears as if from nowhere. Aung San Suu Kyi seemed to be following a particularly Asian pattern of inheritance, where wife or daughter might well pick up the legacy of husband or father: in Sri Lanka Mrs Bandaranaike became prime minister after her husband was assassinated in 1959; in India Mrs Gandhi became prime minister in 1966, pursuing a political career trodden out by her father Nehru before her; in the Philippines Cory Aquino was elected President in 1986 having become her husband's political successor after he was assassinated in 1983; and in 1989 Benazir Bhutto was elected prime minister of Pakistan, a position once held by her father, Zulfikar Ali Bhutto.

The Bhutto comparison is perhaps the closest, although Aung San Suu Kyi herself dismissed all attempts to liken her situation or that of Burma to Benazir Bhutto and Pakistan; she said the two countries had such very different problems that there was no sense in seeking forced similarities. But the Bhutto story does provide some useful contrasts: unlike Benazir Bhutto, Aung San Suu Kyi never really knew her father and she was never groomed for a political life; unlike Bhutto she lived abroad for a great many years, married a foreigner and had a couple of children who had largely been brought up overseas; and, unlike Bhutto, she was struggling not so much to win an election as to alter an entire political system of oppressive, single-party rule.

Almost anywhere else in the world Aung San Suu Kyi's lack of political experience would have been a crippling disadvantage. But in Burma politics had become a very muddy, messy charade; a round of former army officers often discredited, exposed as corrupt and then punished as more army officers rose and fell in turn. Any real opposition both to the army and to Ne Win had been stifled and the country had remained in the hands of ageing leaders who made little apparent attempt to nurture a line of successors. Coming from the world beyond Burma, Aung Sun Suu Kyi was untouched by the blemish of Burmese politics and unintimidated by the Burmese army. It was her defiance and her lack of fear (or, conversely, her marked bravery) that distinguished her from other Burmese people who had lived within the military system for twenty-six years and had become ground down with oppression and despondency. 'After all, who is there capable of running the country?' a diplomat later remarked to me in Rangoon. 'At least Aung San Suu Kyi has got as much chance as anyone else – and certainly the military haven't got things right in the past twenty-six years.'

By the beginning of 1989 there were serious doubts as to whether the SLORC had any intention of holding a general election; no date had been set, no announcements made. But in the meantime an astonishing number of political parties were being spawned. It was as if people had suddenly gone dizzy with the very idea of democracy. Over 230 political parties were registered; along with the NUP, the

NLD and U Nu's Democracy Party, were the re-created AFPFL (formerly the first ruling party of independent Burma), the National Union Democratic Party, the People's Power Party, the Democratic Front for National Construction and even a Young Man's Evergreen Party. Some of the military claimed the sheer number of parties showed that democracy was unsuitable for Burma, but meanwhile many civilians said that a large number of them had been purposefully created by the military themselves so as to cause confusion. In addition, some parties had been set up in a true spirit of Burmese enterprise purely to take advantage of a slight relaxation of restrictions; registered political parties were allowed extra petrol rations and were permitted to hold gatherings in groups of more than five.

Aung San Suu Kyi, meanwhile, had started a series of cross-country tours, not so much to campaign for her party as to explain to those living mainly in the outlying rural areas just what might be understood by democracy. It was over a quarter of a century since the people had been given any real political choice. During her rallies, Aung San Suu Kyi drew vast crowds of people who came out to hear her in defiance of the soldiers and of the martial law. In a single year of political activity (before being held under detention) she made about a thousand speeches up and down the country. Although many of her party were taken into custody, nobody dared to arrest her; she was, after all, the daughter of Aung San. However, the soldiers often did their best to sabotage her speeches by attempting to drown her voice with loud music. On one occasion she came within moments of being shot during a confrontation with an army officer.

'She's got guts and she's also got charisma,' a Burmese friend remarked. 'But at first many people thought her movement was really just a youth movement,' he went on. 'She had tremendous appeal for the students although older people, particularly the professional classes, were fairly cautious.' It was the students, he explained, who protected her, became her self-appointed bodyguards and even camped out around her house in order to guard her from any army action. For them she had become a living myth.

While Aung San Suu Kyi made more and more of an impact throughout the country, the military stepped up their propaganda measures. Government slogans were posted up on huge red boards throughout the country and the *Working People's Daily* was filled with moralistic messages: 'The interests of the State cannot be served and promoted by disturbances and instability. Join hands with the Tatmadaw [the armed forces] in preventing disturbances and acts of instability,' said one such notice on Friday 24 March 1989. Peace, unity, the people and the military working together; it was actually the same sort of message that Aung San Suu Kyi was putting across, but with unnervingly repressive and authoritarian overtones.

On the same day, an editorial in the paper accused the BBC and the Voice of America of broadcasting malicious lies; 'The BBC is not honest, not straightforward at all. It never tells the truth. It takes every opportunity to spread false news . . . It is cunning.' The BBC World Service in particular had inadvertently played an important part in the uprising by managing to broadcast into Burma real news of what was happening within the country. The SLORC retrospectively announced that the news broadcasts had been deliberate attempts to provoke disturbance and cause unrest.

Meanwhile, in a national broadcast on the State radio, the SLORC stipulated that no army personnel would be allowed to stand in the elections, although they still continued to give no date for the event. The lack of military involvement with the future government sounded highly commendable but the SLORC then went on to announce that anyone involved with the recent demonstrations or anyone with 'allegiances to foreign powers' would also be disqualified. This was enough to debar any of the prominent opposition leaders, but in particular Aung San Suu Kyi whose Western links were coming increasingly under attack.

In the meantime, Aung San Suu Kyi continued to emphasize that unity was the way to democracy, that there should be no dissension between the army and the people and that the army should stay out of politics. But in response there were increasing attempts to discredit her with claims that she was reliant on communist advisors, that (with a large leap of logic) she was supported by the West and that she had links with insurgent groups. The fact that she was married to a foreigner provided further ammunition for the more xenophobic of the zealots who even started smear campaigns with obscene rumours of her sexual practices and her Western immorality.

Despite a continued show of wariness about the outside world and despite evident signs of suspicion about foreigners, the SLORC began a desperate bid for foreign business and foreign money. Burma's assets were for sale.

Japan, Australia, the USA and the EC countries had all suspended their aid programmes in protest against the massacres and the military clampdown. The large amount of frozen Japanese aid left the biggest gap. However, in the meantime, having rejected socialism as unworkable and inappropriate, the SLORC started opening Burma's doors to foreign capitalist trade and investment. The country still had much to offer in terms of natural resources; there were areas rich in tin and oil, there were forests of valuable hardwoods and along the coast there were territorial waters of profitable fishing. All these, it seems, were the most readily saleable of Burma's potential wealth and the SLORC began offering up favourable concessions to anybody who would come up with the money. I was told by a despondent Burmese friend that technically, as an interim government, the SLORC was not in a position to do this. He said that they had no right to start selling off Burma's resources. But who could stop them, he added sadly. Quite apart from the fact that the country was bankrupt, the army urgently needed the revenue to buy military provisions in order to keep both the insurgents and the people at bay.

Business is business and despite the studied show of

disapproval by their governments, American and a few British oil companies began signing concessions for inland oil exploration. Coca Cola took a good look at the possibilities of an enormous new market but havered and were outpaced by Pepsi Cola. The Strand Hotel in Rangoon, with all its faded colonialism, was even sold to be revamped for a future, bustling tourist trade. But above all, it was the neighbouring Thais who began making inroads into Burma. Official visits were paid by Thai government ministers and military personnel, deals were struck with Thai companies on the very highest approval of the Thai government and in the meantime Thai policy with regard to Burmese rebels and refugees on their border became increasingly confused. The Thais started chopping down Burmese teak, fishing Burmese waters and even gained concessions to mine for Burmese tin. The Burmese people themselves were appalled at the exploitation of their own natural resources and at the complete lack of conservation measures.

It seemed that foreign money might start to prop up Burma's ailing economy. However, for the average Burmese person life merely got more expensive. Between 1988 and 1989 the cost of living went up an estimated 30 per cent, by 1990 it had increased by at least another 20 per cent. The only signs of government activity and attempts to improve the lot of the people were in the frantic efforts made to reorganize the basic infrastructure of the country. At one point there were even rumours that the government planned to build a whole new city complete with sophisticated technology and advanced telecommunications systems. Although there was evidence to support the speculation, such government plans were clearly beyond the realms of fantasy; Burma had barely reached the age of the basic computer.

By May 1989 Aung San Suu Kyi had started calling for international sanctions to be taken against Burma. Still with no firm date set for a general election, her approach became increasingly confrontational. She began attacking Ne Win by name, although the military continued to maintain that he was no longer responsible for government matters. 'It was perhaps too much of a bold move,' a Burmese friend later said. 'It showed a want of respect for a senior person, which is very much against Burmese tradition and decorum.' However, others increasingly admired her audacity and respected her for daring to do what even the most senior army officer would have found unthinkable. Nobody openly criticized Ne Win and few would even mention him by name.

Tension mounted, particularly towards 19 July and the annual ceremony of Martyrs Day which only a year before Aung San Suu Kyi had attended alongside the military officers. Under martial law, the military announced, the people would not be allowed to attend and pay their respects to Burma's dead heroes since all public gatherings had been banned. But in defiance of these regulations, civil demonstrations and an alternative rally were organized by the NLD. The army retaliated with increasing threats of violence. They warned that they would shoot or arrest anyone found demonstrating and they started deploying troops in readiness. However, Aung San Suu Kyi managed to get word out to cancel the demonstrations and an all-out bloodbath was averted.

The next day troops surrounded Aung San Suu Kyi's home in Rangoon and she was placed under house arrest. The army said that she would remain in custody of her home for at least a year with the possibility of a further, indefinite extension. The reasons for the army's action were not clear and matters became further complicated by the fact that Burma's few international telephone lines were cut for several days. Her family, arriving on a visit from England, were also placed under virtual house arrest with her. They left a few weeks later. (Her sons subsequently had their Burmese passports confiscated and were not allowed to return to the country.)

It was during her family's visit that Aung San Suu Kyi went on hunger strike in protest against the treatment being dished out to some of her young supporters who had been rounded up and thrown into jail. After twelve days of fasting she finally forced the regime to promise that these prisoners would not be tortured.

I get the impression it was only at this juncture that the military had begun to see Aung San Suu Kyi as a very real threat. 'By shutting her away and giving her nothing to do the army simply hoped that she would get bored and agree to go back to England,' one friend explained. 'I think they grossly underestimated her determination.' The gates to Suu's home, meanwhile, became one of the sights of Burma. When I last visited Rangoon every friend I met would insist on making detours around town so as to pass by the outside of the house. They would point out the soldiers, clutching their guns, stationed at the gates and we would peer at other armed soldiers lurking in the bushes. There was no chance even of catching a glimpse of their detainee. One of her supporters told me:

> I'm sure we're supposed to see this as an example of what happens when you try to defy Ne Win – even the daughter of Aung San can be held in custody. But so long as Aung San Suu Kyi stays in the country there's always going to be a residue of hope for the people.

Similar action was taken against Aung San Suu Kyi's colleague Tin U. He was later tried and sentenced to three years hard labour and at about the same time U Nu, the former prime minister of Burma, was also placed under house arrest. Set against increasing reports of arrests and tortures and of ordinary civilians being rounded up and press-ganged into acting as porters for the Burmese army, it seemed depressingly unlikely that any free elections could or would be held in Burma.

It was during the monsoon period of 1989 that the SLORC suddenly changed the name of the country. Even now the reasoning seems confused. The Union of Burma became the Union of Myanmar, Rangoon became Yangon; Maymyo, the former British hill station, became Pyin oo Lwin, among a number of other changes; this was a reversion to Burmese names that had been Anglicized during the days of the British and, by implication, a further mark of paranoia and xenophobia more than forty years after independence. It seemed pointless and a bit silly. The government claimed that the change from Burma to Myanmar had been made specifically to take into account the ethnic minority groups, Burma being the name only of the dominant state of the country. The logic, however, seems curious since Myanmar is merely the Burmese name for Burma.

Any show of acknowledging Burma's ethnic mix, however, did not extend to those areas under the control of rebel forces. I was told by Karen leaders that in December 1989 some of the rebel chiefs sent a letter to Saw Maung asking if they could meet to discuss possible peace negotiations with the Burmese army. Saw Maung, they said, had replied maintaining that as the leader only of an interim government he had no authority to come to any settlement; such talks, he said, would have to wait until a democractically elected government was in position. Meanwhile the Burmese army continued to attack the rebel-held areas.

It is difficult even to think of Burma as one country. So many areas have been at war for so long and so many people from the minority groups have spent whole lifetimes fighting the Burmese army. Even when the people within Burma proper rose up to demand democracy, this bore no relation at all to the struggles of any of the ethnic rebel forces. Within a bankrupt country, the problems of replacing a military dictatorship with a working democratic system might seem formidable enough in themselves, however, the additional question of uniting all the war-torn parts of the region turns the situation into a complex nightmare.

'Actually, we don't want to fight,' I was told by a Karen soldier. 'We just want equal rights and equal status with the Burmans.' But it had been so long since the Karen first took up arms that I wondered how much any young Karen brought up within their rebel territory would really know of the Burmans. And, of course, it wasn't just a question of the Karen, who had merely been the first to set up their own army after independence; there were also the rebel Kachin, Chin, Shan, Karenni, Mon, Wa, Arakanese and many other smaller groups.

Over the years there had been a number of pacts and agreements between the groups. Inevitably there had also been disagreements. By 1989 various of these groups had reached a new understanding and, among other political rebel formations, the Democratic Alliance of Burma (DAB) was formed. There was an important change from some of the past groups, however, in that the new alliance included some organizations set up by Burmese people who had fled from government-controlled areas after the 1988 uprising. It was the first notable link there had been between the ordinary people of Burma proper wanting democracy and the rebel ethnic minority groups wanting their own federal states (within some sort of democratic system).

Visiting a rebel-held area prior to the general elections in Burma, I felt that there was a strength of purpose about these people but that they were motivated almost entirely by their opposition to and their hatred of the Burmese military junta. The DAB, I was told, was a union of twenty-two different groups who had four major objectives: to overthrow Saw Maung's army; to set up an interim government prior to holding general elections within the whole of Burma; to restore democracy to Burma; and to implement a federation of Burmese states. 'Of course we would like to negotiate,' I was told by one of the DAB representatives, 'but realistically we don't see that the Burmese army would ever simply step down. After all, the people tried peaceful protests within Burma and they just got shot.'

Although I knew the Burmese elections would exclude all the rebel-held areas (amounting to over a quarter of the country), I asked the DAB representative what he thought of the politicians within Burma. 'They don't really stand a chance, even Aung San Suu Kyi. She tried, but now that

she's under house arrest she's as powerless as all the others.'
He admired her courage and her determination but he did
not agree with her attempts to win over the Burmese army.
It was simply not feasible, he said. He felt the only option
was a major, all-out civil war despite the strength of the
Burmese army and the fact that it was finding new sources
of revenue through foreign business deals. He was very
earnest and even seemed faintly optimistic about the en-
deavours of the DAB but I couldn't help feeling that the
outlook for Burma, and particularly the rebel minorities,
seemed appallingly gloomy.

Early in 1990 the SLORC finally announced that they
had set the date for the promised general election. It was to
be held on 27 May. I was told that a great deal of serious,
superstitious thought went into the selection of the specific
day and that it all revolved around the number nine; the
number twenty-seven being divisible by nine and the day
itself falling within the fourth week of the fifth month of
the year. So much of Burma seems eccentrically amusing to
an outsider and even to the Burmese people themselves but
on the flip side of all these oddities is a whimsical government who have left the people with no money and no
freedom. Historically, though, government by superstition
is really nothing new in Burma; like Ne Win, the kings of
Burma had been obsessed by the number nine – King
Mindon had nine regal, white umbrellas and nine tiered
roofs to his palace – and U Nu, during Burma's first
independent government after the British, was known to
have carefully observed the presentiments of Burmese astrology and other traditional belief systems.

There was a momentary sigh of relief that, after such a
long struggle and a long wait, there would indeed be an
election, but with two prominent opposition leaders under
house arrest and one sentenced to three years hard labour it
seemed highly unlikely that it would be particularly democratic or fair. Travelling through Burma shortly after
the announcement had been made, there was a depressing
sense of cynicism. The elections would be meaningless and

life would continue just the same, I was told. How could anything change when the military had locked away anybody who could provide a serious alternative to their rule?

However, one prominent opposition leader still remained unshackled. What about Aung Gyi, I wanted to know, he had not been put under arrest and he was freely continuing to head up his own party. Many people, however, had become suspicious of him and felt that he was working too closely with the army. Then what about all the other hundreds of political parties, I asked; I was told that a large number were government backed, some solely represented specific ethnic groups and others were too small and ineffective to be of any national importance. One friend remarked:

> Some people say we should boycott the elections, but if we do that we'll be playing straight into the hands of the military who will merely say that this shows we don't want democracy. Other people say we should all go out on strike and demand the release of our political prisoners, but if we do that we'll just get shot, as we've learnt from experience. We're stuck with a farcical situation.

There was a glimmer of hope when Aung San Suu Kyi sent in her registration and, despite the fact that she was under house arrest, the election commission appeared to rule that she would be allowed to stand in the elections. Nothing was publicly announced but the news got out to the BBC who broadcast it back into the country. There was a feeling of quiet euphoria and also disbelief. The military would find some way round this one, I was told. They did. It was understood that a ruling against Aung San Suu Kyi was duly made on the basis that she was not a proper resident of Burma and that she had been involved in the 1988 'disturbances' although these grounds were never made public. Again, nothing was openly announced and again the news came via the BBC.

In the meantime, surrounded by soldiers, she was still sitting it out in her mother's old house on Inya Lake in Rangoon. She was not permitted to receive visitors (except, on two occasions, some members of the family and, again, on two occasions some Buddhist monks), her telephone was cut off and her letters and books were censored. It is a measure of her self-discipline that under such solitary confinement she is said to have devised strict programmes to keep herself busy: aerobics, practising the piano, reading, listening to news broadcasts. There were rumours (which were possibly rather far-fetched) that she spent time talking to the soldiers by whom she was detained and that she started teaching many of them English; as a consequence many people said that the soldiers were changed on a fairly regular basis. Others rumoured that one of the big fears of the military was that Aung San Suu Kyi would become too popular with members of the army. I heard one story that army officers, anxious to stop their men from becoming too sympathetic, told the young soldiers that Aung San Suu Kyi's marriage to an Englishman had alarming undertones; if she came to power, they warned, the British might come back to Burma.

They say it is a feature of Burmese politics that people out of public view remain just as much in the public mind and are probably more talked about than ever. After all, Burma is a country that reverberates with gossip, myths and legends and the Burmese are delightful storytellers. For all that Ne Win had removed himself from public life and sat in splendid seclusion at his lakeside residence in Rangoon, people would still speak of him elliptically and would still insist that he was really in control of the country. Surrounded by troops, his, however, was a voluntary isolation. But at the other end of the lake, also surrounded by troops, was a woman imprisoned in her own house who many saw as a type of latter-day Joan of Arc come to relieve them from the crushing power and control of Ne Win. No one would forget Aung San Suu Kyi just as no one could forget Ne Win.

Meanwhile news of world events had been very closely monitored by government censors. A revolution had happened in China and, like some bloody re-enactment of

Burma's own uprising, had ended in massacre. Revolutions also happened in Czechoslovakia, Hungary and East Germany. 'We barely heard anything about it through our own Press, but of course we knew what was happening through the BBC,' friends told me. In Mandalay I asked a young shopkeeper if he knew there had been a revolution in Romania. He looked astonished. He knew the Americans had invaded Panama, he said, and that President Bush had taken extreme and foolish measures with Noriega. He should not have been arrested in that way. I asked him (unfairly) what he thought of people being arrested in Burma. He looked embarrassed.

At the beginning of May, Amnesty International published a report on the fate of many known cases of Burma's political prisoners. It read like some of the worst excesses of a horror story; suffocation with plastic bags, iron bars rubbed up and down limbs with increasing pressure while the skin scraped off, hanging by the feet from a ceiling fixture or rotating fan while being beaten, electric shocks to toes, ears, fingertips, even testicles and many additional psychological pressures to break a victim's will and force a confession. In the face of such brutality and such measures of oppression it seemed hardly likely that Burma's long-awaited elections would be either free or fair when the people went to vote later that month.

The main opposition leaders had been locked up, political campaigning had been censored and severely limited and it looked as if no international observers would be allowed into the country. Yet in a totally unexpected twist, Burma's general election on 27 May was a model exercise of peaceful, free choice. At the eleventh hour a few foreign television crews and journalists were invited to Rangoon. There was, they said, no ballot rigging; there were no signs of intimidation. Their pronouncements were borne out by the results that started to trickle through; it seemed that the NLD, headed by a temporary leader in place of Aung San Suu Kyi, was set to win a massive majority.

It was the start of the monsoon. With roads washed away

up country and communications nationwide at a yearly low, counting the votes and registering the results centrally in Rangoon took a long time. It was weeks before a full total could be given. In the meantime the SLORC announced to the world Press that they would hand over power 'according to the law' once they were sufficiently assured of a strong and stable replacement government and once a new constitution had been drawn up and approved. They made it clear that the army would have to retain some power, particularly control over defence. It gave them plenty of loopholes.

The foreign Press departed. The people waited. Thirty-four days after the voting took place the full results were finally announced; the NLD had won 392 of the 485 contested seats in Parliament. Even in some military townships the vote had gone against the SLORC-backed NUP candidate and the soldiers themselves had supported the NLD. There was a mood of quiet and cautious optimism. People began demanding the release of the person the nation had really voted for – Aung San Suu Kyi. But nothing happened.

It is puzzling to figure out what the military authorities had hoped or expected and why they had permitted a free vote to take place at all. Many thought that the SLORC had never anticipated an all out success for the NLD and had imagined that with so many political parties in existence there would not be an overwhelming majority for one single party. But above all, the people had peacefully registered a clear opinion: they no longer wished for the old system of military rule.

The SLORC continued to prevaricate. They announced a sixty-day period to allow people to register complaints about the election procedures and about any unfair conduct; in the interim they said that it would not be possible to start handing over power. The anniversary of Aung San Suu Kyi's house arrest passed. She was not released. The NLD leaders continued to play a patient, waiting game and with them the people waited, growing increasingly tense and wondering if the government they had elected so overwhelmingly would ever be allowed to come to power.

On 7 September 1990 six NLD leaders were arrested on the grounds of spying. (What they were spying on, or for, was not disclosed.) Later the same month the SLORC declared that Aung San Suu Kyi might well remain imprisoned for four years or more. Meanwhile the military refused to hand over any responsibility to a civilian government. They continued to say that a new Parliament could not operate properly until a new constitution had been drawn up, which seemed on the face of it, a fair enough requirement. However, many ordinary people thought that the process of drawing up and agreeing such a constitution would inevitably take at least three years. So the waiting game continued.

For me, it all leaves a whole series of questions and no obvious answers. After years of military domination (and supremacy) would the army, realistically, ever step down? Some of the armed forces might have voted for Aung San Suu Kyi but with all the privileges that military life offered would the army as a whole willingly accept any type of civilian rule at all, however limited? Set against this is Burma's bank balance. With a moribund economy, where would the military government go to find some way of propping up the country? Could they survive as the pariahs of the free, democratic world (even with all the Thai wheeling and dealing)? And, perhaps most importantly of all, for how long would the people of Burma allow their army to carry on torturing and bullying them?

Much, of course, depends on the army and whether they would ever concede to a degree of fair play within the country. However, where the ordinary people of Burma fit in and how they have tolerantly endured an unpopular military dictatorship for so long, are factors that continue to puzzle me. I feel that a great deal must be attributed to Burma's history of authoritarian control (after all they had only fourteen shaky years of democratic government when the British left), but much also rests with the social fabric of the country: the culture, the customs and the long suffering outlook of the people.

PART THREE

CHAPTER SEVEN

BELIEFS:
The Pattern of Living

'Are you interesting the pagoda?' a neatly dressed lady asked me in faltering English. Her dark hair was swept up into a tidy bun and her face was subtly made up with a thin layer of *thanaka*, a powder of finely ground bark used by Burmese women both as a cosmetic and as a way of protecting the skin against the sun. I told the lady that yes indeed, I was interested in the pagoda. 'Come, I want to show you,' she smiled and took my arm.

It was a clear, bright January day in Rangoon, the very best time of year; dry, pleasantly warm, with clean skies of azure blue. Reaching far up above the city, the Shwedagon pagoda sparkled majestically, shimmering in its own intensified light as the gold leaf reflected and refracted the gentle sunshine. It seemed to exude an air of enchantment, drawing people up to the peaceful pagoda platform for contemplation and prayer. It was a tranquil, appealing presence.

I had joined the people visiting the great pagoda that morning. As a requisite show of respect I took my shoes off at the bottom of the main stairway, then I gazed up at the rows of shops and little stalls selling gongs, golden owls (for luck) and, nearer the top, delicate bunches of freshly cut flowers. People were making their way barefoot up the steps, stopping to buy the offerings and mementos on sale. It was at a small owl-stall that I acquired my new companion;

she was passing by and wanted to come to the rescue. Eager to help, she was glad to assist me in making a purchase. Within moments she had also become my self-appointed guide and friend. She was charming and self-confident and she also had a well-developed Burmese sense of the ridiculous. It was not easy to guess her age, although from her determination I reckoned she might have been about forty. (Burmese women under forty generally wear a cloak of submission – although they also manage to make it quite clear that they should never be overlooked.)

But neither the charm nor the pronounced indignation of my new companion made any impression on a couple of officials who appeared as if from nowhere and stood blocking our path. They were firm and faintly apologetic; why had I not visited the special office for foreigners near the bottom of the steps? I turned back perplexed, followed by the officials and my new friend. On reaching the office, I discovered the fuss centred on a question of money that was deemed to be owing; I was duly told to pay five US dollars in cash; a special charge for overseas visitors. My new companion was outraged and defensive; 'This is not good,' she said in a horrified stage-whisper. 'This is not part of any Buddhist practice, nobody should be forced to make a donation.' Of course I had no real objection to making such an offering but I agreed that the obligatory donation was out of kilter with the gentle and gracious atmosphere.

It was 1990. In the build-up to the elections that year a sense of unease permeated everything, especially life at the pagoda. Armed soldiers were very much in evidence, military intelligence officers sneaked around in mufti and the government authorities grasped any opportunity to acquire some foreign currency.

'You are English? Ah, that, at least, is good,' my new friend remarked as I emerged from the office clutching a receipt for five dollars. 'My name is Mya Mya Khin and I listen to the BBC.' She told me she had tuned into a news broadcast the night before; the BBC World Service had

announced that Aung San Suu Kyi was to be allowed to
stand in the elections that May, despite the fact that she
was under house arrest. 'The daughter of Aung San is our
hope for the future. She can bring peace and freedom to
our country,' said Mya Mya Khin with much conviction.
'But of course the military will find some way of dis-
qualifying her from the elections,' she added with a weary
smile.

Following the BBC announcement, that particular morning there was an undercurrent of triumph in Rangoon.
Nothing had been publicly announced within Burma yet all
those who listened to the overseas radio broadcast knew
of the temporary concession on the part of the government. The pagoda was crowded with gentle, smiling
people.

In direct contrast, the soldiers stood around looking
grim. 'Despite all their guns these soldiers are truly
frightened of the people and of what might happen at the
pagoda, it is a symbol of our religion, our independence
and our freedom.' It had been her intention to show me the
pagoda purely as a glorious example of Burmese culture,
but already Daw Mya Mya Khin found herself digressing.
It was almost impossible to avoid some reference to the
government and to the current political situation; in any
case, such matters had become a national obsession. Yet
quite apart from the dangers of anti-government talk, Daw
Mya Mya Khin had taken some risks in befriending me at
all, so she checked herself and with a murmur of 'We
should not talk here,' led me further up the steps.

We stopped to look at a series of pictures illustrating the
legend of the pagoda. The first depicted the story of the
holy hill on which the Shwedagon is built; three sacred
relics of three Buddhas were believed to have been buried
at the top – a rod, a water vessel and a robe. The following
pictures showed the story of the most recent Buddha,
Gautama, and how eight of his sacred hairs were hazardously
carried from India to the holy hill. There they joined the
other relics and were enshrined in a golden stupa – the

beginnings of the great pagoda complex that exists today. The legend was ancient, dating far back beyond my own Western measure of time. The pictures were unappealingly modern. But underlying the contrast was the sense of Burmese myth existing as a fundamental element of life today.

Because of the timeless and isolated nature of Burma, ancient legends have not only been preserved but they also have a function beyond the realms of fantasy and their relevance remains even today. In the meantime, new legends are created that take their place along with other tales of good and evil. Many stories about Aung San Suu Kyi and, indeed, many rumours circulating about Ne Win are now just as much part of Burmese culture as pagoda legends or tales of the Burmese kings. In a land of no real communication, myth and superstition remain an essential part of the Burmese way of life.

As if to illustrate the point, Daw Mya Mya Khin took me to one of the flower stalls at the top of the pagoda steps. She explained that the different types of flower have a particular significance for each day of the week. 'Sunday's flower is the coconut flower,' she told me, 'but look, where are the coconut flowers today?' I confessed I had no idea what a coconut flower even looked like:

> It is a fairly uninteresting spray of white, but what is remarkable is its total absence on this particular morning. In Burma the coconut flower is significant for Sunday but it is also symbolic of victory and today the authorities have banned the sale of this flower at the pagoda. You have to laugh. The BBC announce Aung San Suu Kyi will be allowed to take part in the elections. The government authorities say nothing. Our hopes are raised and meanwhile the sale of coconut flowers is banned, just in case we get any ideas. We have a crazy country.

Daw Mya Mya Khin escorted me around the rest of the pagoda. She told me tales of sacred bells, of spirits and magic stones. But she was careful to impress upon me the strength of Buddhist doctrine and belief; superstition and spirit worship being an entirely separate adjunct of a deeply felt and deeply revered religion. She left me with a sense of the rich web of Burmese spiritual life; the animism, the pure ideals of Theravada Buddhism and the day-to-day preoccupation with Burmese astrology and superstition.

Burmese nats, or spirits, stretch far back in time, pre-dating the introduction of Theravada Buddhism and also the arrival of the Mon and Burman peoples. A form of Bud-dhism was known to have existed in Burma by about 260 BC (Gautama Buddha himself is thought to have visited the country during his lifetime), but over the centuries it increas-ingly lapsed into tantric spirit worship. It was only during the eleventh century that the Burmese King Anawrahta adopted the pure ideals of Theravada Buddhism and ordered his people to follow the teachings of Gautama Buddha. The spirits, meanwhile, were not forgotten or even dismissed; Anawrahta ensured that they were allowed to retain a special place alongside the new belief system. And so it all remains nearly ten centuries later.

Anawrahta, however, tidied up and refined the compo-nent elements of nat worship; out of countless spirits, officially only thirty-six survived and to avoid the possibility of future problems and squabbles among the spirits, An-awrahta introduced a thirty-seventh nat, Thagya, who was made supreme king of the spirits. Over time a number of these nats have been replaced by figures from history – King Tabinshweti from the sixteenth century, even one of the kings of Chiang Mai. I suspect there are actually many more than thirty-seven nats, but that is the official number, and generally the selection of the said thirty-seven varies throughout the country, different spirits being appropriate in different regions.

'I don't know what you find so special about these nats,' one Burmese friend remarked disparagingly when I persisted in questioning him. 'Most educated people have no time for spirit worship – I can't understand why foreigners tend to become fascinated by such an inferior aspect of our culture.' I felt he had a point; I personally knew few Burmese people who admitted they took nats seriously, although I noted that they still regarded them with amused circumspection. There is, however, plenty of evidence of nat worship even in the relative sophistication of Rangoon. Downtown, along Strand Road and Merchant Street, the occasional tree will harbour a little nat house containing images of the spirits and placatory offerings; flowers, tiny paper umbrellas of white and gold. Meanwhile in the rural areas nat worship has a far stronger hold and in a few remote tribal regions entire communities still have no other form of belief.

Despite the apparent incongruity of the folk element of Burmese spirits and the sublime otherworldliness of Theravada Buddhism, nat images are often accorded a place in pagoda precincts. Again, it all dates back to King Anawrahta. In order to encourage his subjects to come to the first great pagoda he built for the new faith, Anawrahta ordered wooden carvings of the thirty-seven nat images to be placed on the platform of the Shwezigon pagoda in Pagan. This, he hoped, would enable the people to worship their old gods and, at the same time, absorb a new belief. Although the nat images have since been removed from the platform, they remain at the pagoda and today they are housed separately in a small building where they are still regularly appeased. Because the nats themselves are considered to be followers of Buddhism, it is neatly deemed to be perfectly acceptable for Buddhists to respect them and to provide them with special places at the pagodas.

But it's not just the nats. Many other aspects of magic and superstition are also manifest at Burmese pagodas. At the Maha Muni pagoda in Mandalay, for example, a side pavilion houses six bronze figures. They were originally temple guardians of Angkor Wat in Cambodia. Seized by the Thais and then captured by the Burmese, these figures were brought into Burma in the sixteenth century and were swiftly considered to have magical properties. There are three *chinthes*, or lions, two warriors and a three-headed elephant and they are all believed to have special healing

powers. Anybody suffering disease or pain in any given
part of the body can be cured by rubbing the corresponding
place on the body of one of the figures. There are some
interesting results; whole areas have become smooth and
shiny after centuries of rubbing, some parts have even been
worn away completely; knees, stomachs, even the groin of
one of the warriors. The figures are entirely secondary to
the religious significance of the pagoda, but they clearly
have an important function even today. During my last
visit to the pagoda I noticed a slender young girl stopping
to stroke the nose and feet of one of the lions. A few
moments later an elderly monk stumbled over to the three-
headed elephant and started vigorously rubbing the second
head. Discretion defied me to ask what was wrong but I did
wonder what the significance of the second head could have
been.

Quite beyond the magic and the nats, however, Burmese
astrology has a vital role in the lives of the people, on both
a domestic and a national level. The professional astrologer
is a rich and respected person. Ne Win himself is considered
to be excessively superstitious and reliant on the delibera-
tions of his astrologers. After he took control of the country
in 1962, he duly held long consultations: the astrologers
are said to have urged that he should move the country
more to the right. This was not, apparently, what Ne Win
wanted to hear, having just swung the country further to
the left in a bid for greater socialism. He therefore chose to
make a broad interpretation of this advice. The result was
that he changed the traffic regulations. The Burmese had
inherited a British system and such traffic as there was
moved on the left-hand side of the road; Ne Win issued a
directive that from then on all traffic should drive on the
right.

The high regard for astrology, however, is not just Ne
Win's personal quirk (although some of the results certainly
show his eccentric and manipulative touch). U Nu before
him was a deeply religious and deeply superstitious leader,
regularly consulting the astrologers about State matters and

taking advice about auspicious occasions. Before the British arrived the Burmese kings had, of course, relied heavily on the court astrologers and many of them would barely set foot beyond their palaces without reference to these counsellors. It is a continuing thread; there seems to be very little difference with Ne Win today.

Burmese astrology has been borrowed and adapted from Hindu origins and was known to have been widely practised long before King Anawrahta united Burma as a single country. The Burmese hold that there are eight planets which shape each person's future. (Nine being a peculiarly mystic number, there is, of course, a ninth planet but this has no direct influence on the fate of men.) As in other countries, the planets are associated with the days of the week, Wednesday being divided into two so that all eight stars are accommodated.

Rather like the signs of the zodiac in the West, in Burma each planet is represented by a particular creature; Sunday's is the mythical *galon* bird, Monday's is a tiger, Tuesday's is a lion, or chinthe, and so on. These creatures are given a place around the base of all the large pagodas and are set at specific posts, or corners; Sunday (the galon bird) in the north-east through to Saturday (a mythical snake, or *naga*) in the south-west. A Buddha image sits above these animals on a small stand or pillar, rather like a solid stamp of approval. Astrology and Buddhism; these two different belief systems that might once have seemed incompatible have become intermingled, much of the one absorbed by the other. Astrology has become a feature of Burmese Buddhism.

Buddhism is not concerned with naming or 'Christening' an individual, so astrology steps smartly in and provides the rough guidelines for the business of acquiring a name. People are simply called according to the day of the week on which they were born and their future is controlled by the planet associated with that day. The letters of the Burmese alphabet are divided up and apportioned among the eight planets; Saturday's planet, for instance, having the consonants ta, hta, da, dha, na. Traditionally every person is given a name that starts with a letter belonging to the birthday; like, for example, Thein, Thant or Nu for someone born on a Saturday. The special birthday name, together with any other names a person might be given, will be selected with great care by an astrologer. Often when a child is born he will be given a name, any name, as a sort of holding measure. Only later will he get his real name after his parents have had due consultations with an astrologer. But if the parents do not care for the astrologer's recommendations they will merely go to another astrologer and perhaps another until they find something to their taste.

Without the convenient hook of a family name, I find that the whole Burmese naming business tends to lead to great confusion. I suppose it all underlies the highly independent, egalitarian nature of the Burmese, but the consequent duplications and repetitions of the same name can be bewildering. In conversation, it is often very difficult to identify who precisely is being referred to simply because so many people tend to have the same names. Added to this is the complication of not immediately knowing who is married or related to whom. Because there are no family names and because women do not change their name on marriage, there are no apparent signs of kinship ties. U Thein Maung, to pick a random name, might be married to Daw Khin Lay with their children, again, called something completely different, and there will be nothing to give even a clue as to the relationship between any of them.

I was told that this system leads to confusion even among the Burmese people themselves. I always found it arduous work mentally plotting out elaborate genealogies and memorizing a complete series of seemingly unrelated names. In some cases the influence of English mission schools has added another naming element and many people have adopted totally different 'Christian' names which, for a foreigner, help to resolve some of the difficulties over identification. So, in a curious mix of East and West, U Thein

Maung and Daw Khin Lay might become Johnny and Pat Thein Maung. Among those of a slightly older generation these adopted names tend to have a distinct ring of the 1940s; Reggie, Gerald, Ruby. Meanwhile some of the younger people I've met will solemnly introduce themselves with such names as Sweetie Pie or Lovely.

One explanation for the general anarchy of Burmese names harks back, once again, to the days of King Anawrahta. The story goes that in his wisdom Anawrahta abolished the use of all union-like, descriptive names; the equivalents, as it might be, of Smith or Carpenter. He was eager to get the great city of Pagan built and built quickly and he wanted his men to be free from the limitations of one particular job. If called Carpenter, a man and his family might stick just to that work so he promptly got rid of the whole idea of such constraints. It's only a theory but it makes some sense.

The magic, the spirits and the dependence on astrology might seem to sit strangely beside Buddhism in Burma, but it is almost precisely because of Buddhism that these pagan beliefs continue. The main drive and preoccupation of Buddhist belief generally involves the life hereafter; the otherworldliness of the religion can leave little room for practical matters of day-to-day living. In Theravada Buddhism there are no immediate solutions. No pleas or prayers can be offered up for this life, man alone is responsible and accountable for his own destiny. So the ancient, pre-Buddhist cults of Burma have been retained and adapted to answer the mundane needs of the people.

Of the forty million people of Burma, the vast majority are Buddhist. It is a religion extremely tolerant of other beliefs and so despite, and perhaps because of, the strength of Buddhism in Burma other faiths have been allowed to develop. But there is something of a paradox here; more recently these other religions have met with a certain amount of repression at the hands of the government. This bears little direct relation to religious conflict; underlying the repression is the fact that it is the minority groups who generally hold these other beliefs. A Muslim minority exists along the Arakanese border with India while some of the tribes to the east are predominantly Christian. It was during the days of the British that missionaries performed whole-sale conversions among many of the Kachin and Karen people who had largely retained ancient animist beliefs. It was probably easier to evangelize among a people who held a primitive and even frightening religious cult. Today, the Baptist tradition seems particularly strong in some of the rebel-held areas.

Theravada Buddhism first came to Burma in the early part of the fifth century and was adopted and absorbed by the Mon people. It was not until some five centuries later that a Burman king was converted. But this single con-version was of the greatest significance in the spread of Buddhism across the country. As King Anawrahta extended his Burman Empire, so he introduced Buddhism and it became the official faith of the new, united nation. I find it an attractive and intriguing religion; at both a literal level, with the outward representation of the pagodas, the flowers and the studied calm of the Buddha images, and at an ideological level – the philosophy and perceptions, which I still struggle to understand.

A division between what are now two schools of Bud-dhism took place way back in the second century BC as Buddhism developed in India. The split developed due to differing interpretations of the Pali scriptures. The broader, Mahayana form of Buddhism is now widely practised in Asia and varies enormously in approach between regions; from Tibet to China, Korea and Japan. Theravada Buddhism is the more orthodox, conservative form which adheres strictly to the original teachings of Gautama Buddha. It is followed within a fairly tight region of South-east Asia: Sri Lanka, Thailand, Cambodia, Laos and, of course, Burma.

Central to Theravada Buddhism is the belief that all life, all existence, is suffering. The ultimate goal of life (a cycle of births and rebirths) is to achieve a state of non-existence or nibbana and thereby to end that suffering. Meditation and the attainment of merit through good deeds are the means of moving up through the cycle of rebirths to escape all suffering and achieve ultimate nothingness.

Within the wheel of life, or the cycle of rebirths, the planes of existence are many and varied and include different spheres for heavenly gods and a section for human life. Below these are four planes of wretchedness; animals, demons, ghosts and finally hell. Movement up or down the cycle is governed by the laws of karma; broadly speaking this means that all action prompted by desire of any form carries some sort of requital bringing merit or demerit to be duly meted out in successive lives. Only by subjugating desire and moving to higher planes of existence can the laws of karma cease to be effective and only after an eternity of rebirths can the cycle of existence finally be escaped.

Of course, in everyday Burma the reality of all this is very different. Most people are mainly preoccupied with improving their immediate lives and preparing for the next one, aspiring to a better life after this and in many cases merely wishing to be reborn as a richer and more powerful person. The Burmese can be very businesslike about the effects of good and bad acts; many will struggle to accumulate merit through good, charitable deeds to atone for any sins they might have committed in this life. In some cases the bad deeds might be directly quantifiable; a man guilty of adultery, for example, could be reborn with a small penis. Meanwhile the ultimate objective of nibbana seems almost irrelevant. It is a long way off and can wait.

The Buddhist way of life is one of tolerance, tranquillity and morality. Bad action causes demerit, good action leads to merit. The doing of good deeds, therefore, is immensely important and effectively centres on acts of giving; as a consequence the Burmese are enormously generous, despite the fact that today most of them have pathetically little left to give. The peace and tranquillity of life is created and maintained by meditation. Ultimately this meditation also leads to the state of inner knowledge and wisdom (or Enlight-enment) that is necessary before attaining nibbana. One result is, broadly, a national temperament of patience and benevolence – a direct contrast, of course, with all the recent displays of brutality and violence.

'We are good Buddhists. So long as we have enough rice in our stomachs we do not complain; we are brought up to accept our fate.' So said one student when I asked if he felt there was any possibility of a further Burmese revolution in the near future. Under the current military regime, one unhappy aspect of Burmese Buddhism is that perhaps the people are too tolerant, they have endured more than twenty-eight years of repressive military rule with surpris-ingly few outbursts of unrest. At the receiving end of the army's bully-boy tactics is a nation of people who simply lie down and take it all.

While tolerance might lead to flaccid acceptance, medita-tion breeds a certain self-absorption and introspection; a convenient defence mechanism against untenable realities of life. It's as if the Burmese people reflect the general isolation of their own country. Historically, geographically and, now, politically Burma has been cut off from the outside world; the experience of colonial rule left the country wary of foreigners and ultimately led to a with-drawal from international affairs. I suspect that as a sort of shadow act the Burmese people have been able to retreat into themselves as life under military rule has become more and more unbearable.

I once asked an official guide if he could tell me how big the Burmese army was. 'We have 170,000 soldiers and we have 170,000 monks,' he promptly volunteered. I'm not at all sure that the figures were correct but the comparison was certainly intriguing. It's the *sangha*, the Buddhist monk-hood, who have perhaps suffered most under military rule. Under the kings of Burma the sangha had a certain degree of power and a great deal of moral influence over the country. Much of this was curbed when the British took control of the country, but after independence Buddhism

and the power of the pungyis were reasserted during U
Nu's government. In a bid to avoid political opposition,
when Ne Win came to power the monks were once again
denied their traditional role of authority.

'I can't believe that many people in the army can be true
Buddhists,' one pungyi remarked sourly when I wanted to
know what the relationship between the sangha and the
government might be. 'When Burma is liberated once
again we will have a tough job in reviving the general
morals of the people.' He explained that the repression, the
intimidation and the wheeler-dealing of the black market
had undermined the moral structure of the country. Whole
generations of people brought up under the military regime
know how to survive through currency fiddles, bribes and
smuggling activities; the traditional, moral Buddhist code
has been eroded. But perhaps most importantly, the policy
and behaviour of the army run directly counter to the basic
Buddhist tenet of non-violence.

Although they provide spiritual and moral leadership,
pungyis are in no way priests nor are they primarily responsible for interpreting or preaching the holy scriptures to the
people. Men become monks and renounce the materialism
of the world chiefly for their own spiritual wellbeing (the
word pungyi literally meaning 'great glory'). Rather than
serving the people, it is the people who serve the monks
and thereby acquire great merit. But it is not necessarily an
élitist or binding order; traditionally all boys should at
some stage be sent to a monastery even for a day or two.
Thereafter they can return to spend varying periods of time
whenever they choose. Those wanting complete spiritual
seclusion are ordained as pungyis and follow the 227 rules
of the Vinaya, the monastic code. They will spend the rest
of their lives in religious contemplation.

On entering the monastery a man will relinquish his
possessions; the only property he is allowed being his saffron robe, a small razor (to keep his head, eyebrows and
face shaved as a measure against vanity), a needle and
thread, a lacquer begging bowl, a fan of palm leaves and a

water strainer (in case he should unwittingly drink and kill any insect life). Each morning he will leave the monastery to collect alms in the form of food – he is never allowed to touch any money. All eating takes place before noon and the rest of the day is spent in prayer, meditation and religious study. It is an austere way of life but for those in the more difficult rural areas it is actually a fairly cushy number. The pungyis do no work and are fed for free; often the standard of living is higher than the ordinary agricultural labourer might be used to. Perhaps the greatest element of self-denial is that the pungyis are celibate, meditation being the way to eliminate all worldly desire and to become closer to the state of nibbana.

When people visit a pagoda they will kneel down in front of a Buddha image to pay their respects. As they venerate the Buddha they will often put their hands together, stretching their five composite fingers apart from each other. These provide five points of reference by which to remember the Five Precepts or moral codes (of which more, later). They will also serve to signify the five objects of reverence within Buddhist thought: it is important for a person to honour the Buddha, the Teaching, the sangha, his parents and his teachers.

The whole concept of teaching and, by extension, learning, lies at the heart of Theravada Buddhism. Buddha was, effectively, a sacred teacher guiding his followers along the path to salvation and release from suffering. Technically it is what Buddha said, rather than what he was, that remains the key element; the teachings rather than the Buddha figure himself. Since Buddha's lifetime, others have taken these teachings and conveyed them to their pupils. In so doing they earn some of the respect accorded to Buddha, the first of the great teachers and the originator of the great teachings themselves.

From the very beginnings of Theravada Buddhism in Burma, young boys entering a monastery for their period of religious initiation would be given a religious education. As a matter of course they would also learn how to read and write. Within the Buddhist tradition, since all boys at some stage become novices, they would therefore all receive some education. Back in the eleventh century, when King Anawrahta first grafted Theravada Buddhism on to what was effectively an animist belief system, he thereby introduced a solid tradition of learning and literacy. For centuries that tradition remained in the hands of the monks.

The pungyis therefore used to have a directly practical, functional role in Burmese society. They were the teachers. At the very least their pupils learnt the three Rs and studied some of the holy texts. The whole pattern of Burmese education, meanwhile, remained an integral part of monastic life. As a direct reflection of this, *kyaung* is the Burmese word for both a school and a monastery. The reverence duly accorded to a pungyi is partly in recognition of his renunciation of worldly matters and partly because of his traditional and quasi-religious status of teacher. Even today the pungyi will be greeted with deep respect as *sayadaw*, literally meaning honoured teacher, although he might never have had much of an opportunity to fill that role. Meanwhile, children are very strictly brought up to show all due reverence to their schoolteachers. Although the majority of Burmese teachers now have no religious function at all, their pupils will still be expected to honour them as they would honour their parents or the pungyis.

While monks have a prominent, respected position, it seems strange that in spite of the egalitarian nature of Burmese society there is no corresponding role for women. Within the lifetime of Gautama Buddha there was, in fact, a special order for women ordained within the sangha but over the centuries this died out. It was replaced by a far more lowly order of nuns which still exists today and which has neither the respect nor the status attributed to the pungyis. Burmese nuns are not, now, ordained, nor is there a tradition of young girls at some stage spending time in a nunnery: only a few women choose to follow a religious life. But since they do not live according to a holy rule they remain, simply, very devout lay people.

The nuns are known as *thilashins*, or keepers of the precepts, the series of moral codes at the heart of Buddhism. There are three sets of these precepts: all Buddhists should observe the Five Precepts, a set of prohibitions against stealing, lying, having illicit sex, killing (anything at all, including tiny insects) and getting drunk. Devout Buddhists will follow the Eight Precepts which include the original five (the rule against illicit sex being extended to a ban against all sex) plus three more prohibitions against eating after noon, sleeping on a high or ornate bed and attending any theatrical entertainment (this, by extension, includes a rule against wearing jewellery and cosmetics). The pungyis will observe the Ten Precepts which include two more prohibitions; a direct veto against wearing any sort of ornament and a ban against handling money.

As devout Buddhists the nuns follow the Eight Precepts and they indicate their removal from worldly matters by shaving their heads and wearing special, apricot-coloured robes. Like the pungyis, they also beg. But this is a very different sort of begging and, as an outside observer, I've always felt that it is the most immediately obvious sign of the nuns' inferior position. Strictly speaking the pungyis do not in fact beg so much as accept charitable donations of food. In the early part of the morning they will leave the monasteries and will often follow a set pattern of visiting the same houses to receive the same quantities of food which are respectfully placed in their begging bowls. It is a neat system; the monks are regularly fed while the donors are regularly able to gain merit. Nuns, however, do not have such an easy time. Very often they have to beg openly and frequently they will have to beg for money. Whereas the pungyis only make their rounds in the mornings and will reverently and willingly be given food, the nuns might sit all day at pagoda steps with their tin begging trays set hopefully in front of them.

During a trip up country I became particularly puzzled by the treatment of these women in apricot robes. A tooth-less nun grinned up at me with gummy gratitude as I deposited one kyat on her sparsely filled tin tray. She was sitting beside the pathway to the Kyauktawgyi pagoda at Amarapura, one of the former capitals of the Burmese kings. I had been taken there by an official tourist guide from Mandalay and while he spoke learnedly about the pagoda, the kings and Burmese Buddhist history, I noticed that he made no attempt to offer any sort of donation to the elderly nun. He walked by, hardly conscious that she was there at all.

I interrupted his scholarly talk to ask why nuns got such a raw deal. He looked confused. 'I don't think many nuns would agree with you there,' he replied. 'They choose to lead a quiet, spiritual life but as women they cannot expect to have the same privileges as pungyis.'

Underlying the status of nuns is, of course, the entire question as to the position of women within Burmese Buddhist society. Historically and traditionally Burmese women have had a high and respected place. During the period of British rule, many of the foreign officials noted that the nineteenth-century Burmese woman had a great deal more independence and liberty than her counterpart in England. Burmese society has not changed radically since then and today women continue to choose who they marry (if they wish to marry at all) and to retain ownership of all their property within the marriage partnership; they even keep their own names. Traditionally Burmese women have made sound business managers and professionally they enjoy a more-or-less equal status with men.

To my mind, though, there is every indication that in the past women came off rather badly. Because, for centuries, education lay in the hands of the monks and because it was only the boys who spent time in the monasteries, women had very little opportunity even for the most rudimentary schooling. I discussed the issue with a Burmese friend who said:

Yes, I suppose women might once have appeared an uneducated lot. Some did learn how to read and write at home of course, but I think that generally while men were getting on with religious matters, the women were far too preoccupied with running the home and organizing other, functional aspects of life to be particularly concerned about this.

She talked about the tradition of men frequently returning to spend time in the monasteries throughout their later life:

I feel that maybe it was because many men tended to get so wrapped up with their religion that Burmese women became so practical. We're excellent managers, you know. For centuries Burmese women have not just been domestic creatures; we've had a great deal of commercial clout, from behind the scenes.

The men in the monasteries while the women got on with things; it was an interesting theory and I felt that what she said made a great deal of sense. It helped to explain why, although women might spiritually be on a lower level to men, they are not apparently held as inferior or lesser beings. 'After all, in Burma we've never really felt the need for women's liberation,' my friend said. 'But then I suppose we don't even have much national liberation at the moment,' she added with a wry laugh.

Perhaps the most marked aspect of women's spiritual inferiority is at the larger pagodas where they are strictly prohibited from entering the upper terraces. (They are not allowed to position themselves higher than the men or the Buddha images because they would thereby pollute the male *hpon* or glory.) This often means that they have to stay some distance away from the more sacred Buddha images around the pagoda platform and that they cannot join the men in making donations of gold leaf which are peeled on to these holy statues.

'It's not really considered to be that much of an important issue,' I was told by one pungyi when I expressed some confusion about the general position of women in Burma. 'The lower status of women is really just a hangover of the Hindu background from which Buddhism developed.' Nevertheless, it still means that within the cycle of existence a woman will have to be reborn as a man in order to reach the next stage nearer nibbana.

There is an apposite reminder of this at Mandalay: immediately above the old capital, Mandalay Hill rises up some 700 feet. It is a sacred place said to contain holy relics and is covered with sheltered stairways that are punctuated at regular intervals by small shrines and Buddha images. About two thirds of the way up one of the main stairways a fairly lurid statue of a woman kneels in front of a Buddha image. Her chest bleeds from self-inflicted mutilation as she offers up her severed breasts to the Buddha in token of her humility and devotion. The statue depicts part of the legend of the ogress Sanda Moke Khit, who became a devout follower of Buddha and cut off her breasts as an offering. She thereby acquired so much merit that despite her unpromising status she was duly reincarnated as a man and was reborn some centuries later as King Mindon himself, the last of the truly great kings of Burma.

There's no implication that women should continue to take such measures but certainly for all Buddhists, men and women, offerings and donations remain an essential feature of religious life. The practice of this gift-giving is another of the more perplexing aspects of Theravada Buddhism. People visiting a pagoda will present offerings of flowers and little umbrellas at their appropriate weekday corner and at the feet of the many Buddha images around the pagoda precincts. It is a ritual that would suggest they are venerating a god-like figure.

'In Burma we have to pray to Buddha to keep us healthy.' This from a government official who was showing me around town. As we passed the Rangoon General Hospital he explained that although Burmese doctors are highly respected, medicines are so scarce that there is often little the doctors can actually do. It was just a passing comment but I felt it spoke volumes. On the one hand it reflected the response, even on the part of officials, to the limitations of the current economic muddle; on the other hand it in turn showed a healthy, if rather confused, respect for Buddhism.

For, strictly speaking, prayers and offerings are totally pointless. In Theravada Buddhism there is no omnipotent god. The Buddhas themselves are enlightened beings who teach men the way to an ultimate release from the suffering of existence. Gautama Buddha was the latest in a long series of twenty-seven of these teachers.

He was born as the Indian Prince Siddhartha in the sixth century BC. He lived a courtly life, married a princess and had a son. Four great signs were revealed to him on one of his princely hunting expeditions (he saw an old man, a leper, a corpse and a religious recluse) and he found himself reconsidering his approach to life. Aged about twenty-nine he abandoned all worldly things. He cast aside his riches and his courtly dress and, wearing only the rough robes of a beggar, he set off on a pilgrimage. He spent a great deal of time in religious contemplation and it was while sitting under a Bo tree one day that he reached an understanding of how to escape the suffering of existence. Having gained Enlightenment he spent the next forty years wandering the earth as a beggar, teaching his disciples how, ultimately, to attain deliverance. These instructions form the vital element of Theravada Buddhism. Meanwhile Buddha himself is the only entity of an otherwise completely abstract religion. But since Buddha attained nibbana centuries ago, technically he is neither a powerful deity nor the saviour of mankind.

Then why pray or make offerings to Buddha? The need for some sort of help here and now makes it tempting to see Buddha as a type of god. I am told, though, that the Buddha statues are there principally as a sort of visual aid, a symbol to help people to concentrate on the holy teachings. The offerings are made to honour and commemorate the life of the great teacher, the apparent act of worship being a form of ritual to assist religious contemplation.

For a foreigner the size of many of these Buddha images is quite staggering: vast seated Buddhas tower above offerings of flowers and candles, huge reclining Buddhas with mirrored soles to their feet lie calmly in special buildings and in Mandalay a whole street of artisans' workshops

churns out quantities of large new statues specially ordered
by those able to pay for the extra merit they hope to acquire.

While Buddha images might be there to help people
concentrate on the holy teachings, the pagodas are places
the people visit not so much to pray as to reflect inwardly
and meditate. Botataung pagoda near Monkey Point in
Rangoon provides perhaps the most obvious facilities for
this sort of religious self-immersion. It is far smaller and far
less romantic than the great Shwedagon pagoda, but it has
been constructed in such a way that visitors can enter the
golden pagoda bell to meditate, absorbed within the quiet-
ness of the pagoda itself. The passageways are lined with
thousands of tiny diamond shapes of mirrored glass so that
people sit surrounded by images that mirror images and by
reflections of reflections of refracted light.

Quite separate from the ritual offerings are the donations
made to the pagoda itself. These are given both to glorify
the pagoda as a religious shrine and to acquire merit. When
a gift of money is deposited in one of many bowls set aside
for the purpose a bell is often struck so that everyone
near by can hear and share in the merit generated by the
good deed. It is as if the virtue of the act reverberates,
creating more merit which flows back to the original donor.

A relatively new mechanism for soliciting pagoda donations had been introduced in Rangoon when I was last
there; electrically powered rotating bowls had become a
feature. I came across the most complex of these in a large
pavilion by the side of Botataung pagoda; it was quite a feat
of engineering. On a platform behind some railings was a
scene from the life of Gautama Buddha; it was as big as a
stage set. The Buddha was sitting under a Bo tree in
discussion with one of his disciples who was holding an
alms bowl which moved up and down. In front of them
more alms bowls popped up from beneath the platform and
moved along the setting, disappearing back into the platform at the far end of the scene and re-emerging behind the
Buddha in constant rotation. A couple of people beside me
were throwing a few coins at the bowls as they passed

along; it was a bit hit and miss. But for all that it was fairly racy stuff and distinctly reminiscent of a fun fair. There seemed, though, to be little interest in making serious donations in this way.

As well as money, people will often donate objects of value to the pagoda. At the larger pagodas these are set aside in glass cases and at the Shwedagon pagoda an entire building set on the pagoda platform acts as a museum for these items. The collection is large and extremely varied, much of it seems faintly Victorian in style. Along one of the walls are rows and rows of little Bo trees, fashioned out of gold and silver, on which dangle coins that were used in colonial days. There are cases of small Buddha images – travelling Buddhas standing up with robes unfurled; meditating Buddhas seated with legs tucked up in the lotus position and a hand, palm upwards, on the lap; pointing Buddhas (a special Burmese variety); and short-necked Buddhas which are said to protect homes from burning down. In a heavily protected case behind some iron railings are the treasures of real monetary value. In pride of place is the old weather vane that has since been replaced at the very top of the pagoda; some of the diamonds still sparkle out of the gold leaf but many of the other jewels have been taken out to be used in the new weather vane. There are great bowls of silver encrusted with huge rubies, sapphires and emeralds and between them are smaller jewelled ornaments. Strangely, among all this is a plastic doll about a foot high; this was the treasured toy of a young girl who died some years ago. A photograph of the little girl still hangs pathetically from its neck. When I last visited the museum there were twelve long pigtails of human hair on display by the entrance. These had recently been donated and each was labelled to identify the original owner; one was still wet from being newly washed.

The very rich, however, will actually cover the cost of building new pagodas as a supreme way of glorifying Buddhism and of gaining merit. It is thought that often men of power also built pagodas to atone for their wrongs. Back in the eleventh century, King Anawrahta started the age of pagoda building in Pagan and it became the great tradition of the first dynasty of Burmese kings whose empire lasted until the thirteenth century. Successive dynasties of Burmese kings continued to mark their faith and their importance by setting up new capitals and constructing new pagodas there. In the eighteenth century King Bodawpaya, the fourth son of the fierce and warlike Alaungpaya, started an ambitious plan to build what might have been the biggest pagoda in the world. The Mingun pagoda remains in ruins on the banks of the Irrawaddy in Central Burma; it was never completed and was largely destroyed by an earthquake early in the nineteenth century. When King Mindon later built Mandalay, he turned the new capital into a religious centre, constructing pagodas and holding the fifth Buddhist synod there. After independence U Nu organized the building of the Kaba Aye, or World Peace, Pagoda, completed with an especially large meeting and meditation centre. (At the time, he was accused by some people of having the same aspirations as the former Burmese monarchy.)

A new pagoda was being built when I last returned to Rangoon. It sat ostentatiously on a small hill directly opposite the ancient Shwedagon pagoda. The large, traditional bell shape had not yet been coated with gold leaf but it promised to look magnificent, like all gilded Burmese pagodas. It was supposedly for the people and it was paid for by the people and by a great many individuals whose donations and gifts were regularly listed in the *Working People's Daily*. But many actually called it Ne Win's pagoda. It was rumoured he was trying to atone for his catalogue of wrongs and to buy his way out of all the demerit he had acquired.

Back in 1960, prior to the general election held that year, Ne Win remarked that the country should make its own choice; 'It will get the government it deserves,' he said. It's an old adage but, for Burma, the implications run particularly deep. The notion of karma and of retribution for past misdeeds is often thought to extend to an entire nation. Many might interpret the suffering brought about by military rule as a direct result of the past sins of the people. I can't think, though, of quite how the Burmese could have deserved their lot. On the contrary, centuries of devout Buddhism have ensured that the people generally adhere to a strict moral code (for all the more recent profiteering on the black market). Buddhism, preaching tolerance and acceptance, has also contributed to the long-suffering outlook of the Burmese. Yet for all that, the pungyis themselves have become one of the most vociferous groups to condemn the actions of the military government.

CHAPTER EIGHT

FESTIVALS AND FEASTING

I once knew a Burmese movie star who tried to teach me how to dance. It was not a great success. I proved to be woefully inadequate at following her intricate movements as she twisted her slender body through tight contortions and wound her hands into impossible, double-jointed positions. She was usually accompanied wherever she went by her father and when she came to visit he came too. He would sit, watch and laugh amicably as we went through our very different motions. 'Don't give up,' he would say. 'My daughter took a long time to learn.' His advice went unheeded.

Burmese dancing is really a series of agile but static postures which require much skill and grace to achieve and hold. As a foreigner, I sometimes find the tautness and rigidity of it all distinctly uncomfortable even to watch. Women dancers have an especially difficult time; the courtly dress they dance in would appear to impede any but the most jerky of actions. It seems against all odds that they manage to move at all. They wear tight tops and tight little jackets below which the *tamein*, a sort of ceremonial skirt, covers the rest of the body. It consists simply of a long length of Mandalay silk which is wound round and tucked securely into the waist, opening out below the knee and extending into a long train behind. It is almost impossible even to walk wearing such a garment; only by bending the knees and kicking back at the train can any sort of forward or backward motion be made. The dancers consequently have to remain in a squatting, crouching position lunging back at the train with their feet and progressing only very slowly across a stage while twisting and turning head, hands and torso.

Male dancers also wear a type of ceremonial courtly dress but this allows them greater scope for mobility and they are able to leap around with some freedom. Their movements, though, are as tense as those of the women; elbows, knees, hands and feet pointing outwards at a series of angles. This jointed, sharp posturing is a very Burmese type of movement. It is not just confined to dancing; *chinlon*, a sort of Burmese football, is played entirely on the basis of such angular action. The ball is a little smaller than the average football and is very light, made of woven bands of wicker. There are no teams or goals; it is essentially a way of exercising the body rather than a game. The object is simply to keep the ball in motion off the ground for as long as possible. It may not touch a player's arms or hands so the ball is hit using the knee, shin, ankle, foot and head. The result is a complicated series of sharp twists and turns and agile, jointed manoeuvres.

I've always felt that all this angular and fitful movement must relate in some way to the love of puppetry in Burma. Traditionally puppet entertainment was more popular than the human counterpart and often the puppet master was accorded just as much prestige and respect as the most talented dancer or actor. Nowadays puppet groups have almost disappeared but the style and motion of Burmese dance still reflects the puppet tradition – from which it all developed. Analogies can be taken to extremes, but it is tempting to see all the puppet play as a sort of symbol of the army rule: awkward posturing, manipulation from behind the scenes and no sign of the person who is really pulling the strings.

The Burmese are past masters of the art of entertainment. Time was when people regularly put together some awning, rigged canopies up outside their houses, called in the dancers, actors and musicians and held their own pwes, or festivals. Until recently, these festivities could last all night, even longer. They would be open to anybody; family, friends, neighbours, even the casual passer-by. The host paid for the whole thing and his expansive circle of guests could just wander in and out at their leisure. A great deal of eating, chatting and smoking of cigarettes and cheroots went on as the orchestra and players performed with much noise, colour and drama. Liberally sprinkled into the performance would be sharp, humorous elements that related to the present day; political lampoon being extremely popular. The pwe in itself was more than a party, more than a play, more than an opera – it was a vibrant Burmese celebration which would take place at even the slightest excuse: getting a new job, making a large pagoda donation, moving house. And of course, pwes would be held for all the serious things in life: births, marriages, deaths.

There aren't so many pwes held nowadays. And they aren't quite the same. People don't have the money, the freedom, nor, probably, the inclination. Over the past twenty-eight years martial law has frequently been imposed, inflicting stifling limitations on the essentially fun-loving and happy-go-lucky Burmese. Under these increased measures of army repression, open gatherings of groups of more than five people are banned and a strict curfew has to be observed. This usually lasts from ten in the evening until four in the morning, although during times of very serious unrest people have to remain immured between 6 a.m. and 6 p.m. It is not wise to be caught out and about at the wrong time; the prisons are full of people who have been thrown in for the most flimsy reasons.

Nevertheless, the Burmese have managed to retain their sense of humour and their sense of theatre. When the curfew is lifted the fanfare does go on but in a more muted manner. Of course nowadays there is also a whole film industry producing romantic, moralistic numbers which are heavily censored. The censorship board has very strict guidelines which determine what may or may not be performed on screen. A film (and also a work of literature) should be edifying and instructive as well as being entertaining.

For all the love of entertainment, though, Burmese festivals bear little direct relation to the Buddhist tradition of contemplation and meditation. The vibrant colour, noise and drama of the pwes reflect the older elements of Burmese nat worship.

Generally, nats are not nice things at all. They are mischievous, impish and aggressive. They are best avoided where possible and indeed the idea behind most nat worship is to keep these spirits at bay. If they are placated and appeased with special offerings they might not cause any trouble. However, nats can also be actively called upon to bring good fortune and to cure ailments. Sometimes they are even asked by special and elaborate invitation to visit particular homes so as to bring luck and prosperity. This, it seems, has become a thriving business.

I was visiting a monastery in Rangoon and conducting a quiet conversation with the head pungyi when the peaceful atmosphere was abruptly shattered by a banging and crashing of gongs some distance away. The young novices at the monastery came dashing out in a state of high excitement and rushed off to see what was happening. There was a nat pwe taking place at a house just outside the monastery, so, at the suggestion of the head pungyi, I went along to take a look. It would be colourful and amusing, he said, a very Burmese sort of entertainment.

The novices, their shaven heads shining at the tops of their saffron robes, were clustered round a doorway at the very edge of the monastery boundaries. They were smiling and giggling, gazing out over a rigged-up shelter where the festivities were taking place. Although nat worship has no connection with monastic life, the young pungyis were as curious as I was to see what was happening on their doorstep. Meanwhile smartly dressed guests, sparkling with gems and wearing crisply ironed lungyis, were arriving. They called out, inviting me to join them.

At one end of the shelter a Burmese orchestra had started

playing, emitting great crescendos of sound as the musicians worked their way vigorously from one climax to the next. To the Western ear Burmese music can seem very noisy and heavily reliant on percussion instruments. Various musicians are usually surrounded by what look like large play-pens full of drums and gongs which are struck with much energy and enthusiasm. There are also xylophones, bamboo clappers, cymbals and occasionally the odd flute. The nat pwe seemed cheerfully loud and as I made my way forward the noise reached deafening heights.

On some matting in front of the orchestra a couple of dancers were leaping around; these were human representatives of the nats, one was a man and one a transvestite. The guests (mainly women) were sitting in a semi-circle on the floor around the dancers and behind them were tables groaning with food, flowers, whisky (bought at great cost on the black market) and other offerings. In a place of honour among these delicacies, a group of nat images looked down on the proceedings.

The lady of the house was more than happy to welcome a foreigner to the pwe; my arrival was something of an auspicious sign. She beckoned me forward and invited me to sit by her side while we watched as the dancers and the music became more and more frenetic. Suddenly the transvestite stopped and began trembling from head to toe; 'A nat has arrived and is entering the human body,' someone hissed at me by way of explanation. Then the money and the whisky began to flow. The nat dancers gulped down large tumblers of whisky and began to make increasingly outrageous demands for gifts. But the lady of the house seemed very happy to oblige. She was duly rewarded for her efforts; the visiting nat, speaking through the medium of the transvestite dancer, declared that the lady of the house was a fortunate lady, she was rich; next year she would be even richer and she would be able to buy a new car (in Burma a new car involves a very serious outlay of money). The lady glowed with smiles of delight.

As a foreigner I was fair game, and the dancers switched their attention to me: would I like to give some money, and some more, and some more – I began to suspect that this was really why my presence was considered so auspicious (I was never even rewarded with optimistic tales of my future prosperity). Finally I removed myself as gracefully as possible before I was left with nothing at all.

As I retreated from the nat pwe and the cacophony of the orchestra I looked back to the monastery and saw the young novices doubled up with laughter, great white teeth gleaming. How much was I forced to pay, they asked. 'These dancers really know how to make money,' they remarked between bursts of giggles. They clearly felt nats were a lot of nonsense. Later, a friend explained:

> Nat dancers are not always men, in fact technically a nat will only enter a woman's body. Many women nat dancers have considerable talent. It's a shame because they often ruin their reputations by becoming involved with the nats. Mind you, they can earn a fortune. For those who are prepared to believe in spirits and that sort of thing, the nat pwes are quite some business. They are mainly held by the richer people who have to hire the orchestra, the dancers and all the other paraphernalia at vast expense, to say nothing of the size of the so-called gifts they have to make.

I asked about the transvestite dancers. There was a short laugh. 'Oh, those homosexuals are an odd bunch. I don't think we have many in Burma. But already we do have what-do-you-call-it, AIDS – I believe there are thirty known cases of it in the country.'

While pwes tend to be noisy and even raucous, Buddhist celebrations are tempered with decorum and restraint. Despite the popularity of show business and revelry there are surprisingly few personal festivities in religious life. Even when a pwe is held for a marriage or a birth it will have no connection with any sort of religious ritual or ceremony. Buddhist festivities, meanwhile, centre largely around feasting. The Burmese are great eaters. It's a serious business (even when meals are so costly to produce) and, as a mark of this, I've always noted that very little conversation tends to take place when people sit down with a plate of food. Eating precludes talking. Feasting takes place quietly and earnestly, it's a way of marking an important occasion and also of gaining merit. With few formal religious ceremonies, progression through life is signified with a series of special meals.

There is no formal religious wedding ceremony. Marriage is constituted by a couple simply living and eating together. Often, though, permission will first be obtained from a group of elders or relatives to whom much respect will be shown and with whom a meal will be eaten to mark the occasion. Sometimes the couple will be given a type of blessing by the pungyis. These will be the only formalities although parties, pwes and elaborate celebrations might well take place later. Within Theravada Buddhist belief it is possible to take several wives, but in Burma polygamy is normally viewed as a social scandal and it very rarely occurs. Meanwhile, divorce takes place without elaborate procedure and simply by mutual consent. Each partner will take back his or her own property and will claim roughly half of everything jointly acquired. To an outsider, Burmese marriage sounds like a remarkably relaxed arrangement; no formal vows, no formal promises and an easy release if things go wrong. But the Burmese tend to take marriage very seriously and there are relatively few divorces.

While marriage, birth and the giving of names are not marked with a stamp of any religious significance, death and burial are quite a different matter. Since Theravada Buddhism is principally concerned with the life hereafter, death is of great importance in the next stage along the cycle of existence. Often prayer-like, religious sayings will be chanted over the deathbed and the Three Gems of Buddhism will be enumerated: to honour the Buddha, to honour the *Dhamma*, or sacred teachings and to honour the sangha, the monkhood. These will be repeated over and over again to help the dying person concentrate on the basis of Theravada Buddhist thought; the instructions of Gautama Buddha. Sometimes pungyis will be asked to come and contribute their chants and devotions.

After death the body will probably lie in state for a few days, dressed in special burial clothes. During this time the pungyis might be invited back to make more devotions. Finally, the monks will perform a special ceremony and the body will be taken to the cemetery for burial or cremation. (Most people are buried.)

'When we were rich we used to put a gold coin or a gold ornament in the coffin,' I was told by an elderly friend. 'Most people cannot afford this any more and it is a practice that has all but stopped.' He also told me that during the rioting of 1988 many of the older graves in the cities were broken open and robbed. This was not done by the ordinary people but by prisoners, the convicted criminals who were set loose by government troops in order to create havoc and terror among the demonstrators. The desecration of the burial grounds was particularly hard to bear.

Throughout the period from death to burial, the attending pungyis will probably be offered food whenever possible by the dead person's family. A particularly important feast will be held on the morning of the burial day. Like the food that is given to the pungyis on their begging rounds every morning, these meals are perhaps one of the most effective ways of gaining merit. The idea is that the merit gained before a burial will be transferred directly to the dead person to help in his future existence.

But generally, the feeding of monks is a much practised and accepted way of gaining merit principally for the individual donor and his family, who will inevitably be called upon to help. I remember attending a great feast once where about a hundred monks were being fed; vast vats of noodles and *mohinga* (a traditional Burmese fish dish) were stirred with huge paddles by a plump and jolly lady and she slopped large helpings into rows of tin bowls that were then served to the monks and other guests. Her husband, the donor, hovered near by issuing a few orders and checking that all was proceeding smoothly. The lay people attending the feast took their food at the same time as the pungyis but remained at a distance from them. We all sat on the ground on matting made from bamboo and ate silently from small low tables. As the monks finished their meal they got up and left separately while more monks arrived to take their place. They were all ages and sizes in a medley of saffron robes of different shades. It was very peaceful and quiet and as some of the monks left the room they were clearly in a state of near meditation.

On marriage, birth, death, or taking a driving test, passing an exam and so on, it might be customary to feed the pungyis but, as on this occasion, there needs to be no reason as to why someone should produce a vast meal for great numbers of monks. Most of the time the pungyis do not actually need the food; they will probably get more than enough to eat from their morning rounds and from other food donations made to the monastery. But they will always eat the special feasts so that the donors will duly acquire merit.

While the feasts for the monks are a way of acquiring merit and a frequent form of religious gathering, there are other annual festivals which mark the progression of the year and the life of Gautama Buddha. Confusingly, the Buddhist year is solar while the months of the year are measured according to the state of the moon.

Buddha Day during the full moon of May is the day that Gautama Buddha was born and also died. It serves, as well, to mark the day on which all Buddhas gain Enlightenment. Since Gautama Buddha gained Enlightenment while he was sitting under a Bo tree, these trees have a deep religious significance and will be ceremoniously watered on Buddha Day. People will also treat this day as a special sabbath day, visiting the pagoda, making donations and offerings and perhaps even ceremoniously releasing trapped fish or birds as an extra way of acquiring merit.

The year is punctuated by Buddhist Lent which lasts for three months from the full moon of July to the full moon of October, roughly the same period as the monsoon. During this time monks are not permitted to travel and technically marriages and pwes should not take place.

The First Festival of Lights marks the end of Lent;

according to myth, after gaining Enlightenment Buddha ascended into the sphere of the gods for the period of Lent and here he held discussions on Buddhist teaching and Buddhist thought. At the end of Lent he descended back into the sphere of men, surrounded by the light of heavenly torches. Masses of oil lamps are therefore lit in front of Buddha images and all around the pagoda. The cities also blaze with flashing electric lights.

Later in October the Robe Giving ceremonies start and they continue for about a month; saffron robes are publicly presented to the monasteries and, inevitably, there are great celebrations and feasts for the monks. These ceremonies are succeeded by the Second Festival of Lights to mark the time that Buddha set aside wordly garments and first put on his saffron robes.

The biggest and the most vibrant of the annual celebrations is the Burmese New Year (*Thingyan*) which takes place over a period of about three days in April. It is both a Buddhist and a nat celebration (with much consequent noise and colour), for while Thingyan brings in the new year it also marks the descent to earth of Thagyamin, the king of the nats. He makes a two-day visit to bless the people, and also to check up on them; he carries with him two books: one bound in gold recording the names of all good children and one in dog skin with the names of all bad children. During the two days of Thagyamin's visit the Burmese Water Festival takes place; literally and figuratively the washing away of the dirt and impurities of the year. Traditionally, water jugs are respectfully given to older relatives while the younger people will splash each other in fun. However, today things have become rather more lively and most people will spend the two days drenched to the skin. The final day of the New Year celebrations is a time for religious contemplation; food will be served to the monks and offerings will be made. (A similar sort of festival happens in Thailand, these Buddhist celebrations undoubtedly having their origins in the Hindu festival of Holi.)

Generally, there is a great love of water in Burma; it is, after all, a land of many rivers. And it is not just the Burmans themselves who show signs of this aqueous pleasure. To my mind, the national delight in the splashing and drenching of the Water Festival, and the background to it all, have interesting repercussions on the Karen and Kachin Christians. It is purely a piece of speculation, but the ready acceptance of Christianity through baptism and total immersion in water seems to have a direct correlation with the former animist beliefs of these people and the animist background to the water festivities.

In the cities, the two days of the Water Festival have developed into a boisterous carnival. Everything comes to a stop. It is impossible to avoid the festivities; anybody, anywhere is likely to get soaked with water. We used to join friends who responded to the whole occasion with studied enthusiasm and hired an uncovered truck which was loaded with exuberant passengers and driven around town. I never really knew where we were going or where we had been because the volumes of water being constantly chucked at us made it impossible to see very clearly. We sat sodden and smiling with a film of water almost permanently over our eyes. But anyway, the route was irrelevant, the object of the drive was simply to get as wet as possible.

Ours was by no means the only truck in town. Most young people either hired or clambered aboard some form of moving vehicle which cruised around, the passengers getting progressively wetter and wetter. Other people would line the streets, stopping all the cars and trucks as they came along and yelling out jokes and mock insults as they doused everybody inside. There were fire hoses at most street corners shooting out great jets of water which were usually aimed at the largest and noisiest of the truckloads. Sometimes things got out of hand; fights would break out between rival trucks and balloons filled with water would be hurled between feuding parties. These were rather like liquid hand grenades and would explode forcefully on landing; it could be very painful if a victim was hit directly on the skin.

Looking back on it all, it seems a remarkably pointless activity; two days when the entire nation comes to a halt and everyone rushes out to get wet. But the weather is almost unbearably hot at that time of year and it is a relief to be able, literally, to cool down. Despite the soldiers hanging round, it is also a relief, on the more abstract level, to be able to let go, to feel the tension in the country suddenly relax as the people's true festive character emerges from behind all the intimidation.

In the evening the water-throwing stops, it is safe to venture out without getting wet and the cities become alive with pwes; much colour, much dancing and much extremely loud music. If the country is not under curfew, the celebrations will continue all night. The Water Festival pwes are renowned for their political satire. It is all too easy to make fun of Burmese politics and the Burmese people themselves are very good at it: the country, after all, has a government that nervously and superstitiously bans certain flowers from pagodas, that abruptly alters the entire currency system to comply with whimsical numerology and that blithely bends all its own rules so as to stay in power. Then there's the scandal of all the political prisoners and the stories that leak out.

I heard of one very popular clown who regularly went in and out of jail on account of his satirical antics. He developed an act based on his prison experiences; 'I'm asked if life behind bars is rough,' he says. 'I always reply, "Oh no."' He laughs.

'I'm asked if my head has been shaved. I reply, "Oh no."' He then takes off his hat to reveal a bald head.

'I'm asked if I have been beaten. I reply, "Oh no."' He then lifts up his shirt to reveal a bruised back.

'I'm asked if my teeth are still good. I reply, "Oh yes."' He then spits out his false teeth (Burmese political prisoners are frequently made to chew stones and often lose their teeth in this way). The crowd laughs uproariously, delighted with the daring and the exposure of such hypocrisy, brutality and attempted intimidation.

Last time I was in Burma, I was surprised to see that the Rangoon authorities had not stopped a pagoda festival from taking place. It was just prior to the elections in 1990, the atmosphere was particularly tense and, technically, the martial law in force banned gatherings of groups of more than five people. I think, perhaps, it was an attempt to show a degree of liberality. By comparison with other festivities it was a pretty subdued event but it was better than nothing.

Pagoda festivals are a mix of refined religious celebration and zestful pwe. They can last for two or three evenings. The pagoda will be lit and decorated, offerings will be made and donations given. Around the pagoda there will also be an open-air fête with stalls selling food and trinkets and a stage will be set up for entertainment. Each pagoda normally has a festival once a year to mark the day on which it was founded.

Sule pagoda in Rangoon had recently been regilded and the golden bell was still under protective matting as the annual festival took place. 'The civic authorities are really trying hard at the moment,' I was quietly told by a young Burmese man who came up to me in the street and accompanied me to the pagoda. By way of introduction he had swiftly said that his name was Ronny and that he did not want me, as a foreigner, to be duped. All was not as festive as it seemed:

> This year they've spent a fortune from public funds on new gold leaf not just for Sule pagoda but also the Shwedagon pagoda. It's all part of their cleaning-up programme and I think it's supposed to impress us. Of course most of the gold will wash off in the monsoon but fortunately we are practical people and there are special sieves at the base of the pagodas to catch all the gold so that it can be recycled.

Ronny pointed out the new walkways that had been built over the wide road around Sule pagoda:

> They look as if they are pedestrian passes, but why should we need these when we have hardly any traffic on our roads?

Many people say the walkways have really been constructed for crowd control. If we have any more public riots the soldiers will be able to stand at a vantage point and shoot at people demonstrating below.

As we walked on to the pagoda, truckloads of soldiers rumbled past us and Ronny melted away into the crowds. Despite his original intentions to show me around, his nerve failed. It was clearly not a good idea to be seen by soldiers talking so openly with a foreigner.

There was a sense of muted enjoyment at the pagoda. Coloured lights festooned the area. Men were wandering around selling balloons, toys and sweets. There were crowded little food stalls from which a peculiarly Burmese smell emanated (a mixture, I think, of garlic, coriander and chillies) and at one of them I saw bits of pig strung up, snout and all. Looking up the entrances to the pagoda platform, mirrors twinkled and neon lights of red and green pulsed around the head of each Buddha. Throngs of people were making their way up the pagoda steps, carrying bunches of gladioli and chrysanthemums for their offerings. The soldiers lingering around appeared to be alarmingly young, none of them looked over eighteen. They stood strung about with guns, looking shy and frightened of the people, and of each other. As an orchestra on the far side of the pagoda struck up, heralding the start of the entertainment, more trucks of soldiers arrived. I felt a distinct sense of menace in the air. There was not long to go, however, before the festivities for that evening ended. At 9.30 everyone packed up and began to slink away, disappearing off the streets before the curfew fell at 10.00.

Above and beyond all the annual festivals and ceremonies for the dead, Buddhist initiation is by far the most significant religious occasion in Burma. Spiritually, it is certainly the most important event of a man's life. It entails costly and elaborate ceremony as a young boy prepares to learn the holy scriptures and enter a monastery, wearing the saffron robes of a pungyi for the first time in his life. Technically, as lesser beings, women are not afforded the same treatment. They are not offered any religious initiation and they do not, unless they make a specific choice, enter a nunnery to acquire a spiritual education. There are, though, two parallel ceremonies that mark the coming maturity of a girl and a boy: while Burmese boys are given a *shin pyu*, or initiation, ceremony to mark their spiritual coming of age, the *na-twin*, or 'ear-boring' ceremony will be performed for Burmese girls.

In a sense, the girls are fobbed off with a worldly and rather superficial event that leads only to furthering their feminine charms: their ears are pierced, giving them greater scope to wear the rubies, sapphires, pearls and jade which are the glittering riches of Burma. But it is an elegant and courtly occasion and it is typical that the Burmese, with their sense of equality and fair play, have developed a secular tradition for females that corresponds with the religious ceremony of male initiation.

When we lived in Burma, I thought there might be a certain logic in having my ears pierced there. Because the ear-piercing ceremony is frequently performed, I felt there would be people well practised and well qualified to tackle my requirements. Our friend Daw Khin Kyi had often asked me why my ears were not pierced, she felt it was rather unfitting for me to have two unpunctured ears. I asked if she could recommend anybody who would do the job well. 'It will be arranged,' she replied.

You did not question or argue with Daw Khin Kyi. She could be a commanding person, both because of her own achievements and because she was the widow of Burma's national hero. I wanted to know what, exactly, would be arranged, but I reckoned I would find out soon enough. In fact I heard nothing more for at least two weeks and I began to think that Daw Khin Kyi had forgotten. Then she phoned up one morning. 'Saturday is the auspicious day,' she said. 'You must come at 7 a.m. and bring your family.'

We were used to obeying the dictates of Burmese astrology and were touched that Daw Khin Kyi should have gone to some lengths to ascertain the correct moment for me to have my ears pierced, however, we never imaged that she would lay on a full ceremony. We duly arrived at 7 o'clock to find a number of Burmese friends had already gathered at her house. They were all wearing their very best.

I was immediately taken off and squeezed into some of Daw Khin Kyi's own ceremonial clothes; a lungyi of Mandalay silk, an engyi of the finest cotton and a tiny jacket that went with it. My hair was garlanded with jasmine flowers strung together in delicate bunches and a rope of pearls was fastened around my neck. Then, as if part of the whole procedure, came the photograph session; a group picture in the drawing room, a group picture on the porch, a group picture in the garden. Finally it was time for the ceremony itself. The occasion was orchestrated by a soothsayer and a doctor. First came the soothsayer's rites. At the appointed hour, a small bowl was brought in filled with water and rose petals. Hidden among the petals at the bottom of the bowl were five auspicious gems and nestling in one of the petals at the top were two gold pins. The soothsayer muttered some prayers over the pins, dipped two fingers in the bowl and chanted some more prayers as he flicked a few drops of water over each of my shoulders. Then the doctor, the professional 'ear-borer', stepped forward. Having anaesthetized my ear lobes, he simply picked up the pins and skewered them into my ears at two previously marked points. The sharp ends of the pins were then chopped off with special wire-cutters and the lengths of gold left at the backs of my ears were bent round so that the pins would not fall out as the wounds of the holes healed. The ceremonies over, a large meal was then produced as if from nowhere and we sat down to eat together.

Of course, most Burmese girls will have their own horoscopes carefully drawn up and consulted by the soothsayer at their ear-boring ceremony. It is not a religious event but it is the one occasion that marks a girl's coming of age and

it should take place only at the most auspicious moment.
Gifts of gems will often be presented after a ceremony, and
when I had my ears 'bored' people dropped by our house
over the next few days bringing presents of pearls and jade.
In the past, women would often extend the holes in their
ears so that they were big enough to take ear cylinders,
large tubes of gold with plugs of diamonds and rubies at
one end. Sometimes the holes would become so big that
they would even be used to carry around a spare cheroot. A
girl's ear-boring ceremony might well take place at the same
time as her brother's or cousin's shin pyu ceremony. Although it will be a festive, joyful occasion, her moment of
glory will be swiftly eclipsed by all the proceedings for the
boy's initiation.

The shin pyu ceremony follows elements from the early
life of Gautama Buddha. It will last about three days and it
is on the first and second day that the initiation rites take
place. Like Gautama Buddha in his courtly state as the
Prince Siddharta, the boy will be dressed up and treated
like royalty. His feet will not be allowed to touch the
ground and he will have white umbrellas held over him
wherever he goes. In his princely state he will be taken on a
triumphant journey to visit relatives and people of seniority,
technically to make his farewells since he will shortly be
leaving the material world but I suspect this is also a way of
getting additional funds to pay for the ceremony; the relatives will, of course, make donations when the boy visits
them. He will then be taken to make offerings at various
pagodas and perhaps also at the monastery to which he is
designated. Then comes the induction proper, prayers will
be chanted, sermons will be made and there will be a great
feast when the monks (and guests) will be fed. After this,
the boy will have his courtly clothes removed and replaced
by saffron robes and his head and eyebrows will be shaved.
(The hair becomes sacred once the boy becomes a novice.
It is therefore not allowed to fall to the ground but is
caught instead with a sheet.) The next day, after more food
for the monks and more prayers, the boy will enter the

monastery. He will remain there for as little as a day or as long as a few years. Should he then decide to become a full monk he will be fully ordained and will abide by the 227 rules of the Vinaya.

When a shin pyu ceremony took place within our household everybody was involved. Full invitations were sent out a few weeks beforehand (these often looked a bit like wedding invitations and were specially printed for the occasion). Formal replies were expected. In his full princely glory, the novice-to-be would pay a formal visit to our house and later the entire household joined a crowd of other guests at the shin pyu feasts. There was a particularly flamboyant occasion when the two sons of our cook were given their shin pyu. I was back in England at the time, but I received a vivid report:

> The shin pyu family had announced they wished to come and pay their respects at the house in the afternoon between pagoda visits. Just after 4.30 there was a commotion outside and we found a wonderful combination of the jumblies and a vintage car rally awaiting us when we got down the stairs. There seemed to be hundreds of people popping out of ancient cars, most of them were members of Aung Htin's abundant family. They were escorting two young boys, dressed to the nines in silk lungyis and gilded cardboard crowns and wristlets. Everyone was typically jolly and gentle, and they all seemed to be moving at top speed. In fact the whole thing appeared to move like a film run through at twice the normal pace.
>
> When we suggested that photos would be better taken in a patch of sun by the orchids, the whole gang set off at a run, carrying the shin pyuites (who evidently were not allowed to set foot to earth) and leaping the flower beds. Still at top speed, an old curtain was spread ceremoniously on the grass and the boys were stood on it while various attendants very rapidly arranged their finery. Then we clicked away, and so did the professional photographer who tore along with them. We took photographs of the boys, of the parents, of about half a hundred assorted members of the family of all ages and sizes, of the bevy of girl attendants each bearing strange gilt objects. Then the professional photographer took photos of us with the boys,

with the parents, with about half a hundred of the assorted members of the family – and so on. After that they all rushed off swiftly with delighted waves of the hand and golden umbrellas poking from the windows of the vintage cars.

We attended the ceremony at the pungyi kyaung [monastery] the next day. There we were greeted with cries of delight and ushered to the upper floor where we found the whole gang reassembled plus another half-hundred friends and relations. We were sat on bamboo mats, were shaken warmly (in every sense of the word) by the hand and given food and drink. We drove off later in a positive gale of handwaving and goodwill.

Such vivacity and generosity set against the harsh repression of the military regime, strike me as some of the biggest discrepancies of life in Burma today. I feel one of the saddest things about the situation today is that all the generosity, conviviality and good spirits are constantly ground down by economic depression and restrictive military action. Burmese culture has distinctive and inimitable qualities that reflect the country's historical and current day isolation. But it seems ironic that the very measures taken by a government anxious to preserve such seclusion and cultural integrity have increasingly removed the sense of joy and richness that characterize many of the customs.

CHAPTER NINE

YOUTH:
Tradition and Protest

Boredom and frustration; the lot of the youth of Burma today. Some might find the odd job, some might pass the time by starting up a band, others simply sit around in tea-shops. It is not that they lack initiative, it is just that they frequently have nothing to do (unless, perhaps, they join the army). During the lengthy period of military rule, life at universities and even schools has hiccupped along in a series of jolts; academic study intermittently comes to a complete halt in nervous reaction to political unrest. Rather like the sensitive fright of the sea anenome that grows in profusion along the coasts of Burma, at any outburst of trouble these institutions are closed down and stay firmly shut until all hint of danger has passed. Between 1974 and 1978, for example, universities were open only for brief periods due to the frequent student protests. More recently, during the 1988 disturbances universities were swiftly shut down and have now remained out of operation for nearly three years. Under the military regime pupils and students have frequently been deprived of the facilities to study. During these periods they will hang around wearily waiting until the authorities feel they have crushed all potential dissidence and finally the young people will be allowed to limp back. There will be a few empty spaces; some of their classmates might have fled to jungle areas, others might have been chucked into prison. The crippling effects of all this on the long-term future of the country and the distressing waste of human resources are bad enough in themselves, but the situation is made even more pitiful by the fact that education has been a strong and proud tradition for centuries within Burmese Buddhist society.

Of course there is another side to the picture. The military authorities would argue that the problems are brought about specifically by the students themselves and even by the schoolchildren. Not all of them, of course, but activists from underground opposition groups, particularly the (former) Communist Party of Burma. Communist infiltration had given rise to the student unrest of 1962, so they said at the time. Again, the communists were purportedly behind more student riots in 1974 and the further, intermittent, simmering unease through to the mass demonstrations in 1988. (These were, of course, started and led by a student movement.) To some extent the military authorities are probably right. There would undoubtedly be an element of underground subversion in any of the student riots; a university anywhere, even in the richest capitalist country, is a seedbed for young idealist thought and it seems almost inevitable that when basic freedom of speech and action is severely repressed, many young idealists will go underground and become revolutionary.

The Communist party was once a powerful and very real threat to the government; it was presented as the big bad wolf of the people, their number one enemy. And indeed it probably was. But certainly today it can no longer be held responsible for radical student action. By early 1989, about six months after the Burmese army's violent suppression of the public demonstrations, the Burma Communist Party as such ceased to be. Overrun with internal problems, the party tore itself to pieces as the rank and file soldiers mutinied and left the ageing leaders politically impotent.

Despite the reactions of the ruling military and their attempts to pin the reasons for student unease on the enemies of the people, dissidence at the universities is tacitly associated with public heroism. It is still an essential part of

the legendary story of Burma's independence. Looking back
to the start of the 'Thakin' independence movement, it was
at Rangoon University that Aung San became involved in
politics and took the first of his daring and dramatic actions
against the British authorities. His was essentially a youth
movement and his status today as Burma's national,
martyred hero gives great popular credence to other current-
day student action. The students have remained the freedom fighters of Burma but today they fight for a different
sort of cause against a different sort of enemy: it is ironic
that they are up against the very army Aung San effectively
created.

The periodic closure of schools and universities, though,
has become more than just a measure of reprisal and repression against student activism. It is almost as if education
in Burma has become too much of a dangerous thing.

'Look at those soldiers, they are so young, so ignorant
and so uneducated,' a friend remarked as we passed an
army truck near a market one morning. It was just prior to
the recent elections in 1990 and the military were to be seen
around in great number. Several khaki-clad orderlies were
lolling around smoking cheroots and one of the soldiers
shouted out at us as we walked by – it was clearly some sort
of quip. The others burst out laughing at his apparent wit
and bravado. My friend hurried on and refused to translate
fully. 'Those boys are really just uninformed, simple farm
workers. They have no idea of anything beyond Burma and
they are appallingly rude about foreigners. What they just
said is so offensive that I really cannot repreat it. You
wouldn't want to know anyway.' I did of course, but I
knew I would upset Burmese decorum by admitting this.
Despite the current political xenophobia, individually the
Burmese are almost overwhelmingly hospitable and courteous
to outsiders (and also to each other); for my friend, it
was a mark of embarrassing backwardness that the soldiers
had been quite so insolent. 'What future is there for our
poor country when we have boorish, unschooled people like
this in control?' he asked dismally.

We walked on into the market, passing by a clutch of giggling schoolgirls. 'The soldiers are particularly tense at the moment because of the schoolchildren,' he went on. 'Exams will be starting very soon,' he added by way of explanation. I was confused. I could not see a connection between soldiers and school exams. 'Oh, I'm sorry, of course for outsiders this is not obvious,' he smiled sadly. 'Exams are being held some months earlier than usual so that the government can close all the schools down well ahead of the elections. They are likely to remain closed for some time. In the meantime the soldiers have become especially nervous of crowds of outspoken schoolchildren.'

It seemed scarcely believable that men with guns should quail at the sight of children with books. The schools themselves had not even been in operation for a full year since the 1988 uprising; they had only opened in June 1989 having been shut for over twelve months as a measure against the mass unrest. All universities, meanwhile, had remained firmly locked up.

Set in direct contrast to the anti-intellectual stance of the army is the deep and revered background of Buddhist thought and Buddhist learning. Even though religious matters might have been slightly undermined today, the teachings of Buddha still form an integral part of the whole make-up of Burmese society. Since the eleventh century, the tradition of monastic schools admirably ensured a very high rate of literacy among the male population. But girls were only occasionally able to attend some of the monastic schools. It was not until the arrival of the British in the nineteenth century that schooling became widely available and that girls had a real opportunity for national education in Burma. As the British variously took control of the country, missionary schools were introduced and over time non-religious, government-assisted schools became increasingly popular. Meanwhile the Buddhist monastic schools continued to operate as well.

While the role and power of the pungyis was not overtly

challenged by the British, their status was inevitably weakened under a foreign and non-Buddhist government. Education, which had for centuries remained almost entirely under their management as a religious function, abruptly broadened. Sir Arthur Phayre, the first Chief Commissioner of British Lower Burma, at first tried to use and modernize the existing monastic structure. He had wanted to widen and add to a well-respected educational system, introducing a variety of new subjects like higher level science, geography and even English. However, the pungyis would have none of it; they were used to running their own show and would tolerate no interference.

Greater emphasis was consequently given to the few secular schools that were already in existence. More were encouraged and were given government grants. These schools had previously been set up outside the monasteries by rich lay people who gained a great deal of merit through such good acts. Since the schools were a sort of charity, like the monastic schools, the education they provided was free. However, as the British became more involved these lay schools started to charge fees. They became known as the Anglo-Vernacular schools and as they developed they started to offer a very different sort of education to the traditional monastic schools.

People went to Anglo-Vernacular schools principally to learn English. There was a slight Catch 22 situation about the whole thing: in order to get a good, relatively well-paid clerical job you needed to speak and write English. In order to learn English you needed to go to the Anglo-Vernacular school. But in order to attend the school you needed to come from a fairly rich family who were able to afford the fees in the first place.

The British concentrated on bringing their own form of primary and secondary education to Burma. This developed alongside the old monastic schools. Higher education, in the meantime, only gradually started up. Rangoon University itself was, after all, not fully established until the 1920s. Although this provided the genesis of the independence movement in the 1930s, nationalist feeling had been awoken long before then. This earlier sense of nationalism, in fact, related directly to the whole question of education in Burma. By the early 1900s a growing body of opinion was starting to object to the erosion of traditional Burmese teaching in the face of élitist Western education. It was the Young Men's Buddhist Association (YMBA) which became the most vocal group to criticize the spread of foreign learning and the way it was usurping the integrity of Burmese Buddhism and Burmese education. However, as nationalist thought deepened and increased the independence leaders were forced to take on board a series of complex and conflicting ideas; while Western education effectively challenged a Burmese tradition and a Burmese way of life, it was necessary to absorb that educational system in order to achieve independence and look to the future. By the 1930s they had accepted that English was the language of modern development and of communication with the world beyond Burma.

After independence, it was U Nu who started to restore the Theravada Buddhist tradition within Burmese society. The Sixth World Buddhist Synod was held in 1951 and the Kaba Aye or World Peace Pagoda was finished in early 1952. Following the split in his party, the AFPFL, and the subsequent military caretaker government, U Nu based much of his campaign for the general election of 1960 on the promise of formally making Buddhism the State religion. He won an overwhelming majority.

But the practical difficulties of instituting Buddhism as a national religion within a socialist state and also of allowing for the Christian and Muslim beliefs of some of the minority groups were never fully resolved. The whole issue was overtaken by events when Ne Win and the army seized power in 1962. In the meantime, within the socialist ideology of the new Burma, education had largely become State controlled. I can't help feeling that there must have been some clash of interests here: while the U Nu administration was following socialist principles of providing free, government-controlled schooling, U Nu in particular was also trying to revive the role of Buddhism and the role of the pungyis within Burmese society. Education had been a central part of that role.

How U Nu might have resolved such matters within the ideal of a Buddhist socialist state can only remain a matter of conjecture. When Ne Win took over he rapidly put into operation a programme of sweeping changes that established his far stricter and far more authoritarian interpretation of socialism. While the extensive measures of nationalization affected all walks of life and put paid to much Burmese enterprise, the State educational system moved from being government controlled to geing government directed.

Under the new system of military socialism, education was restructured with the aim of meeting conjectured demand; if it was anticipated that, say, the State would need a set quota of doctors, dentists and engineers, then the government would dictate that the appropriate quantity of people should be trained to meet those requirements. Such demand-led education sounds beautifully logical in theory, but in practice, of course, it is impossibly despotic and extreme. Freedom of choice gets chucked out and is replaced by a set of dreary regulations and a series of government objectives. It was all part of Ne Win's master plan of 'The Burmese Way to Socialism' and it sat at direct odds with the relaxed and individual nature of the Burmese. In the 1970s, it was a mark of achievement if you were training to be a doctor (Ne Win, himself, of course, remains preoccupied with medicine). Those with the highest grades from school automatically went to medical school quite regardless of any vocational concern. I was told that those of the next grade went into engineering, and so on.

Meanwhile Ne Win also stymied the efforts that had been made to put the Burmese clergy back in a position of respected authority. In 1964 all political groups other than the government-run BSPP were banned. Shortly after that a law was passed which demanded that all organizations should be registered with the government; this specifically, and pointedly, included those of a religious nature. It was not just the monks who resented this State interference; many ordinary people were outraged.

Over the next few years the military government took action against false monks and purged the monasteries. People actively working against the government who wore the saffron robes of monkhood principally to take refuge with the pungyis, as well as the corrupt monks living with women, running their own business or generally failing to comply with the Ten Precepts, were all exposed. Many were arrested and locked up in prison. Meanwhile, measures were taken to curb the activities of the surviving monastic schools.

The link though, between the pungyis and the students, the traditional teachers and their former pupils, has remained particularly strong. For the past quarter of a century these have been the two most volatile groups. Angry and outspoken, they have been by far the biggest source of public dissidence and opposition to military rule.

The army's efforts to curb the authority of the pungyis was a way of establishing control over the only formal organization left that might provide a dangerous and potentially powerful source of political opposition. There is a school of thought, however, that interprets all these acts in a more positive light: before the days of the British, it was a tradition that the kings of Burma would periodically purify the sangha; bogus monks (or 'humans in yellow robes') would be expelled and the monkhood would be given an opportunity to reassess itself in terms of the pure ideals of Theravada Buddhism. It could be argued that Ne Win's actions were entirely in keeping with this royal custom – although such a theory would, conversely, bring into play all the suspicions of Ne Win's kingly delusions.

Some of the monkhood might well have been corrupt or politically active when Ne Win's government stepped in, but the military also deliberately made moves to discredit the sangha and undermine their authority in the eyes of the people. To some extent it was an attack on the very nature of things Burmese. Meanwhile Ne Win himself was eager to be seen as the champion of Burmese culture.

It was in a bid to purify and revitalize the Burmeseness of Burma that Ne Win kicked all foreigners out of the country during the first few years of full military rule. The Indians left in droves. In a further fever of xenophobic activity Ne Win then banned the teaching of English in schools in 1965. This was a major blow to many learned and erudite Burmese. English had gradually been established as the language of modern education and a great number of Burmese both spoke and wrote it fluently. Suddenly, seventeen years after independence, English was outlawed from the school curriculum. By the end of the 1970s this effectively left many young people of Burma without the ability to communicate with the wider world and without the faculty to keep up with academic or scientific developments beyond their country.

When I first went to Burma I used to be approached by numerous middle-aged Burmese ladies who would beg me to come and meet their children so that they could learn some English. I never really understood why they thought it was so important until I began to learn a little more about the Burmese respect for knowledge and teaching. English had at one time been absorbed into a developing Burmese culture but, having acquired a place of its own, it was then abruptly cut out and thrown to one side. Many parents felt that their children were growing up with a serious disability; they were called 'the Ne Win generation' (and also, perhaps, 'the No Win generation') and they felt embarrassed by their limitations.

Then, unexpectedly, in 1981 English came back in again and was reinstated on the national curriculum. The story went that Sanda Win, Ne Win's doctor daughter, went over to England to further her medical training. She failed some qualifying English exams and returned to Burma in humiliation. Ne Win acted promptly.

Many younger people can now speak English. They are not very good at it but it does give them a wider scope for the future. Their knowledge of the world beyond, meanwhile, tends to be slightly eccentric. When I last visited

Mandalay, a young trishaw driver asked me where I came from. 'England. Ah, yes, Duran Duran and also *Wuthering Heights*,' he commented. 'We read the book at our school; I liked it very much. Cathy and Heathcliffe, it's a good story.' *Wuthering Heights*, I later discovered, was among the first of the English books to be reintroduced to Burmese schoolchildren after 1981. It has remained one of the only readily available English-language school texts and is now widely studied in Burma.

I asked the trishaw driver if he knew anything about England other than a pop group and a nineteenth-century novel. (He was in fact a student who had taken a temporary job because his academic life had come to a sudden halt with the closure of the universities.) 'Yes, I know of the BBC,' he said. 'It has a bad reputation here; it does not tell the truth.' Did he ever listen to the World Service, I wanted to know. No, he said, he did not. Why should foreigners tell the Burmese people what was happening in their own country, he asked.

Here was someone who actually reflected the views of government. I was surprised. Most people I met talked to me with whispered gratitude about the vital importance of overseas news broadcasts. Meanwhile the government-run *Working People's Daily* had even started producing scathing attacks on individual foreign journalists. Flying out of Burma some days later, I bought a government publication that was prominently on sale at the airport. Written in English, it had the catchy title 'The Conspiracy of Treasonous Minions within the Myanmar Naing-Ngan [Burma] and their Treacherous Cohorts Abroad'. On the plane I leafed through it in disbelief; it was such crude propaganda, such an insult to the inherent intelligence of the Burmese, and such an extraordinary show of government paranoia. Among mug shots and case histories of insurgents and a few former politicians who had fled the country, were details and even photographs of foreign journalists judged to be the enemies of the State.

It was not always the case, however, that Western Press

reports reflected badly on the Burmese military government. To some extent lack of knowledge bred lack of
interest and during the late sixties and the seventies there
were very few international reports on Burmese matters.
Within the country all privately run newspapers had been
banned by the end of 1966, and it was at about the same
time that most foreign correspondents were expelled; a few
Burmese journalists were subsequently allowed to report to
the international Press but they had first to be approved by
the government. Meanwhile, Vietnam and Cambodia were
set on a course of gunfire and devastation. In comparison to
the bloodshed and human misery of these nearby parts of
Southeast Asia, the situation in Burma appeared placid and
controlled. The plight of the minority peoples and the rebel
action against the central government remained a relatively
obscure issue and was given little if any international news
coverage. In the meantime, the Burmese army's stance
against communism gained a favourable reaction in the free
and democratic West.

It was against this background that I first read the Western Press reports of the events of 1974. It was bewildering
later to arrive in Burma and find that in reality matters
were very different. Following a poor harvest and rising
inflation, a series of rice riots in June 1974 were violently
put down. The international Press simply reported that
unrest in Burma had been quietened after emergency rations
of food were dished out to querulous office and factory
workers. Then, after months of simmering unease, came
the major troubles: at the end of November, U Thant,
senior Burmese statesman and former Secretary-General to
the United Nations, died in New York. His body was flown
back to be buried in Burma where it met with studied
disregard from the government authorities. Outraged, the
students rioted. The outcome was messy, with particularly
harsh reprisals on the part of the army. The reports I read
in the Western Press led me to understand that the riots
concerning U Thant's body had taken place against the
wishes of his family and that mob disorder was being

controlled by the army. That was just about it. But when I arrived in Rangoon I found a city reeling from the shock of brutality, bloodshed and severe measures of repression.

U Thant had become the Burmese representative to the United Nations during U Nu's government. By most accounts he was an erudite, warm and modest person but it was well known that Ne Win viewed him with suspicion and even distrust. After the military *coup* of 1962, he was seen by many within Burma as a national hero and the one effective link Burma had with the outside world. He was internationally admired and respected for his work at the UN. On his death his body lay in state for a few days at the UN headquarters in New York and was duly honoured before being despatched with all ceremony back to Burma.

I was told of the arrival of his coffin in Burma by people who happened, purely by chance, to be at Rangoon Airport at the time. They said they saw a huge black box being thrown out with other baggage from the hold of a plane. It sat on the tarmac for a while and was then casually loaded on to an airport luggage trolley and taken to the main building. Only when they saw a United Nations vehicle waiting to collect it did they realize that this was U Thant's ceremonial coffin. They were astonished that no government official had been there to receive the body and that it had been treated with such complete lack of decorum.

U Thant's family held their own lying-in-state for the body. The government, meanwhile, had no plans for holding a funeral nor for providing a special burial place; the body was to be placed in a public cemetery in Rangoon. For the students and many pungyis, this was intolerably disrespectful. As U Thant's body was being taken to be buried a group of people intercepted, kidnapped the body and took it to the Rangoon University campus.

At this point the government were forced to react and to show some interest in U Thant's remains. Soldiers surrounded the campus as the students and the pungyis held another lying-in-state for U Thant. Thousands of civilians came to pay their respects, and also by implication to show their support for the action. A mausoleum was even built for U Thant within the confines of the University campus. However, a few days later government troops stormed the area and removed the body. It was finally buried by the government authorities in a place of honour at the foot of the Shwedagon pagoda.

It's a macabre story of a dead body dumped in one place, kidnapped by a party of outraged youths and then seized amid increasing violence by men with guns. The clashes between the army and the students were particularly bloody; on an official count nine civilians were killed and seventy-four were wounded, although this was undoubtedly a very conservative estimate. The repercussions continued for quite some time; the universities were closed down, martial law was imposed and thousands of students were arrested and made to stand trial. Many people disappeared and were never seen by their families again. In a curious and paranoid reaction to the student movement, Western clothes and Western fashions were suddenly banned; students were prohibited from wearing trousers (and particularly jeans) and all male students had to have their hair cut short. I suppose the human mind can't cope with the reality of too much violence. The abiding image I have of the U Thant riots is not of demonstrations or wounded people but of a student friend with his hair cut off in tufts. It was a detail, but the violence was implicit. He had been dragged from the street by soldiers who had forcibly hacked off his hair with their bayonets.

Many students (and some pungyis) were held in detention for a number of years, others went underground and a few ethnic Karen, Shan and Kachin fled into jungle areas where they joined the revolutionary movements of their groups. Some students who had lain low for a number of years re-emerged during the 1988 demonstrations and helped lead the democracy movement that at one stage looked so likely to succeed.

The 1988 demonstrations were started by a new generation of students who, like the veterans of the U Thant riots, found a great deal of support among the people, particularly the pungyis. What began as a series of student riots became a mass movement. However, when the movement was crushed it was the students who seemed particularly certain to suffer harsh reprisals at the hands of the military. The prevailing mood rapidly switched from euphoria to panic as thousands of people were killed and many of the defeated students took to their heels and fled.

They did not know exactly where they were going or what they would do, they only knew that they had to get away from the army. Tales of execution, rape and unspeakable torture circulated in the cities so they headed away from regions controlled by the Burmese army and made for jungle areas occupied by rebel forces. These exiles on the run were largely Burmese students and schoolchildren, some of them as young as fifteen or sixteen. They came from Rangoon, Mandalay, Toungoo, Moulmein and other cities; urban people with no knowledge of basic jungle survival and with an inbuilt horror of the insurgent armies who, historically, were their enemies. A background of over twenty-six years of government propaganda about the evils of the rebel troops added to their apprehension of the ethnic minority people.

Over 10,000 of these young Burmese people ended up in Karen-held territory along the Burma – Thai border. In spite of the inherent suspicion between the two different ethnic groups, the Karen immediately responded to the predicament of the Burmese exiles. The students had no food, no medicines and no resistance to the type of malaria endemic in that region. The Karen people helped them to build camps, fed them and gave them medical aid. But 10,000 urban students proved to be a heavy burden on their own, already limited, supplies.

Despite their initial panic, many of the students were bolstered by a great sense of optimism. For a while they felt that it would not be long before they could all go home again. With the sheer numbers of people arriving at the border it was unthinkable that their democracy movement

had been completely crushed and they expected that international pressure would come to bear on the Burmese
military who would surely have to relent. Meanwhile they
had to contend with the jungle and jungle diseases; thousands went down with malaria and many died.

Within Burma proper, the government claimed to be
horrified by the mass exodus. 'These are our sons and
daughters,' they said, and indeed many of them literally
were; among the young people at the border were the
children of army colonels and other government officials. It
was openly agreed that the students were not hard-line
rebels; they were representatives of an entire generation of
Burma's future leaders and professionals. Overtures were
made, amnesties were offered and the students were encouraged to return.

Towards the end of 1988 it became clear that the military
authorities had no intention of relinquishing any hold over
the country and many students sitting it out on the border
became increasingly disillusioned. They felt also that the
West had let them down and had forgotten about their
struggle for democracy. Tired of the rough life in the
jungle, several thousand of them gave up the cause and
agreed to go home. More rumours of execution, torture and
beatings followed. In January 1989, three months after
foreign journalists had been banned from the country, a
group of foreign correspondents arrived in Burma on special
invitation from the government. During carefully ordered
sessions that were filmed by government authorities they
were allowed to meet some of the students who had
returned. It seems this was an attempt to persuade the
outside world that the students were not being badly treated
when they came back.

Later in the year the military began to claim that the
students who remained on the border were dissidents and
had become the enemies of the people. In the meantime the
Burmese army's campaign against the Karen rebel forces
was stepped up. This, it seems, was partly with a view to
showing their military strength prior to the general elections

they had promised, partly because they wanted the rich teak land held by the Karen but also because of the embarrassing existence of the student camps scattered along the border area.

By April 1990 many of the camps had fallen to the Burmese army. Generally the students managed to pull out in time but thereafter they led an increasingly nomadic existence. Thai authorities allowed some camps to be shifted on to their soil but other students had to resort to a peripatetic existence, hopping between Thailand and Burma as and when they could. Many gave up and headed for a very uncertain future in Bangkok. In the meantime, a few international emergency-relief programmes had been set up to provide medicines and food for the students so that they no longer relied on the Karen for their subsistence. However, it was ironic that these Burmese students remained largely dependent on Karen troops for protection against the Burmese army.

'Do the people in Rangoon know the student army is coming to help them?' a young Burmese student asked me when I met him at his camp on the Burmese side of the border. 'We've now learnt how to fight properly and we're going to beat Ne Win's army.' (None of the students I met on the border ever referred to the Burmese military as anything other than Ne Win's or Saw Maung's personal army.) He was dressed in khaki and wore heavy jackboots but he did not have a gun. I learnt they had one rifle between about four students.

They were all full of bravado, posing as guerrilla rebels, anxious to persuade visitors of their strength and their militancy. The Karen in nearby settlements, however, were more realistic. The students were young and hot-headed, Karen leaders told me. They did not have the training to be effective fighters although they were certainly learning how to defend themselves.

When the students first arrived at the border they sat miserably in their camps with very little to do. Rather like the classmates they had left behind in the cities of Burma, they had no way of continuing their studies and they faced hours of boredom. Military training and vengeful ideas of fighting the Burmese army kept them occupied, but they also set up their own education programmes to learn how to cope with their new environment and some even started up a few basic primary schools for Karen children. It was the first time many of these students had actually been exposed to the problems of the minority peoples of Burma and how, through opposing and fighting the Burmese army, the rebel groups had been left with almost nothing; there was little possibility of setting up schools, of providing teachers or even of training doctors.

The students I met at the border seemed deeply earnest and totally dedicated to the struggle for Burma's democracy. I suppose it was all they had. Unlike the oppressed people within Burma proper, here were a group of Burmese people with a sense of purpose. Ironically, in their state of exile they had more freedom than they had ever known before. They were uncrushed and felt strongly that they had a mission to keep their movement alive.

There was something of a boy-scout atmosphere as I was proudly shown around one of their camps. It was a miserable collection of thatched shelters accommodating about 150 young people. These were the dormitories, I was told, looking at a series of roofed bamboo platforms. Here was the hospital area (a few wan students on drips, a few others sweating and shivering with malaria), here was the store hut and here was the assembly hall; the students stopped, stiffened and formally saluted their flag, the traditional Burmese emblem of the fighting peacock. Having been denied democracy back home, they rigorously and scrupulously held ballots in their assembly hall, voting for anything going; their committee members, their camp leaders, their union representatives.

The place seemed strangely empty. 'Many members of the camp have gone to the front line,' I was told. 'It's about four or five days' walk away.' Although this sounded like some military offensive, I later established that it was actually a method of getting real information into Burma. The students would go out into territory controlled by the Burmese military and make contact with villagers and with members of underground movements. It was effectively a publicity exercise to keep people within Burma aware of what the students were doing and how the cause for democracy was not lost.

Did students in the West know about their predicament, the Burmese students wanted to know. Did the Western countries care about their continued struggle for democracy? I told them that there was some concern for their survival but that, because little was generally known about Burma, it was difficult to sustain a wide level of interest.

However, at that stage a degree of international concern about the Burmese students had also drawn attention to the general plight of the minority peoples in the border area. The issue was one that had long been overlooked. Because of well-documented problems on the Thai–Cambodia border and the general sparsity of world knowledge about Burmese matters, human rights issues and the predicament of refugees on the Thai–Burma border for years have not received much international recognition. During periods of heavy fighting between the Burmese army and the rebel troops as many as 100,000 people are likely to come flooding across the border to take refuge in Thailand. (Those caught by the Burmese troops are killed, raped or forced to serve as porters in the Burmese army while villages are looted and farmlands burned.) In time the Burmese troops are often forced to withdraw from rebel areas and the people are able to return, but the situation has continued to be extremely volatile. In the midst of all this, the Burmese students have become just a tiny part of the problem.

When I visited a rebel area I found it difficult to see how circumstances could possibly improve. The Burmese army continued to attack the rebel bases, the rebels demanded negotiations for federalism but got nowhere and in the meantime a small population of Burmese students were stuck on the border, little more than an emblem of the sad waste of their country. Of course, the general elections of 1990 had very little impact on the border situation. Even on the day of voting within Burma proper, fighting continued between the Burmese army and the rebel forces. When the results were announced, the exiled students remained extremely sceptical; they maintained that of course the Burmese army would find a way of keeping their power, of course the soldiers would continue to oppress the people and inevitably it would be a very long time before any of the students still living in the jungle would be able to go home again.

If it seemed a bleak outlook for the students on the border, life for those students within Burma proper offered nothing very much better. While education had been left in check, thousands hung around with nothing to do, waiting while nothing happened. It was a stroke of tragic mismanagement that a country once so proud of its education and literacy had closed down all its universities and schools for an unspecified period and had effectively outlawed a large group of its university students who sat in exile in the jungle.

CHAPTER TEN

WHAT HAPPENS NEXT?

Never travel in Burma without a spare sixty-watt light bulb; a useful piece of advice offered to me by a Burmese friend when I last visited the country. But at that stage it was too late for me to act upon it to any great effect. It is difficult to acquire light bulbs even in Rangoon and those available on the black market tend mainly to be of the forty-watt variety which shed only a dim reassurance of light and leave little possibility of reading or writing with any degree of ease after the tropical sun sinks at about 5.30. With a curfew enforced every evening from 10 o'clock, books might seem a worthy resource, but few can enjoy such luxuries because of the hefty censorship of written material and also the lack of light.

On my last trip, I returned to the Strand Hotel one evening at about 9.30. It seemed too early to go to bed but there was no prospect of curling up with the cockroach resident in my vast room and settling down to a good read (I had brought books from England). The darkness in the room was broken only by a small pool of light from a huge Victorian standard lamp which merely cast disproportionate shadows and added to the pervading sense of gloom. Downstairs, there were some neon lights in the bar, so congratulating myself on a neat move I took my book and headed for the light. I had anticipated the chance of at least half an hour's reading but I got no further than the first paragraph.

'What a godforsaken country!' exclaimed a fellow guest,

interrupting the quiet and pulling up a chair beside me. 'I've travelled to some pretty miserable places in my time, but this really beats the lot.' In need of company to unburden his frustration and dispel his feelings of depression, he was clearly determined to talk. I glumly put down my book and listened to his monologue.

He was a Thai businessman in the travel industry and had come to Burma to negotiate over various tourist ventures. He had, he said, spent the day plying numerous Burmese officials with bottles of whisky and packets of foreign cigarettes in order to create 'the right impression'. Undoubtedly there was tourist money to be made out of Burma, he told me, but he failed to understand what the big attraction was. 'There's nothing much to do, the food is no good, the best hotels are third rate and there's no entertainment,' he complained. He felt distinctly worried by the lack of consumerism in Burma, probably the most striking contrast with his own country. 'What can I buy?' he wailed. 'There aren't really any shops and tourists visiting the country could well come away empty-handed. The people here are hopeless. They have nothing and it seems as if they're all just waiting to die; all they want to do is to go to heaven.'

I could see his point. The Burmese have been left with very little but their religion, teaching tolerance, acceptance and an ultimate goal of nibbana, the release from suffering. And, as the Burmese are well aware, suffering is what life is all about. It was a strange reflection, however, that a Thai, who was after all a fellow Buddhist, saw the Burmese in this particular light. It emphasized the enormous differences between the businesslike thrust of Thailand and the sad, rather hopeless, stagnation of its neighbour Burma.

Yet, for the moment it seems that Thai involvement will continue to play a significant part in the future of Burma. SLORC, the governing military body, badly need foreign money. But while they conjure up obstacles that attempt to justify why they have not handed over power to a civilian government, many foreign governments refuse to have much to do with Burma. The Thais, on the other hand, have maintained fairly cordial relations with the Burmese military, their eyes firmly fixed on all the business opportunities the country has to offer. Quite apart from smaller tourist ventures, Thai companies have continued to fish Burmese waters and to set up joint mining operations. In June 1990 one Thai firm even signed an agreement with the Burmese ministry of trade to start a joint venture for a retail store in Rangoon (which would, I thought, please the Thai businessman at the Strand Hotel; at last he would have something to buy).

After years of self-imposed seclusion, Burma is being forced to come out of isolation because the country has gone broke. But while SLORC are criticized by many foreign governments and also by the UN, they continue to insist that they are performing their 'duties concerning the United Nations'. For what it was worth, they announced in August 1990 that they were complying with United Nations economic sanctions against Iraq and Kuwait. Meanwhile reports of human rights abuses mounted: thousands of people were said to have been arrested and many were believed to have died in prison. In November 1990 two representatives from the UN Human Rights Commission arrived in Rangoon to investigate the situation. They had hoped to get a balanced view by meeting members of the military and also many of the political detainees. More reports circulated of how Insein prison had been repainted and how the prisoners there had been given new blankets and better food just prior to the UN visit. The delegates, however, remained heavily guarded thoughout their stay in Burma and their efforts to interview many political prisoners (including Aung San Suu Kyi) were blocked. The army officials, instead, began calling on the representatives to investigate Japanese and British wartime atrocities of the 1940s.

SLORC now need the outside world although they brook no criticism. Conversely, Burma has never played a significant role in world affairs and for the general international community it is of little real interest. But to my mind, increasing concern over environmental issues and also over the drug trade will have more and more of an impact. Although Thai companies have continued to chop down Burmese trees, it seemed that towards the end of 1990 the Burmese military were actually becoming a little embarrassed by the environmental horror stories in circulation. To some extent outside pressure seemed to be working for it was rumoured that SLORC would not be renewing many of their forestry concessions with foreign logging companies. Meanwhile, the opium trade flourished (I was told that there was a bumper crop in 1990). Much of it continues to be exported and an estimated 50 per cent of the heroin flowing into the USA is said to come from the Golden Triangle, of which Burma is by far the biggest producer.

The Americans, in the meantime, have been perhaps the most vociferous in objecting to the actions of the Burmese military junta. In August 1990 an article in the *Far Eastern Economic Review* reported that a new US ambassador had been appointed to Burma; however, he was said to have been instructed not to take up his post until Burma's democratically elected government had come to power. He ran the risk of waiting around for a long time. The EC countries, meanwhile, continued to voice their objections and to withhold their aid and Japan (which had shown a tendency to waver) also joined the long list of those condemning the actions of the Burmese military.

For all the years of anti-communist propaganda, SLORC, meanwhile, were turning their attentions to China. Of course, both governments now had something in common in that they had recently shown themselves to be quite capable of shooting thousands of their own, unarmed, people. For the Burmese military it seems that the attraction of China lay largely with its supply of arms and ammunition which SLORC were busily buying up in order to keep the general population under control.

By the end of the monsoon in 1990 public 'disturbances'

had become a very real threat to the military regime. In Mandalay the monks organized a series of peaceful demonstrations to coincide with the second anniversary of the public strikes of 8 August 1988. They were, of course, demanding that the civilian government the people had elected in May should be allowed to come to power. Diplomats resident in Burma said that at least two monks and two students were killed in clashes with the army although these claims were hotly denied by the authorities. A Press release issued by the Burmese Embassy in Bangkok stated that 'it is necessary for the people to realize that unscrupulous persons, as a rule, will try to spread . . . rumours and create unrest and harm the country.' More demonstrations took place throughout August and September but these were swiftly quelled and did not generate a mass movement. Many monks, meanwhile, began boycotting the military by refusing to perform religious ceremonies for them and by rejecting alms and donations offered by soldiers. It was, effectively, a humiliating excommunication for the army and SLORC retaliated by ordering that all Buddhist organizations connected with anti-government action should be dissolved. Monks not complying with the government directives were to be de-robed and local army officers were given special powers enabling them to arrest and even execute dissident pungyis. In the face of such repression, the boycott largely came to an end but the military action against the monks sent shock waves through neighbouring Buddhist organizations in Thailand.

If there was a clampdown even on the monks, what hope was there for the people? But one Burmese refugee student told me at the time:

Although people are still very scared, I think there's a discernible change of heart. Before the elections nobody knew for sure how strong the support was for the opposition and how deeply national feeling went against the army. They would have been too afraid to discuss such matters openly. Now that over 80 per cent of the electorate has shown beyond a shadow of doubt that military rule is no longer acceptable, it's a very different story.

But could there be another revolution, I wanted to know. 'It's possible; people are continuing to demonstrate. We'll have to wait and see.'

I couldn't help feeling, though, that the real issue was not so much over the action of the people as over the action of the army. Democratic elections might have taken place but the military clearly still had the upper hand and would do everything within their power to retain this position – and for the Burmese their power is formidable. It seemed scarcely believable that after years of absolute control the army had allowed free and fair elections to be held at all. They had not rigged the votes and had announced that the NLD had gained an overwhelming majority. But then the sudden show of free choice had been abruptly checked. Having been so roundly defeated, the military fudged the issue and continued to insist that a new constitution had to be drawn up and approved before any sort of Parliament could convene – a process that could take years. In the meantime the number of NLD members arrested reached at least 400, including most of the party's leaders.

National feelings of frustration and desperation mounted. With an assembly elected in May but still unable to convene, over 100 of the elected candidates held secret meetings during October in a monastery in Mandalay. They apparently drew up plans to set up a parallel government but it was suspected that these plans leaked out for more arrests swiftly followed. In the meantime, several of the candidates from the NLD and other allied opposition parties fled to the Thai border. They were headed by Sein Win, a cousin of Aung San Suu Kyi and a member of the PND (a smaller political party affiliated with the NLD). On 18 December they announced that with the support of the DAB, the umbrella organization for many of the rebel groups, they were setting up a parallel government on Burmese soil in rebel-held territory.

The reaction back home was fairly swift. The PND was deregistered by SLORC and in order to continue their struggles as a viable political party within Burma, the surviving NLD central committee had little option but to expel those of its members who fled to take part in the border operation. The irony was, though, that the members of the parallel government were legally elected by the people; SLORC were not.

Many think that the May elections were really just a big blunder on the part of the military. Desperate for foreign exchange, they had to hold some sort of national vote in an attempt to gain credibility with the rest of the world. But with candidates from at least eighty different political parties registered for the election, the army authorities probably never expected one single party to win such a large majority. As I have mentioned in a previous chapter, one theory is that the military had simply anticipated mass confusion, with parliamentary candidates elected from numerous different parties and with their own party, the NUP, gaining a majority, however small. But they grossly underestimated the popular support for the NLD and their charismatic leader, Aung San Suu Kyi, who although silenced under house arrest continued to be seen by the people as their hope for the future, the liberating alternative to military dictatorship.

What might happen next is really open to wide speculation although there are some distinct alternatives: The military will undoubtedly continue their delaying tactics and once a new constitution is finally agreed they might well hold another election, this time ensuring that their own party wins a clear majority. In the meantime, there still remains a possibility that the simmering anger of the people could lead to another mass uprising. Then there's a question as to whether elements of the army might defect and the military split; after all, the election results showed strong support for the NLD from some military townships. But many think it is highly unlikely that the army will show any real signs of division while Ne Win is still alive. However old and ill he might be, he will undoubtedly continue to command enormous loyalty from his troops.

What happens when Ne Win dies is quite another matter. This is the most obvious point at which the country might change radically. As with the kings of Burma back in the eighteenth and nineteenth centuries, there is no clear line of succession within the army. Saw Maung, the current President, is widely held to be something of a puppet figure. Khin Nyunt, head of the secret police, undoubtedly has greater power and control but officially he ranks only eighteenth within the military council. It is likely that Ne Win's death will lead to particularly nasty struggles among those angling to take control of the army. While the kings of Burma frequently used to massacre their kinsmen in order to safeguard their own positions, it seems possible that a bloodbath could precede the emergence of a new military leader. Taking an optimistic view, such a leader could well be one of the younger, more liberal members of the army, willing to gain popular support by allowing greater civilian control. On the other hand, if Khin Nyunt takes over it seems probable that the military stranglehold of Burma will continue for a great deal longer.

Then what of the minority groups, particularly those in armed rebellion, and the growing number of Burmese in exile around the border areas? While SLORC refused to hand over power to an elected government they also refused to hold any official dialogue with many of the armed rebels, particularly the Karen. 'The State Law and Order Restoration Council is not a political government,' one of their declarations proclaimed in their own sort of military double-speak. 'It has no reason at all to negotiate by political means with any armed insurgent organization.' The DAB, in the meantime, welcomed the parliamentary candidates who had fled from the government-controlled part of Burma and offered them support. Their objectives, they announced, were to remove the governing military body, to establish democratic rights and to rebuild Burma as a federal republic.

It sounds workable in theory, but in practice how could they remove a military dictatorship that had been in power for over twenty-eight years? It seems, to my mind, rather unlikely that the military could be overthrown even by a combination of total war from the insurgents and revolution within Burma proper. (It seems, also, equally unlikely that sufficiently regular contact could be established between those in the government-controlled areas and those in rebel-held territory.) Any lasting change will surely have to take place either with the backing of the army or with the support of some of the military if the army does indeed split. The interim prospects for the rebels and those in exile in their territory seem depressingly dismal; for the time being they are unable to negotiate with the military government (I can't think they would want to anyway), they certainly would not give up their cause for democracy and greater federalism but they can only continue their struggle in the hinterland of the country, far from the central government where the crucial decisions are made.

What, also, of Aung San Suu Kyi? It seems more than likely that she will be kept under house arrest for quite some time unless, as the military keep stipulating, she either gives up politics (they suggest she takes up literature instead) or leaves the country. It is doubtful that she would do either. She remains the linchpin of a free Burma, and, like her father before her, she is the one figure in the country with enough mass appeal to unite the Burmese people and rise above the factionalism that has been the blight of multi-party politics in Burma since the days of the British. While she stays in the country, even under house arrest, she remains a focus for a democratic future.

Before she was silenced, Aung San Suu Kyi's insistence that the people and the army should work together was in many ways a move to smooth the antagonistic division between oppressor and oppressed. It was probably also a tacit recognition that within a free Burma the army would continue to have a large administrative role to play, whatever the wishes of the people. After years of military domination, there simply isn't the infrastructure and there aren't sufficient civilians trained for a full alternative to army government. Should Aung San Suu Kyi finally be allowed to hold some power, I can't help feeling that this would be when her problems really begin. Uniting the country and bringing Burma out of the gloom would be a task enough in itself. Maintaining real control over a national army that could quite simply turn round and stage another military *coup* or conjure up a reason for removing the national leader (even one with as much popular support as Aung San Suu Ki) would be a daunting challenge even for the most experienced of politicians. Analogies can be misleading; however, recent events in Pakistan where Benazir Bhutto was forced out of office while the army stepped in (albeit temporarily) do seem to underline the very real dangers a civilian government would face in Burma. Pakistan is a reminder that military regimes don't like relinquishing power.

But for all the immediate problems in Burma there is still a real prospect of change and a real chance that the country might yet emerge as a democratic federation of states with a discernible position in the international community. Since 1988 the people have shown in every way possible that they do not want to be ruled by the army. They have also acquired a national leader who appears sufficiently determined to continue the struggle for Burma's second independence. Under the military the country has become virtually bankrupt but Burma still has a wealth of natural resources and, given help and investment, these could well turn round the dwindling economy. Burma could yet become a free, prosperous country. For the moment, though, the future remains in the hands of the army. After all, they are the men with the guns.

BIBLIOGRAPHY

Aye Saung, *Burman in the Back Row: Autobiography of a Burmese Rebel* (Asia 2000, 1989)

Braund, H. E. W., *Calling To Mind: Steel Brothers and Co. Ltd* (Pergamon, 1975)

Butwell, Richard, *U Nu of Burma* (Stanford, 1963)

Donnison, F. S. V., *Burma* (Ernest Benn, 1970)

Furnival, J. S., *Colonial Policy and Practice: A Comparative Study of Burma and Netherlands India* (Cambridge University Press, 1948)

Harvey, G. E., *History of Burma* (Longmans, 1925)

Jesse, F. Tennyson, *The Lacqueur Lady* (Virago, 1979)

Khaing, Mi Mi, *The World of Burmese Women* (Zed Books, 1984)

Lehman, F. K. (ed.), *Military Rule in Burma Since 1962* (Mauruzen Investment, 1981)

Linter, Bertil, *Outrage: Burma's Struggle for Democracy* (Review Publishing, 1989)

Lewis, Norman, *Golden Earth: Travels in Burma* (Eland Books, 1984)

Maung Maung, *Aung San of Burma* (Martinus Nijhof, 1962)

Maung Maung, *Burma and General Ne Win* (Asia Publishing House, 1969)

Nisbet, John, *Burma Under British Rule and Before* (Constable, 1901)

O'Connor, V. S., Scott, *Mandalay and Other Cities of the Past in Burma* (Hutchinson & Co., 1907)

Orwell, George, *Burmese Days* (Penguin, 1978)

Shway Yoe (Sir George James Scott), *The Burman: His Life and Notions* (The Norton Library, 1963)

Spiro, Melford, E., *Buddhism and Society: A Great Tradition and its Burmese Vicissitudes* (University of California Press, 1970)

Tinker, Hugh, *The Union of Burma* (Oxford University Press, 1967)

Tinker, Hugh (ed.), *Burma: The Struggle for Independence 1944–48* (documents from official and private sources). Vol. 1: *From Military Occupation to Civil Government*, Jan. 1, 1944 to Aug. 31, 1946. Vol. 2: *From General Strike to Independence*, Aug. 31, 1946 to Jan. 4, 1948 (HMSO 1983 & 1984)

U Nu, *Saturday's Son: Memoirs of the Former Prime Minister of Burma* (New Haven, 1975)

Ziegler, Philip, *From Shore to Shore: The Diaries of Earl Mountbatten of Burma 1953–59* (Collins, 1979)

INDEX